PROBLEM-SOLVING CASES IN MICROSOFT® ACCESS™ AND EXCEL®

PROBLEM-SOLVING CASES IN MICROSOFT® ACCESS™ AND EXCEL®

Fifteenth Annual Edition

Ellen F. Monk

Joseph A. Brady

Emilio I. Mendelsohn

CENGAGE
Learning·

Australia · Brazil · Mexico · Singapore · United Kingdom · United States

CENGAGE
Learning·

**Problem-Solving Cases in Microsoft®
Access™ and Excel®, 15th Annual Edition**

Ellen F. Monk, Joseph A. Brady,
Emilio I. Mendelsohn

Vice President, General Manager, Science,
Math & Quantitative Business: Balraj Kalsi

Senior Product Director: Kathleen McMahon

Product Team Manager: Kristin McNary

Associate Product Manager: Kate Mason

Senior Director, Development:
Julia Caballero

Senior Content Development Manager:
Leigh Hefferon

Senior Content Developer: Michelle Ruelos
Cannistraci

Development Editor: Dan Seiter

Marketing Manager: Scott Chrysler

Marketing Coordinator: Cassie Cloutier

Content Project Manager: Michele Stulga

Art and Cover Direction, Production
Management, and Composition:
Lumina Datamatics, Inc.

Manufacturing Planner: Ron Montgomery

Cover Design: Lumina Datamatics

Cover Image Credits:
Omelchenko/Shutterstock.com
ESB Essentials/Shutterstock.com
mrmohock/Shutterstock.com
Monkey Business Images/Shutterstock.com

For product information and technology assistance, contact us at
Cengage Learning Customer & Sales Support, 1-800-354-9706
For permission to use material from this text or product,
submit all requests online at **www.cengage.com/permissions**
Further permissions questions can be e-mailed to
permissionrequest@cengage.com

Library of Congress Control Number: 2017931021

Student Edition ISBN: 978-1-337-10133-2

Cengage Learning
20 Channel Center Street
Boston, MA 02210
USA

Cengage Learning is a leading provider of customized learning solutions, with employees residing in nearly 40 different countries and with sales in more than 125 countries around the world. Find your local representative at **www.cengage.com**.

Cengage Learning products are represented in Canada by Nelson Education, Ltd.

To learn more about Cengage Learning, visit **www.cengage.com**.

Purchase any of our products at your local college store or at our preferred online store: **www.cengagebrain.com**.

Printed in the United States of America
Print Number: 02   Print Year: 2017

BRIEF CONTENTS

Part 3: Data Analysis Cases in Microsoft Access and Excel

Part 4: Decision Support Case Using Basic Excel Functionality

Part 5: Integration Cases Using Microsoft Access and Excel

Part 6: Advanced Skills Using Excel

Part 7: Presentation Skills

PREFACE

For more than two decades, we have taught MIS courses at the university level. From the start, we wanted to use good computer-based case studies for the database and decision-support portions of our courses.

At first, we could not find a casebook that met our needs! This surprised us because we thought our requirements were not unreasonable. First, we wanted cases that asked students to think about real-world business situations. Second, we wanted cases that provided students with hands-on experience, using the kind of software that they had learned to use in their computer literacy courses—and that they would later use in business. Third, we wanted cases that would strengthen students' ability to analyze a problem, examine alternative solutions, and implement a solution using software. Undeterred by the lack of casebooks, we wrote our own for Cengage.

This is the fifteenth casebook we have written for Cengage. The cases are all new, and the tutorials have been updated using Microsoft Office 2016.

As with our prior casebooks, we include tutorials that prepare students for the cases, which are challenging but doable. The cases are organized to help students think about the logic of each case's business problem and then about how to use the software to solve the business problem. The cases fit well in an undergraduate MIS course, an MBA information systems course, or a computer science course devoted to business-oriented programming.

To date we have written nearly 200 cases. We are proud to say that all of them have tried to teach students how to use software to help them make good business decisions. The business computing environment continues to evolve, and our cases should follow that evolution. To stay current, students need to learn a broader range of data analysis activities. Starting with this edition, therefore, we have increased the range of topics covered in our casebook. This edition includes instructions and a case on data cleaning, a necessary step before data can be used in operations. This edition also contains instruction and a case on the differences between handling operational data and analytical data. We have added data analysis sections to the database cases and placed greater emphasis throughout the text on the various uses of pivot tables. In the future, we intend to further increase the range of data analysis topics we cover. We welcome feedback from instructors on this process. If there are data analysis topics you want to see covered, or covered differently, let us know! Please contact Kate Mason, our Associate Product Manager at Cengage.

BOOK ORGANIZATION

The book is organized into seven parts:

- Database cases using Access
- Decision support cases using the Excel Scenario Manager
- Data analysis using Access and Excel
- A decision support case using basic Excel functionality
- Integration cases using Access and Excel
- Advanced Excel skills
- Presentation skills

Part 1 begins with two tutorials that prepare students for the Access case studies. Parts 2 and 3 each begin with a tutorial that prepares students for the Excel case studies. All four tutorials provide students with practice in using the software's features—the kind of support that other books about Access and Excel do not provide. Part 4 asks students to use Excel's basic functionality for decision support. Part 5 challenges students to use both Access and Excel to find a solution to a business problem. Part 6 is a tutorial about advanced skills students might need to complete some of the Excel cases. Part 7 is a tutorial that hones students' skills in creating and delivering an oral presentation to business managers. The next sections explore these parts of the book in more depth.

Part 1: Database Cases Using Access

This section begins with two tutorials and then presents five case studies.

Tutorial A: Database Design

This tutorial helps students understand how to set up tables to create a database without requiring students to learn formal analysis and design methods, such as data normalization.

Tutorial B: Microsoft Access

The second tutorial teaches students the more advanced features of Access queries and reports—features that students will need to know to complete the cases.

Cases 1–5

Five database cases follow Tutorials A and B. The students must use the Access database in each case to create forms, queries, and reports that help management. The first case is an easier "warm-up" case. The next four cases require more effort to design the database and implement the results. New in this edition is an assignment to explore data analysis within the context of the cases.

Part 2: Decision Support Cases Using Excel Scenario Manager

This section has one tutorial and two decision support cases that require the use of the Excel Scenario Manager.

Tutorial C: Building a Decision Support System in Excel

This section begins with a tutorial that uses Excel to explain decision support and fundamental concepts of spreadsheet design. The case emphasizes the use of Scenario Manager to organize the output of multiple "what-if" scenarios.

Cases 6–7

Students can complete these two cases with Scenario Manager. In each case, students must use Excel to model two or more solutions to a problem. Students then use the model outputs to identify and document the preferred solution in a memo.

Part 3: Data Analysis Cases in Microsoft Access and Excel

This section has one tutorial and two cases that emphasize the fundamentals of data analysis.

Tutorial D: Data Analytics

This section begins with a tutorial about two topics related to data analysis: data cleaning and the importance of separating analytical data from operational data.

Cases 8–9

Case 8 illustrates the basic differences between operational and analytical data and how to minimize operational impacts during data analysis. In Case 9, students are asked to clean an Excel file and get rid of unusable data, leaving a data set that can be processed.

Part 4: Decision Support Case Using Basic Excel Functionality

Case 10

The book continues with a case that uses basic Excel functionality. The case does not require Scenario Manager. Excel is used to test students' analytical skills in a "what-if" analysis.

Part 5: Integration Cases Using Microsoft Access and Excel

Cases 11 and 12

These cases integrate Access and Excel. The cases show students how to share data between Access and Excel to solve problems.

Part 6: Advanced Skills Using Excel

This part contains one tutorial that focuses on using advanced techniques in Excel.

Tutorial E: Guidance for Excel Cases

Some cases may require the use of Excel techniques that are not discussed in other tutorials or cases in this casebook. For example, techniques for using data tables and pivot tables are explained in Tutorial E rather than in the cases themselves. ·

Part 7: Presentation Skills

Tutorial F: Giving an Oral Presentation

Cases may include an optional assignment that lets students practice making a presentation to management to summarize the results of their case analysis. This tutorial gives advice for creating oral presentations. It also includes technical information on charting, a technique that is useful in case analyses or as support for presentations. This tutorial will help students to organize their recommendations, to present their solutions both in words and graphics, and to answer questions from the audience. For larger classes, instructors may want to have students work in teams to create and deliver their presentations, which would model the team approach used by many corporations.

INDIVIDUAL CASE DESIGN

The format of the cases uses the following template:

- Each case begins with a *Preview* and an overview of the tasks.
- The next section, *Preparation*, tells students what they need to do or know to complete the case successfully. Again, the tutorials also prepare students for the cases.
- The third section, *Background*, provides the business context that frames the case. The background of each case models situations that require the kinds of thinking and analysis that students will need in the business world.
- The *Assignment* sections are generally organized to help students develop their analyses.
- The last section, *Deliverables*, lists the finished materials that students must hand in: printouts, a memorandum, a presentation, and files. The list is similar to the deliverables that a business manager might demand.

USING THE CASES AND TUTORIALS

We have successfully used cases like these in our undergraduate MIS courses. We usually begin the semester with Access database instruction. We assign the Access database tutorials and then a case to each student. Then, to teach students how to use the Excel decision support system, we do the same thing: We assign a tutorial and then a case.

Some instructors have asked for access to extra cases, especially in the second semester of a school year. For example, they assigned the integration case in the fall, and they need another one for the spring. To meet this need, we have set up an online "Hall of Fame" that features some of our favorite cases from prior editions. These password-protected cases are available to instructors on the Cengage Web site. Go to *www.cengage.com/login* and search for this textbook by title, author, or ISBN. Note that the cases are in Microsoft Office 2016 format.

TECHNICAL INFORMATION

The cases in this textbook were written using Microsoft Office 2016, and the textbook was tested for quality assurance using the Windows 10 operating system, Microsoft Access 2016, and Microsoft Excel 2016.

Data Files and Solution Files

We have created "starter" data files for the Excel cases, so students need not spend time typing in the spreadsheet skeleton. Cases 11 and 12 also ask students to load Access and Excel starter files. All these files are on the Cengage Web site, which is available both to students and instructors. Instructors should go to *www.cengage.com/login* and search for this textbook by title, author, or ISBN. Students will find the files at *www.cengagebrain.com/login*. You are granted a license to copy the data files to any computer or computer network used by people who have purchased this textbook.

Solutions to the material in the text are available to instructors at *www.cengage.com/login*. Search for this textbook by title, author, or ISBN. The solutions are password protected.

ACKNOWLEDGMENTS

We would like to give many thanks to the team at Cengage, including our Associate Product Manager, Kate Mason; our Development Editor, Dan Seiter; and our Content Project Manager, Michele Stulga. As always, we acknowledge our students' diligent work.

PART 1

DATABASE CASES USING ACCESS

TUTORIAL A

DATABASE DESIGN

This tutorial has three sections. The first section briefly reviews basic database terminology. The second section teaches database design. The third section features a database design problem for practice.

REVIEW OF TERMINOLOGY

You will begin by reviewing some basic terms that will be used throughout this textbook. In Access, a **database** is a group of related objects that are saved in one file. An Access **object** can be a table, form, query, or report. You can identify an Access database file by its suffix, .accdb.

A **table** consists of data that is arrayed in rows and columns. A **row** of data is called a **record**. A **column** of data is called a **field**. Thus, a record is a set of related fields. The fields in a table should be related to one another in some way. For example, a company might want to keep its employee data together by creating a database table called Employee. That table would contain data fields about employees, such as their names and addresses. It would not have data fields about the company's customers; that data would go in a Customer table.

A field's values have a **data type** that is declared when the table is defined. Thus, when data is entered into the database, the software knows how to interpret each entry. Data types in Access include the following:

- *Text* for words
- *Integer* for whole numbers
- *Double* for numbers that have a decimal value
- *Currency* for numbers that represent dollars and cents
- *Yes/No* for variables that have only two values (such as 1/0, on/off, yes/no, and true/false)
- *Date/Time* for variables that are dates or times

Each database table should have a **primary key** field—a field in which each record has a *unique* value. For example, in an Employee table, a field called Employee Identification Number (EIN) could serve as a primary key. (This assumes that each employee is given a number when hired and that these numbers are not reused later.) Sometimes, a table does not have a single field whose values are all different. In that case, two or more fields are combined into a **compound primary key**. The combination of the fields' values is unique.

Database tables should be logically related to one another. For example, suppose a company has an Employee table with fields for EIN, Name, Address, and Telephone Number. For payroll purposes, the company has an Hours Worked table with a field that summarizes Labor Hours for individual employees. The relationship between the Employee table and Hours Worked table needs to be established in the database, so you can determine the number of hours worked by any employee. To create this relationship, you include the primary key field from the Employee table (EIN) as a field in the Hours Worked table. In the Hours Worked table, the EIN field is then called a **foreign key** because it's from a "foreign" table.

In Access, data can be entered directly into a table, or it can be entered into a form, which then inserts the data into a table. A **form** is a database object that is created from an existing table to make the process of entering data more user-friendly.

A **query** is the database equivalent of a question that is posed about data in a table (or tables). For example, suppose a manager wants to know the names of employees who have worked for the company for more than five years. A query could be designed to search the Employee table for the information. The query would be run, and its output would answer the question.

Queries can be designed to search multiple tables at a time. For this to work, the tables must be connected by a **join** operation, which links tables on the values in a field that they have in common. The common field acts as a "hinge" for the joined tables; when the query is run, the query generator treats the joined tables as one large table.

In Access, queries that answer a question are called *select queries* because they select relevant data from the database records. Queries also can be designed to change data in records, add a record to the end of a table, or delete entire records from a table. These queries are called **update**, **append**, and **delete** queries, respectively.

Access has a **report** generator that can be used to format a table's data or a query's output.

DATABASE DESIGN

Designing a database involves determining which tables belong in the database and then creating the fields that belong in each table. This section begins with an introduction to key database design concepts, then discusses design rules you should use when building a database. First, the following key concepts are defined:

- Entities
- Relationships
- Attributes

Database Design Concepts

Computer scientists have highly formalized ways of documenting a database's logic. Learning their notations and mechanics can be time-consuming and difficult. In fact, doing so usually takes a good portion of a systems analysis and design course. This tutorial will teach you database design by emphasizing practical business knowledge; the approach should enable you to design serviceable databases quickly. Your instructor may add more formal techniques.

A database models the logic of an organization's operation, so your first task is to understand the operation. You can talk to managers and workers, make your own observations, and look at business documents, such as sales records. Your goal is to identify the business's "entities" (sometimes called *objects*). An **entity** is a thing or event that the database will contain. Every entity has characteristics, called **attributes**, and one or more **relationships** to other entities. Let's take a closer look.

Entities

As previously mentioned, an entity is a tangible thing or an event. The reason for identifying entities is that *an entity eventually becomes a table in the database*. Entities that are things are easy to identify. For example, consider a video store. The database for the video store would probably need to contain the names of DVDs and the names of customers who rent them, so you would have one entity named Video and another named Customer.

In contrast, entities that are events can be more difficult to identify, probably because they are more conceptual. However, events are real, and they are important. In the video store example, one event would be Video Rental and another event would be Hours Worked by employees.

In general, your analysis of an organization's operations is made easier when you realize that organizations usually have physical entities such as these:

- Employees
- Customers
- Inventory (products or services)
- Suppliers

Thus, the database for most organizations would have a table for each of these entities. Your analysis also can be made easier by knowing that organizations engage in transactions internally (within the company) and externally (with the outside world). Such transactions are explained in an introductory accounting course, but most people understand them from events that occur in daily life. Consider the following examples:

- Organizations generate revenue from sales or interest earned. Revenue-generating transactions include event entities called Sales and Interest Earned.
- Organizations incur expenses from paying hourly employees and purchasing materials from suppliers. Hours Worked and Purchases are event entities in the databases of most organizations.

Thus, identifying entities is a matter of observing what happens in an organization. Your powers of observation are aided by knowing what entities exist in the databases of most organizations.

Relationships

As an analyst building a database, you should consider the relationship of each entity to the other entities you have identified. For example, a college database might contain entities for Student, Course, and Section to contain data about each. A relationship between Student and Section could be expressed as "Students enroll in sections."

An analyst also must consider the **cardinality** of any relationship. Cardinality can be one-to-one, one-to-many, or many-to-many:

- In a one-to-one relationship, one instance of the first entity is related to just one instance of the second entity.
- In a one-to-many relationship, one instance of the first entity is related to many instances of the second entity, but each instance of the second entity is related to only one instance of the first.
- In a many-to-many relationship, one instance of the first entity is related to many instances of the second entity, and one instance of the second entity is related to many instances of the first.

For a more concrete understanding of cardinality, consider again the college database with the Student, Course, and Section entities. The university catalog shows that a course such as Accounting 101 can have more than one section: 01, 02, 03, 04, and so on. Thus, you can observe the following relationships:

- The relationship between the entities Course and Section is one-to-many. Each course has many sections, but each section is associated with just one course.
- The relationship between Student and Section is many-to-many. Each student can be in more than one section, because each student can take more than one course. Also, each section has more than one student.

Thinking about relationships and their cardinalities may seem tedious to you. However, as you work through the cases in this text, you will see that this type of analysis can be valuable in designing databases. In the case of many-to-many relationships, you should determine the tables a given database needs; in the case of one-to-many relationships, you should decide which fields the tables need to share.

Attributes

An attribute is a characteristic of an entity. You identify attributes of an entity because *attributes become a table's fields*. If an entity can be thought of as a noun, an attribute can be considered an adjective that describes the noun. Continuing with the college database example, consider the Student entity. Students have names, so Last Name would be an attribute of the Student entity and therefore a field in the Student table. First Name would be another attribute, as well as Address, Phone Number, and other descriptive fields.

Sometimes it can be difficult to tell the difference between an attribute and an entity, but one good way is to ask whether more than one attribute is possible for each entity. If more than one instance is possible, but you do not know the number in advance, you are working with an entity. For example, assume that a student could have a maximum of two addresses—one for home and one for college. You could specify attributes Address 1 and Address 2. Next, consider that you might not know the number of student addresses in advance, meaning that all addresses have to be recorded. In that case, you would not know how many fields to set aside in the Student table for addresses. Therefore, you would need a separate Student Addresses table (entity) that would show any number of addresses for a given student.

Database Design Rules

As described previously, your first task in database design is to understand the logic of the business situation. Once you understand this logic, you are ready to build the database. To create a context for learning about database design, look at a hypothetical business operation and its database needs.

Example: The Talent Agency

Suppose you have been asked to build a database for a talent agency that books musical bands into nightclubs. The agent needs a database to keep track of the agency's transactions and to answer day-to-day questions. For example, a club manager often wants to know which bands are available on a certain date at a certain time, or wants to know the agent's fee for a certain band. The agent may want to see a list of all band members and the instrument each person plays, or a list of all bands that have three members.

Suppose that you have talked to the agent and have observed the agency's business operation. You conclude that your database needs to reflect the following facts:

1. A booking is an event in which a certain band plays in a particular club on a particular date, starting and ending at certain times and performing for a specific fee. A band can play more than once a day. The Heartbreakers, for example, could play at the East End Cafe in the afternoon and then at the West End Cafe on the same night. For each booking, the club pays the talent agent. The agent keeps a 5 percent fee and then gives the remainder of the payment to the band.

2. Each band has at least two members and an unlimited maximum number of members. The agent notes a telephone number of just one band member, which is used as the band's contact number. No two bands have the same name or telephone number.

3. Band member names are not unique. For example, two bands could each have a member named Sally Smith.

4. The agent keeps track of just one instrument that each band member plays. For the purpose of this database, "vocals" are considered an instrument.

5. Each band has a desired fee. For example, the Lightmetal band might want $700 per booking and would expect the agent to try to get at least that amount.

6. Each nightclub has a name, an address, and a contact person. The contact person has a telephone number that the agent uses to call the club. No two clubs have the same name, contact person, or telephone number. Each club has a target fee. The contact person will try to get the agent to accept that fee for a band's appearance.

7. Some clubs feed the band members for free; others do not.

Before continuing with this tutorial, you might try to design the agency's database on your own. Ask yourself: What are the entities? Recall that business databases usually have Customer, Employee, and Inventory entities, as well as an entity for the event that generates revenue transactions. Each entity becomes a table in the database. What are the relationships among the entities? For each entity, what are its attributes? For each table, what is the primary key?

Six Database Design Rules

Assume that you have gathered information about the business situation in the talent agency example. Now you want to identify the tables required for the database and the fields needed in each table. Observe the following six rules:

Rule 1: You do not need a table for the business. The database represents the entire business. Thus, in the example, Agent and Agency are not entities.

Rule 2: Identify the entities in the business description. Look for typical things and events that will become tables in the database. In the talent agency example, you should be able to observe the following entities:

- *Things*: The product (inventory for sale) is Band. The customer is Club.
- *Events*: The revenue-generating transaction is Bookings.

You might ask yourself: Is there an Employee entity? Isn't Instrument an entity? Those issues will be discussed as the rules are explained.

Rule 3: Look for relationships among the entities. Look for one-to-many relationships between entities. The relationship between those entities must be established in the tables, using a foreign key. For details, see the following discussion in Rule 4 about the relationship between Band and Band Member.

Look for many-to-many relationships between entities. Each of these relationships requires a third entity that associates the two entities in the relationship. Recall the many-to-many relationship from the college database scenario that involved Student and Section entities. To display the enrollment of specific students in specific sections, a third table would be required. The mechanics of creating such a table are described in Rule 4 during the discussion of the relationship between Band and Club.

Rule 4: Look for attributes of each entity and designate a primary key. As previously mentioned, you should think of the entities in your database as nouns. You should then create a list of adjectives that describe those nouns. These adjectives are the attributes that will become the table's fields. After you have identified fields for each table, you should check to see whether a field has unique values. If such a field exists, designate it as the primary key field; otherwise, designate a compound primary key.

In the talent agency example, the attributes, or fields, of the Band entity are Band Name, Band Phone Number, and Desired Fee, as shown in Figure A-1. Assume that no two bands have the same name, so the primary key field can be Band Name. The data type of each field is shown.

BAND	
Field Name	Data Type
Band Name (primary key)	Text
Band Phone Number	Text
Desired Fee	Currency

FIGURE A-1   The Band table and its fields

Two Band records are shown in Figure A-2.

Band Name (primary key)	Band Phone Number	Desired Fee
Heartbreakers	981 831 1765	$800
Lightmetal	981 831 2000	$700

FIGURE A-2   Records in the Band table

If two bands might have the same name, Band Name would not be a good primary key, so a different unique identifier would be needed. Such situations are common. Most businesses have many types of inventory, and duplicate names are possible. The typical solution is to assign a number to each product to use as the primary key field. A college could have more than one faculty member with the same name, so each faculty member would be assigned an EIN. Similarly, banks assign a personal identification number (PIN) for each depositor. Each automobile produced by a car manufacturer gets a unique vehicle identification number (VIN). Most businesses assign a number to each sale, called an invoice number. (The next time you go to a grocery store, note the number on your receipt. It will be different from the number on the next customer's receipt.)

At this point, you might be wondering why Band Member would not be an attribute of Band. The answer is that, although you must record each band member, you do not know in advance how many members are in each band. Therefore, you do not know how many fields to allocate to the Band table for members. (Another way to think about band members is that they are the agency's employees, in effect. Databases for organizations usually have an Employee entity.) You should create a Band Member table with the attributes Member ID Number, Member Name, Band Name, Instrument, and Phone. A Member ID Number field is needed because member names may not be unique. The table and its fields are shown in Figure A-3.

BAND MEMBER	
Field Name	Data Type
Member ID Number (primary key)	Text
Member Name	Text
Band Name (foreign key)	Text
Instrument	Text
Phone	Text

FIGURE A-3   The Band Member table and its fields

Note in Figure A-3 that the phone number is classified as a Text data type because the field values will not be used in an arithmetic computation. The benefit is that Text data type values take up fewer bytes than Numerical or Currency data type values; therefore, the file uses less storage space. You should also use the Text data type for number values such as zip codes.

Five records in the Band Member table are shown in Figure A-4.

Member ID Number (primary key)	Member Name	Band Name	Instrument	Phone
0001	Pete Goff	Heartbreakers	Guitar	981 444 1111
0002	Joe Goff	Heartbreakers	Vocals	981 444 1234
0003	Sue Smith	Heartbreakers	Keyboard	981 555 1199
0004	Joe Jackson	Lightmetal	Sax	981 888 1654
0005	Sue Hoopes	Lightmetal	Piano	981 888 1765

FIGURE A-4   Records in the Band Member table

You can include Instrument as a field in the Band Member table because the agent records only one instrument for each band member. Thus, you can use the instrument as a way to describe a band member, much like the phone number is part of the description. Phone could not be the primary key because two members might share a telephone and because members might change their numbers, making database administration more difficult.

You might ask why Band Name is included in the Band Member table. The common-sense reason is that you did not include the Member Name in the Band table. You must relate bands and members somewhere, and the Band Member table is the place to do it.

To think about this relationship in another way, consider the cardinality of the relationship between Band and Band Member. It is a one-to-many relationship: one band has many members, but each member in the database plays in just one band. You establish such a relationship in the database by using the primary key field of one table as a foreign key in the other table. In Band Member, the foreign key Band Name is used to establish the relationship between the member and his or her band.

The attributes of the Club entity are Club Name, Address, Contact Name, Club Phone Number, Preferred Fee, and Feed Band?. The Club table can define the Club entity, as shown in Figure A-5.

CLUB	
Field Name	**Data Type**
Club Name (primary key)	Text
Address	Text
Contact Name	Text
Club Phone Number	Text
Preferred Fee	Currency
Feed Band?	Yes/No

FIGURE A-5   The Club table and its fields

Two records in the Club table are shown in Figure A-6.

Club Name (primary key)	Address	Contact Name	Club Phone Number	Preferred Fee	Feed Band?
East End	1 Duce St.	Al Pots	981 444 8877	$600	Yes
West End	99 Duce St.	Val Dots	981 555 0011	$650	No

FIGURE A-6   Records in the Club table

You might wonder why Bands Booked into Club (or a similar name) is not an attribute of the Club table. There are two reasons. First, you do not know in advance how many bookings a club will have, so the value cannot be an attribute. Second, Bookings is the agency's revenue-generating transaction, an event entity, and you need a table for that business transaction. Consider the booking transaction next.

You know that the talent agent books a certain band into a certain club for a specific fee on a certain date, starting and ending at a specific time. From that information, you can see that the attributes of the Bookings entity are Band Name, Club Name, Booking Date, Start Time, End Time, and Fee. The Bookings table and its fields are shown in Figure A-7.

BOOKINGS	
Field Name	**Data Type**
Band Name (foreign key)	Text
Club Name (foreign key)	Text
Booking Date	Date/Time
Start Time	Date/Time
End Time	Date/Time
Fee	Currency

FIGURE A-7   The Bookings table and its fields—and no designation of a primary key

Some records in the Bookings table are shown in Figure A-8.

Band Name	Club Name	Booking Date	Start Time	End Time	Fee
Heartbreakers	East End	11/21/16	21:30	23:30	$800
Heartbreakers	East End	11/22/16	21:00	23:30	$750
Heartbreakers	West End	11/28/16	19:00	21:00	$500
Lightmetal	East End	11/21/16	18:00	20:00	$700
Lightmetal	West End	11/22/16	19:00	21:00	$750

FIGURE A-8   Records in the Bookings table

Note that no single field is guaranteed to have unique values, because each band is likely to be booked many times and each club might be used many times. Furthermore, each date and time can appear more than once. Thus, no one field can be the primary key.

If a table does not have a single primary key field, you can make a compound primary key whose field values will be unique when taken together. Because a band can be in only one place at a time, one possible solution is to create a compound key from the Band Name, Booking Date, and Start Time fields. An alternative solution is to create a compound primary key from the Club Name, Booking Date, and Start Time fields.

If you don't want a compound key, you could create a field called Booking Number. Each booking would then have its own unique number, similar to an invoice number.

You can also think about this event entity in a different way. Over time, a band plays in many clubs, and each club hires many bands. Thus, Band and Club have a many-to-many relationship, which signals the need for a table between the two entities. A Bookings table would associate the Band and Club tables. You implement an associative table by including the primary keys from the two tables that are associated. In this case, the primary keys from the Band and Club tables are included as foreign keys in the Bookings table.

Rule 5: Avoid data redundancy. You should not include extra (redundant) fields in a table. Redundant fields take up extra disk space and lead to data entry errors because the same value must be entered in multiple tables, increasing the chance of a keystroke error. In large databases, keeping track of multiple instances of the same data is nearly impossible, so contradictory data entries become a problem.

Consider this example: Why wouldn't Club Phone Number be included in the Bookings table as a field? After all, the agent might have to call about a last-minute booking change and could quickly look up the number in the Bookings table. Assume that the Bookings table includes Booking Number as the primary key and Club Phone Number as a field. Figure A-9 shows the Bookings table with the additional field.

BOOKINGS	
Field Name	Data Type
Booking Number (primary key)	Text
Band Name (foreign key)	Text
Club Name (foreign key)	Text
Club Phone Number	Text
Booking Date	Date/Time
Start Time	Date/Time
End Time	Date/Time
Fee	Currency

FIGURE A-9   The Bookings table with an unnecessary field—Club Phone Number

The fields Booking Date, Start Time, End Time, and Fee logically depend on the Booking Number primary key—they help define the booking. Band Name and Club Name are foreign keys and are needed to establish the relationship between the Band, Club, and Bookings tables. But what about Club Phone Number? It is not defined by the Booking Number. It is defined by Club Name—*in other words, it is a function of the club, not of the booking.* Thus, the Club Phone Number field does not belong in the Bookings table. It is already in the Club table.

Perhaps you can see the practical data-entry problem of including Club Phone Number in Bookings. Suppose a club changed its contact phone number. The agent could easily change the number one time, in the Club table. However, the agent would need to remember which other tables contained the field and change the values there too. In a small database, this task might not be difficult, but in larger databases, having redundant fields in many tables makes such maintenance difficult, which means that redundant data is often incorrect.

You might object by saying, "What about all of those foreign keys? Aren't they redundant?" In a sense, they are. But they are needed to establish the one-to-many relationship between one entity and another, as discussed previously.

Rule 6: Do not include a field if it can be calculated from other fields. A calculated field is made using the query generator. Thus, the agent's fee is not included in the Bookings table because it can be calculated by query (here, 5 percent multiplied by the booking fee).

The Talent Agency Tables in Microsoft Access

The previous sections and figures describe the talent agency database tables, but the relationships between the tables might be more clear in a graphical representation, which you can create in Microsoft Access (see Figure A-10).

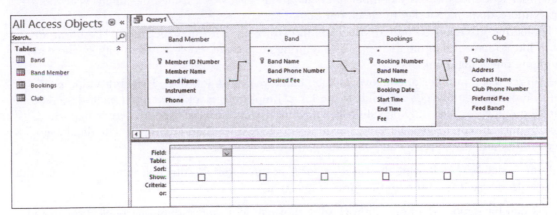

FIGURE A-10   Graphical view of talent agency tables

In Tutorial B, you will learn how to define a table in Access—in other words, you will input the fields and their data types and designate the table's primary key. Tutorial B also explains how to query tables graphically in Access.

Figure A-10 shows the talent agency's tables as they would be used in the Access query generator. The relationships between tables are indicated by the links between the tables. For example, the Band Name field is the primary key in the Band table and a foreign key in the Band Member table. The two tables are linked by a common field to demonstrate that a band member is partially described by the name of a band. In a similar way, a club's name partially describes Bookings, and the two tables can be linked by a common field, Club Name.

PRACTICE DATABASE DESIGN PROBLEM

Imagine that your town library wants to keep track of its business in a database, and that you have been called in to build the database. You talk to the town librarian, review the old paper-based records, and watch people use the library for a few days. You learn the following about the library:

1. Any resident of the town can get a library card simply by asking for one. The library considers each cardholder a member of the library.

2. The librarian wants to be able to contact members by telephone and by mail. She calls members when books are overdue or when requested materials become available. She likes to mail a thank-you note to each patron on his or her anniversary of becoming a member of the library. Without a database, contacting members efficiently can be difficult; for example, multiple members can have the same name. Also, a parent and a child might have the same first and last name, live at the same address, and share a phone.

3. The librarian tries to keep track of each member's reading interests. When new books come in, the librarian alerts members whose interests match those books. For example, long-time member Sue Doaks is interested in reading Western novels, growing orchids, and baking bread. There must be some way to match her interests with available books. One complication is that, although the librarian wants to track all of a member's reading interests, she wants to classify each book as being in just one category of interest. For example, the classic gardening book *Orchids of France* would be classified as a book about orchids or a book about France, but not both.

4. The library stocks thousands of books. Each book has a title and any number of authors. Also, more than one book in the library might have the same title. Similarly, multiple authors might have the same name.

5. A writer could be the author of more than one book.

6. A book will be checked out repeatedly as time goes on. For example, *Orchids of France* could be checked out by one member in March, by another member in July, and by another member in September.

7. The library must be able to identify whether a book is checked out.

8. A member can check out any number of books in one visit. Also, a member might visit the library more than once a day to check out books.

9. All books that are checked out are due back in two weeks, with no exceptions. The librarian would like to have an automated way of generating an overdue book list each day so she can telephone offending members.

10. The library has a number of employees. Each employee has a job title. The librarian is paid a salary, but other employees are paid by the hour. Employees clock in and out each day. Assume that all employees work only one shift per day and that all are paid weekly. Pay is deposited directly into an employee's checking account—no checks are hand-delivered. The database needs to include the librarian and all other employees.

Design the library's database, following the rules set forth in this tutorial. Your instructor will specify the format of your work. Here are a few hints in the form of questions:

- A book can have more than one author. An author can write more than one book. How would you describe the relationship between books and authors?

- The library lends books for free, of course. If you were to think of checking out a book as a sales transaction for zero revenue, how would you handle the library's revenue-generating event?

- A member can borrow any number of books at one checkout. A book can be checked out more than once. How would you describe the relationship between checkouts and books?

MICROSOFT ACCESS

Microsoft Access is a relational database package that runs on the Microsoft Windows operating system. There are many different versions of Access; this tutorial was prepared using Access 2016.

Before using this tutorial, you should know the fundamentals of Access and know how to use Windows. This tutorial explains advanced Access skills you will need to complete database case studies. The tutorial concludes with a discussion of common Access problems and how to solve them.

To prevent losing your work, always observe proper file-saving and closing procedures. To exit Access, click the File tab and select Close, then click the Close button in the upper-right corner. Always end your work with these steps. If you remove your USB key or other portable storage device when database forms and tables are shown on the screen, you will lose your work.

To begin this tutorial, you will create a new database called Employee.

AT THE KEYBOARD

Open Access. Click the Blank desktop database icon from the templates list. Name the database Employee. Click the file folder next to the filename to browse for the folder where you want to save the file. Click the new folder, click Open, and then click OK. Otherwise, your file will be saved automatically in the Documents folder. Click the Create button.

A portion of your opening screen should resemble the screen shown in Figure B-1.

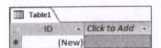

FIGURE B-1   Entering data in Datasheet view

When you create a table, Access opens it in Datasheet view by default. Because you will use Design view to build your tables, close the new table by clicking the X in the upper-right corner of the table window that corresponds to Close "Table1." You are now on the Home tab in the Database window of Access, as shown in Figure B-2. From this screen, you can create or change objects.

FIGURE B-2   The Database window Home tab in Access

CREATING TABLES

Your database will contain data about employees, their wage rates, and the hours they worked.

Defining Tables

In the Database window, build three new tables using the following instructions.

AT THE KEYBOARD

Defining the Employee Table

This table contains permanent data about employees. To create the table, click the Create tab and then click Table Design in the Tables group. The table's fields are Last Name, First Name, Employee ID, Street Address, City, State, Zip, Date Hired, and US Citizen. The Employee ID field is the primary key field. Change the lengths of Short Text fields from the default 255 spaces to more appropriate lengths; for example, the Last Name field might be 30 spaces, and the Zip field might be 10 spaces. Your completed definition should resemble the one shown in Figure B-3.

Field Name	Data Type	Description (Optional)
Last Name	Short Text	
First Name	Short Text	
Employee ID	Short Text	
Street Address	Short Text	
City	Short Text	
State	Short Text	
Zip	Short Text	
Date Hired	Date/Time	
US Citizen	Yes/No	

FIGURE B-3   Fields in the Employee table

When you finish, click the File tab, select Save As, select Save Object As, click the Save As button, and then enter a name for the table. In this example, the table is named Employee. (It is a coincidence that the Employee table has the same name as its database file.) After entering the name, click OK in the Save As window. Close the table by clicking the Close button (X) that corresponds to the Employee table.

Defining the Wage Data Table

This table contains permanent data about employees and their wage rates. The table's fields are Employee ID, Wage Rate, and Salaried. The Employee ID field is the primary key field. Use the data types shown in Figure B-4. Your definition should resemble the one shown in Figure B-4.

Field Name	Data Type	Description (Optional)
Employee ID	Short Text	
Wage Rate	Currency	
Salaried	Yes/No	

FIGURE B-4   Fields in the Wage Data table

Click the File tab and then select Save As, select Save Object As, and click the Save As button to save the table definition. Name the table Wage Data.

Defining the Hours Worked Table

The purpose of this table is to record the number of hours that employees work each week during the year. The table's three fields are Employee ID (which has a Short Text data type), Week # (number–long integer), and Hours (number–double). The Employee ID and Week # are the compound keys.

In the following example, the employee with ID number 08965 worked 40 hours in Week 1 of the year and 52 hours in Week 2.

Employee ID	Week #	Hours
08965	1	40
08965	2	52

Note that no single field can be the primary key field because 08965 is an entry for each week. In other words, if this employee works each week of the year, 52 records will have the same Employee ID value at the end of the year. Thus, Employee ID values will not distinguish records. No other single field can distinguish these records either, because other employees will have worked during the same week number and some employees will have worked the same number of hours. For example, 40 hours—which corresponds to a full-time workweek—would be a common entry for many weeks.

All of this presents a problem because a table must have a primary key field in Access. The solution is to use a compound primary key; that is, use values from more than one field to create a combined field that will distinguish records. The best compound key to use for the current example consists of the Employee ID field and the Week # field, because as each person works each week, the week number changes. In other words, there is only *one* combination of Employee ID 08965 and Week # 1. Because those values *can occur in only one record*, the combination distinguishes that record from all others.

The first step of setting a compound key is to highlight the fields in the key. Those fields must appear one after the other in the table definition screen. (Plan ahead for that format.) As an alternative, you can highlight one field, hold down the Control key, and highlight the next field.

AT THE KEYBOARD

In the Hours Worked table, click the first field's left prefix area (known as the row selector), hold down the mouse button, and drag down to highlight the names of all fields in the compound primary key. Your screen should resemble the one shown in Figure B-5.

Field Name	Data Type	Description (Optional)
Employee ID	Short Text	
Week #	Number	
Hours	Number	

FIGURE B-5 Selecting fields for the compound primary key for the Hours Worked table

Now click the Key icon. Your screen should resemble the one shown in Figure B-6.

Field Name	Data Type	Description (Optional)
Employee ID	Short Text	
Week #	Number	
Hours	Number	

FIGURE B-6 The compound primary key for the Hours Worked table

You have created the compound primary key and finished defining the table. Click the File tab and then select Save As, select Save Object As, and click the Save As button to save the table as Hours Worked.

Adding Records to a Table

At this point, you have set up the skeletons of three tables. The tables have no data records yet. If you printed the tables now, you would only see column headings (the field names). The most direct way to enter data into a table is to double-click the table's name in the navigation pane at the left side of the screen and then type the data directly into the cells.

NOTE

To display and open the database objects, Access 2016 uses a navigation pane, which is on the left side of the Access window.

AT THE KEYBOARD

In the navigation pane, double-click the Employee table. Your data entry screen should resemble the one shown in Figure B-7.

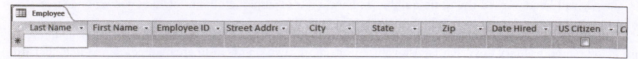

FIGURE B-7   The data entry screen for the Employee table

The Employee table has many fields, some of which may be off the screen to the right. Scroll to see obscured fields. (Scrolling happens automatically as you enter data.) Figure B-7 shows all of the fields on the screen.

Enter your data one field value at a time. Note that the first row is empty when you begin. Each time you finish entering a value, press Enter to move the cursor to the next cell. After you enter data in the last cell in a row, the cursor moves to the first cell of the next row *and* Access automatically saves the record. Thus, you do not need to click the File tab and then select Save after entering data into a table.

When entering data in your table, you should enter dates in the following format: 6/15/10. Access automatically expands the entry to the proper format in output.

Also note that Yes/No variables are clicked (checked) for Yes; otherwise, the box is left blank for No. You can change the box from Yes to No by clicking it.

Enter the data shown in Figure B-8 into the Employee table. If you make errors in data entry, click the cell, backspace over the error, and type the correction.

Last Name	First Name	Employee ID	Street Address	City	State	Zip	Date Hired	US Citizen	Click to Add
Howard	Jane	11411	28 Sally Dr	Glasgow	DE	19702	6/1/2017	☑	
Johnson	John	12345	30 Elm St	Newark	DE	19711	6/1/1996	☑	
Smith	Albert	14890	44 Duce St	Odessa	DE	19722	7/15/1987	☑	
Jones	Sue	22282	18 Spruce St	Newark	DE	19716	7/15/2004	☐	
Ruth	Billy	71460	1 Tater Dr	Baltimore	MD	20111	8/15/1999	☐	
Add	Your	Data	Here	Elkton	MD	21921		☑	
								☐	

FIGURE B-8   Data for the Employee table

Note that the sixth record is *your* data record. Assume that you live in Elkton, Maryland; were hired on today's date (enter the date); and are a U.S. citizen. Make up a fictitious Employee ID number. For purposes of this tutorial, the sixth record has been created using the name of one of this text's authors and the employee ID 09911.

After adding records to the Employee table, open the Wage Data table and enter the data shown in Figure B-9.

Employee ID	Wage Rate	Salaried
11411	$10.00	☐
12345	$0.00	☑
14890	$12.00	☐
22282	$0.00	☑
71460	$0.00	☑
Your Employee ID	$8.00	☐
	$0.00	☐

FIGURE B-9   Data for the Wage Data table

In this table, you are again asked to create a new entry. For this record, enter your own employee ID. Also assume that you earn $8 an hour and are not salaried. Note that when an employee's Salaried box is not checked (in other words, Salaried = No), the implication is that the employee is paid by the hour. Because salaried employees are not paid by the hour, their hourly rate is 0.00.

When you finish creating the Wage Data table, open the Hours Worked table and enter the data shown in Figure B-10.

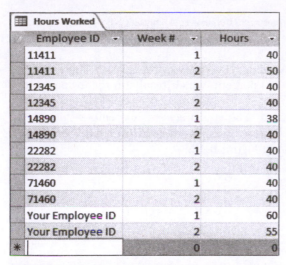

FIGURE B-10   Data for the Hours Worked table

Notice that salaried employees are always given 40 hours. Nonsalaried employees (including you) might work any number of hours. For your record, enter your fictitious employee ID, 60 hours worked for Week 1, and 55 hours worked for Week 2.

CREATING QUERIES

Because you know how to create basic queries, this section explains the advanced queries you will create in the cases in this book.

Using Calculated Fields in Queries

A **calculated field** is an output field made up of *other* field values. A calculated field can be a field in a table; here it is created in the query generator. The calculated field here does not become part of the table—it is just part of the query output. The best way to understand this process is to work through an example.

AT THE KEYBOARD

Suppose you want to see the employee IDs and wage rates of hourly workers, and the new wage rates if all employees were given a 10 percent raise. To view that information, show the employee ID, the current wage rate, and the higher rate, which should be titled New Rate in the output. Figure B-11 shows how to set up the query.

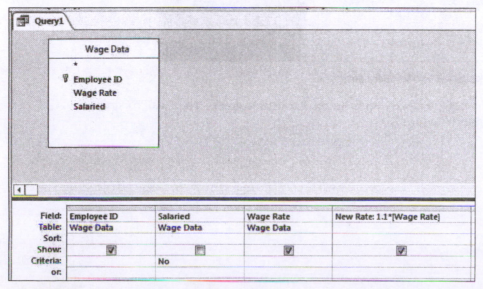

FIGURE B-11   Query setup for the calculated field

To set up this query, you need to select hourly workers by using the Salaried field with Criteria = No. Note in Figure B-11 that the Show box for the field is not checked, so the Salaried field values will not appear in the query output.

Note the expression for the calculated field, which you can see in the far-right field cell:

New Rate: 1.1 * [Wage Rate]

The term *New Rate:* merely specifies the desired output heading. (Don't forget the colon.) The rest of the expression, 1.1 * [Wage Rate], multiplies the old wage rate by 110 percent, which results in the 10 percent raise.

In the expression, the field name Wage Rate must be enclosed in square brackets. Remember this rule: *Any time an Access expression refers to a field name, the field name must be enclosed in square brackets.*

If you run this query, your output should resemble the one in Figure B-12.

Employee ID	Wage Rate	New Rate
11411	$10.00	11
14890	$12.00	13.2
09911	$8.00	8.8
*	$0.00	

FIGURE B-12   Output for a query with calculated field

Notice that the calculated field output is not shown in Currency format but as a Double—a number with digits after the decimal point. To convert the output to Currency format, select the output column by clicking the line above the calculated field expression. The column darkens to indicate its selection. Your data entry screen should resemble the one shown in Figure B-13.

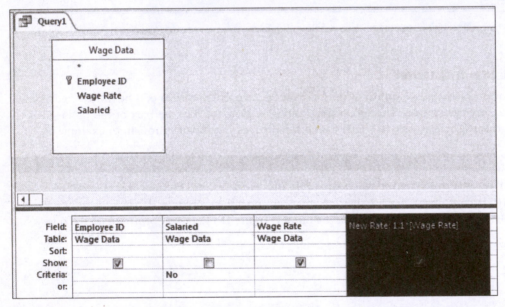

FIGURE B-13   Activating a calculated field in query design

Then, on the Design tab, click Property Sheet in the Show/Hide group. The Field Properties sheet appears, as shown on the right in Figure B-14.

FIGURE B-14   Field properties of a calculated field

Click Format and choose Currency, as shown in Figure B-15. Then click the X in the upper-right corner of the window to close it.

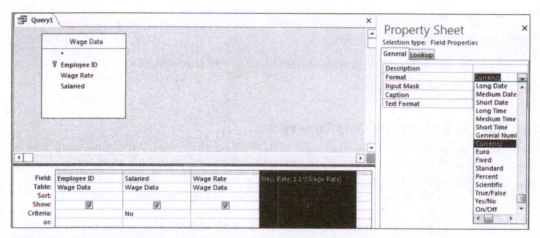

FIGURE B-15   Currency format of a calculated field

When you run the query, the output should resemble the one in Figure B-16.

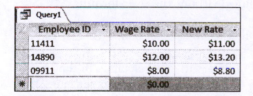

FIGURE B-16   Query output with formatted calculated field

Next, you examine how to avoid errors when making calculated fields.

Avoiding Errors When Making Calculated Fields

Follow these guidelines to avoid making errors in calculated fields:

- Do not enter the expression in the *Criteria* cell as if the field definition were a filter. You are making a field, so enter the expression in the *Field* cell.

- Spell, capitalize, and space a field's name *exactly* as you did in the table definition. If the table definition differs from what you type, Access thinks you are defining a new field by that name. Access then prompts you to enter values for the new field, which it calls a Parameter Query field. This problem is easy to debug because of the tag *Parameter Query*. If Access asks you to enter values for a parameter, you almost certainly misspelled a field name in an expression in a calculated field or criterion.

  For example, here are some errors you might make for Wage Rate:

  Misspelling: (Wag Rate)

  Case change: (wage Rate/WAGE RATE)

  Spacing change: (WageRate/Wage Rate)

- Do not use parentheses or curly braces instead of the square brackets. Also, do not put parentheses inside square brackets. You *can*, however, use parentheses outside the square brackets in the normal algebraic manner.

  For example, suppose that you want to multiply Hours by Wage Rate to get a field called Wages Owed. This is the correct expression:

  Wages Owed: [Wage Rate] * [Hours]

  The following expression also would be correct:

  Wages Owed: ([Wage Rate] * [Hours])

  But it would *not* be correct to omit the inside brackets, which is a common error:

  Wages Owed: [Wage Rate * Hours]

"Relating" Two or More Tables by the Join Operation

Often, the data you need for a query is in more than one table. To complete the query, you must **join** the tables by linking the common fields. One rule of thumb is that joins are made on fields that have common *values*, and those fields often can be key fields. The names of the join fields are irrelevant; also, the names of the tables or fields to be joined may be the same, but it is not required for an effective join.

Make a join by bringing in (adding) the tables needed. Next, decide which fields you will join. Then click one field name and hold down the left mouse button while you drag the cursor over to the other field's name in its window. Release the button. Access inserts a line to signify the join. (If a relationship between two tables has been formed elsewhere, Access inserts the line automatically, and you do not have to perform the click-and-drag operation. Access often inserts join lines without the user forming relationships.)

You can join more than two tables. The common fields *need not* be the same in all tables; that is, you can daisy-chain them together.

A common join error is to add a table to the query and then fail to link it to another table. In that case, you will have a table floating in the top part of the query by example (QBE) screen. When you run the query, your output will show the same records over and over. The error is unmistakable because there is *so much* redundant output. The two rules are to add only the tables you need and to link all tables.

Next, you will work through an example of a query that needs a join.

AT THE KEYBOARD

Suppose you want to see the last names, employee IDs, wage rates, salary status, and citizenship only for U.S. citizens and hourly workers. Because the data is spread across two tables, Employee and Wage Data, you should add both tables and pull down the five fields you need. Then you should add the Criteria expressions. Set up your work to resemble the one in Figure B-17. Make sure the tables are joined on the common field, Employee ID.

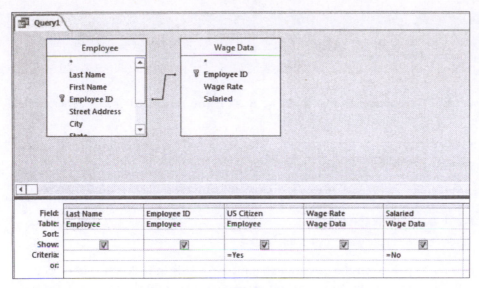

FIGURE B-17 A query based on two joined tables

You should quickly review the criteria you will need to set up this join: If you want data for employees who are U.S. citizens *and* who are hourly workers, the Criteria expressions go in the *same* Criteria row. If you want data for employees who are U.S. citizens *or* who are hourly workers, one of the expressions goes in the second Criteria row (the one with the or: notation).

Now run the query. The output should resemble the one in Figure B-18, with the exception of the name "Brady."

Last Name	Employee ID	US Citizen	Wage Rate	Salaried
Howard	11411	☑	$10.00	☐
Smith	14890	☑	$12.00	☐
Brady	09911	☑	$8.00	☐

FIGURE B-18 Output of a query based on two joined tables

You do not need to print or save the query output, so return to Design view and close the query. Another practice query follows.

AT THE KEYBOARD

Suppose you want to see the wages owed to hourly employees for Week 2. You should show the last name, the employee ID, the salaried status, the week #, and the wages owed. Wages will have to be a calculated field ([Wage Rate] * [Hours]). The criteria are No for Salaried and 2 for the Week #. (This means that another "And" query is required.) Your query should be set up like the one in Figure B-19.

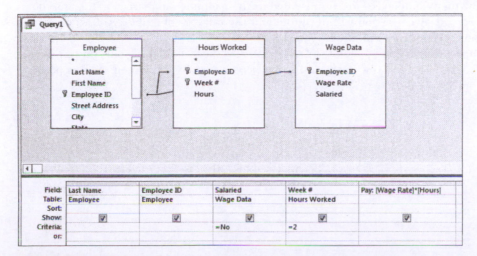

FIGURE B-19 Query setup for wages owed to hourly employees for Week 2

NOTE

In the query in Figure B-19, the calculated field column was widened so you could see the whole expression. To widen a column, click the column boundary line and drag to the right.

Run the query. The output should be similar to that in Figure B-20, if you formatted your calculated field to Currency.

Query1				
Last Name	Employee ID	Salaried	Week #	Pay
Howard	11411	☐	2	$500.00
Smith	14890	☐	2	$480.00
Brady	09911	☑	2	$440.00
*		☐		

FIGURE B-20   Query output for wages owed to hourly employees for Week 2

Notice that it was not necessary to pull down the Wage Rate and Hours fields to make the query work. You do not need to save or print the query output, so return to Design view and close the query.

Summarizing Data from Multiple Records (Totals Queries)

You may want data that summarizes values from a field for several records (or possibly all records) in a table. For example, you might want to know the average hours that all employees worked in a week or the total (sum) of all of the hours worked. Furthermore, you might want data grouped or stratified in some way. For example, you might want to know the average hours worked, grouped by all U.S. citizens versus all non-U.S. citizens. Access calls such a query a **Totals query**. These queries include the following operations:

Sum	The total of a given field's values
Count	A count of the number of instances in a field—that is, the number of records. In the current example, you would count the number of employee IDs to get the number of employees.
Average	The average of a given field's values
Min	The minimum of a given field's values
Var	The variance of a given field's values
StDev	The standard deviation of a given field's values
Where	The field has criteria for the query output

AT THE KEYBOARD

Suppose you want to know how many employees are represented in the example database. First, bring the Employee table into the QBE screen. Because you will need to count the number of employee IDs, which is a Totals query operation, you must bring down the Employee ID field.

To tell Access that you want a Totals query, click the Design tab and then click the Totals button in the Show/Hide group. A new row called the Total row opens in the lower part of the QBE screen. At this point, the screen resembles the one in Figure B-21.

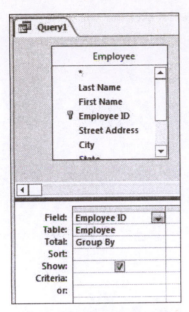

FIGURE B-21   Totals query setup

Note that the Total cell contains the words *Group By*. Until you specify a statistical operation, Access assumes that a field will be used for grouping (stratifying) data.

To count the number of employee IDs, click next to Group By to display an arrow. Click the arrow to reveal a drop-down menu, as shown in Figure B-22.

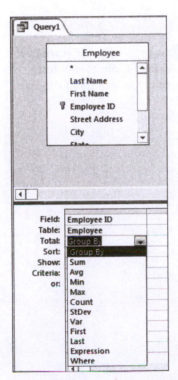

FIGURE B-22   Choices for statistical operation in a Totals query

Select the Count operator. (You might need to scroll down the menu to see the operator you want.) Your screen should resemble the one shown in Figure B-23.

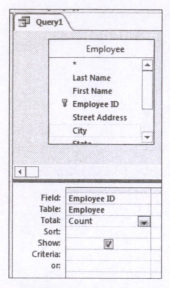

FIGURE B-23   Count in a Totals query

Run the query. Your output should resemble the one in Figure B-24.

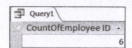

FIGURE B-24   Output of Count in a Totals query

Notice that Access created a pseudo-heading, "CountOfEmployee ID," by splicing together the statistical operation (Count), the word Of, and the name of the field (Employee ID). If you wanted a phrase such as "Count of Employees" as a heading, you would go to Design view and change the query to resemble the one shown in Figure B-25.

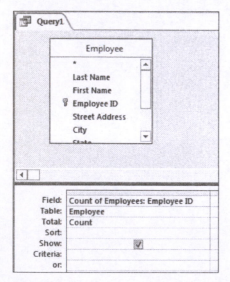

FIGURE B-25   Heading change in a Totals query

When you run the query, the output should resemble the one in Figure B-26.

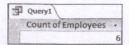

FIGURE B-26   Output of heading change in a Totals query

You do not need to print or save the query output, so return to Design view and close the query.

AT THE KEYBOARD

As another example of a Totals query, suppose you want to know the average wage rate of employees, grouped by whether the employees are salaried. Figure B-27 shows how to set up your query.

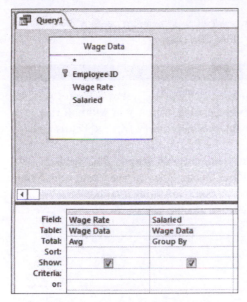

FIGURE B-27 Query setup for average wage rate of employees

When you run the query, your output should resemble the one in Figure B-28.

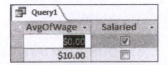

FIGURE B-28 Output of query for average wage rate of employees

Recall the convention that salaried workers are assigned zero dollars an hour. Suppose you want to eliminate the output line for zero dollars an hour because only hourly-rate workers matter for the query. The query setup is shown in Figure B-29.

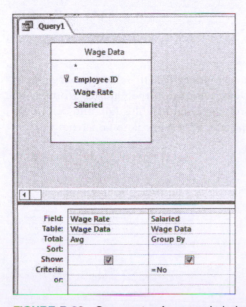

FIGURE B-29 Query setup for nonsalaried workers only

When you run the query, you will get output for nonsalaried employees only, as shown in Figure B-30.

FIGURE B-30   Query output for nonsalaried workers only

Thus, it is possible to use Criteria in a Totals query, just as you would with a "regular" query. You do not need to print or save the query output, so return to Design view and close the query.

AT THE KEYBOARD

Assume that you want to see two pieces of information for hourly workers: (1) the average wage rate, which you will call Average Rate in the output, and (2) 110 percent of the average rate, which you will call the Increased Rate. To get this information, you can make a calculated field in a new query from a Totals query. In other words, you use one query as a basis for another query.

Create the first query; you already know how to perform certain tasks for this query. The revised heading for the average rate will be Average Rate, so type *Average Rate: Wage Rate* in the Field cell. Note that you want the average of this field. Also, the grouping will be by the Salaried field. (To get hourly workers only, enter *Criteria: No.*) Confirm that your query resembles the one in Figure B-31, then save the query and close it.

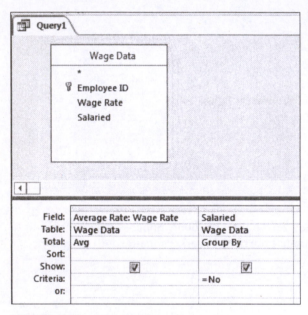

FIGURE B-31   A totals query with average

Now begin a new query. However, instead of bringing in a table to the query design, select a query. To start a new query, click the Create tab and then click the Query Design button in the Queries group. The Show Table window appears. Click the Queries tab instead of using the default Tables tab, and select the query you just saved as a basis for the new query. The most difficult part of this query is to construct the expression for the calculated field. Conceptually, it is as follows:

Increased Rate: 1.1 * [The current average]

You use the new field name in the new query as the current average, and you treat the new name like a new field:

Increased Rate: 1.1 * [Average Rate]
The query within a query is shown in Figure B-32.

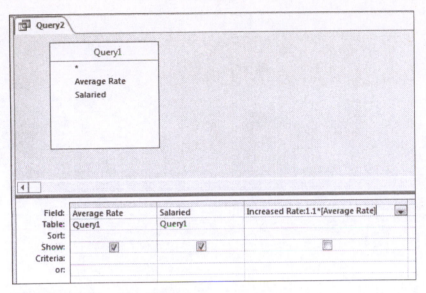

FIGURE B-32   A query within a query

Figure B-33 shows the output of the new query. Note that the calculated field is formatted.

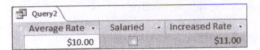

FIGURE B-33   Output of an Expression in a Totals query

You do not need to print or save the query output, so return to Design view and close the query.

Using the Date() Function in Queries

Access has two important date function features:

- The built-in Date() function gives you today's date. You can use the function in query criteria or in a calculated field. The function "returns" the day on which the query is run; in other words, it inserts the value where the Date() function appears in an expression.
- Date arithmetic lets you subtract one date from another to obtain the difference—in number of days—between two calendar dates. For example, suppose you create the following expression:
  10/9/2012 – 10/4/2012
  Access would evaluate the expression as the integer 5 (9 minus 4 is 5).

As another example of how date arithmetic works, suppose you want to give each employee a one-dollar bonus for each day the employee has worked. You would need to calculate the number of days between the employee's date of hire and the day the query is run, and then multiply that number by $1.

You would find the number of elapsed days by using the following equation:

Date() – [Date Hired]

Also suppose that for each employee, you want to see the last name, employee ID, and bonus amount. You would set up the query as shown in Figure B-34.

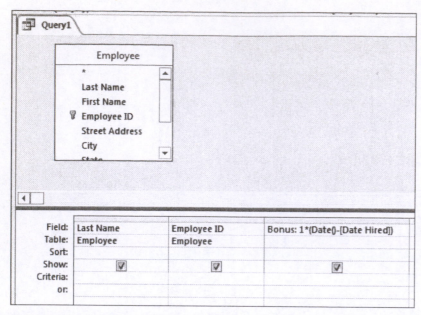

FIGURE B-34   Date arithmetic in a query

Assume that you set the format of the Bonus field to Currency. The output will be similar to that in Figure B-35, although your Bonus data will be different because you used a different date.

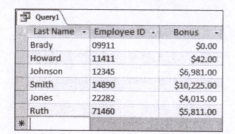

FIGURE B-35   Output of query with date arithmetic

Using Time Arithmetic in Queries

Access also allows you to subtract the values of time fields to get an elapsed time. Assume that your database has a Job Assignments table showing the times that nonsalaried employees were at work during a day. The definition is shown in Figure B-36.

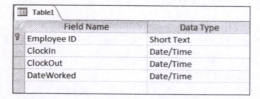

FIGURE B-36   Date/Time data definition in the Job Assignments table

Assume that the DateWorked field is formatted for Long Date and that the ClockIn and ClockOut fields are formatted for Medium Time. Also assume that for a particular day, nonsalaried workers were scheduled as shown in Figure B-37.

Employee ID	ClockIn	ClockOut	DateWorked	Click to Add
09911	8:30 AM	4:30 PM	Friday, September 29, 2017	
11411	9:00 AM	3:00 PM	Friday, September 29, 2017	
14890	7:00 AM	5:00 PM	Friday, September 29, 2017	

FIGURE B-37   Display of date and time in a table

You want a query showing the elapsed time that your employees were on the premises for the day. When you add the tables, your screen may show the links differently. Click and drag the Job Assignments, Employee, and Wage Data table icons to look like those in Figure B-38.

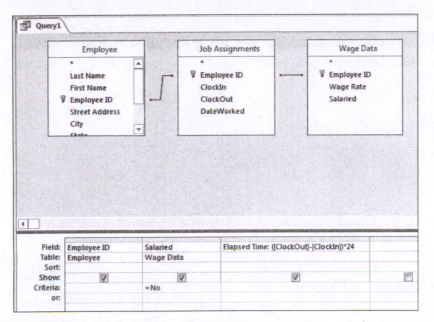

FIGURE B-38 Query setup for time arithmetic

Figure B-39 shows the output, which looks correct. For example, employee 09911 was at work from 8:30 a.m. to 4:30 p.m., which is eight hours. But how does the odd expression that follows yield the correct answers?

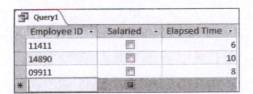

FIGURE B-39 Query output for time arithmetic

([ClockOut] – [ClockIn]) * 24

Why wouldn't the following expression work?

[ClockOut] – [ClockIn]

Here is the answer: In Access, subtracting one time from the other yields the *decimal* portion of a 24-hour day. Returning to the example, you can see that employee 09911 worked eight hours, which is one-third of a day, so the time arithmetic function yields .3333. That is why you must multiply by 24—to convert from decimals to an hourly basis. Hence, for employee 09911, the expression performs the following calculation: $1/3 \times 24 = 8$.

Note that parentheses are needed to force Access to do the subtraction *first*, before the multiplication. Without parentheses, multiplication takes precedence over subtraction. For example, consider the following expression:

[ClockOut] – [ClockIn] * 24

In this example, ClockIn would be multiplied by 24, the resulting value would be subtracted from ClockOut, and the output would be a nonsensical decimal number.

Deleting and Updating Queries

The queries presented in this tutorial so far have been Select queries. They select certain data from specific tables based on a given criterion. You also can create queries to update the original data in a database. Businesses use such queries often, and in real time. For example, when you order an item from a Web site, the company's database is updated to reflect your purchase through the deletion of that item from the company's inventory.

Consider an example. Suppose you want to give all nonsalaried workers a $0.50 per hour pay raise. Because you have only three nonsalaried workers, it would be easy to change the Wage Rate data in the table. However, if you had 3,000 nonsalaried employees, it would be much faster and more accurate to change the Wage Rate data by using an Update query that adds $0.50 to each nonsalaried employee's wage rate.

AT THE KEYBOARD

Now you will change each of the nonsalaried employees' pay via an Update query. Figure B-40 shows how to set up the query.

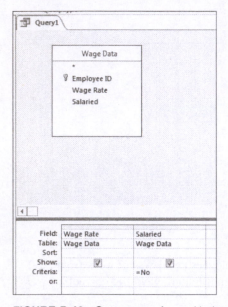

FIGURE B-40   Query setup for an Update query

So far, this query is just a Select query. Click the Update button in the Query Type group, as shown in Figure B-41.

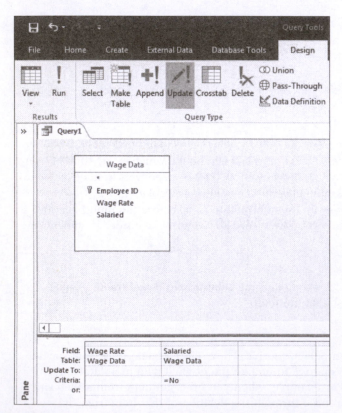

FIGURE B-41   Selecting a query type

Notice that you now have another line on the QBE grid called Update To:, which is where you specify the change or update the data. Notice that you will update only the nonsalaried workers by using a filter under the Salaried field. Update the Wage Rate data to Wage Rate plus $0.50, as shown in Figure B-42. Note that the update involves the use of brackets [ ], as in a calculated field.

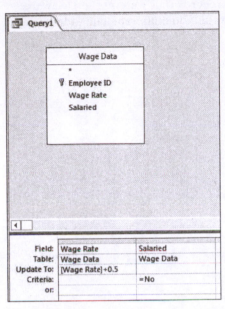

FIGURE B-42   Updating the wage rate for nonsalaried workers

Now run the query by clicking the Run button in the Results group. If you cannot run the query because it is blocked by Disabled Mode, click the Enable Content button on the Security Warning message bar. When you successfully run the query, the warning message in Figure B-43 appears.

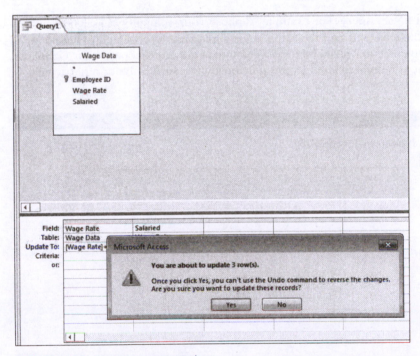

FIGURE B-43   Update query warning

When you click Yes, the records are updated. Check the updated records by viewing the Wage Data table. Each nonsalaried wage rate should be increased by $0.50. You could add or subtract data from another table as well. If you do, remember to put the field name in square brackets.

Another type of query is the Delete query, which works like Update queries. For example, assume that your company has been purchased by the state of Delaware, which has a policy of employing only state residents. Thus, you must delete (or fire) all employees who are not exclusively Delaware residents. To do that, you would create a Select query. Using the Employee table, you would click the Delete button in the Query Type group, then bring down the State field and filter only those records that were not in Delaware (DE). Do not perform the operation, but note that if you did, the setup would look like the one in Figure B-44.

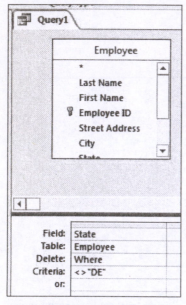

FIGURE B-44   Deleting all employees who are not Delaware residents

Using Parameter Queries

A **Parameter query** is actually a type of Select query. For example, suppose your company has 5,000 employees and you want to query the database to find the same kind of information repeatedly, but about different employees each time. For example, you might want to know how many hours a particular employee has worked. You could run a query that you created and stored previously, but run it only for a particular employee.

AT THE KEYBOARD

Create a Select query with the format shown in Figure B-45.

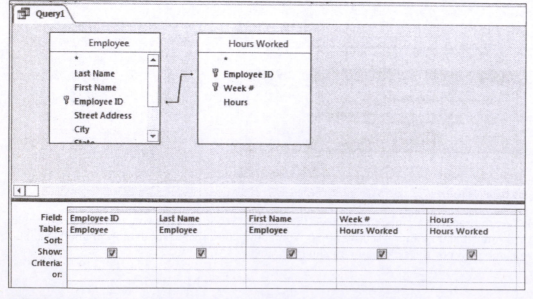

FIGURE B-45   Design of a Parameter query beginning as a Select query

In the Criteria line of the QBE grid for the Employee ID field, type what is shown in Figure B-46.

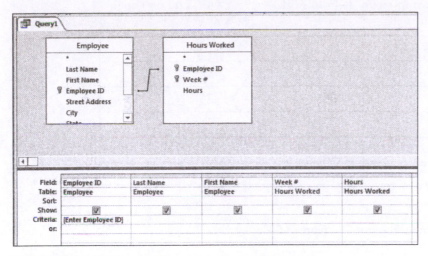

FIGURE B-46   Design of a Parameter query, continued

Note that the Criteria line uses square brackets, as you would expect to see in a calculated field. Now run the query. You will be prompted for the employee's ID number, as shown in Figure B-47.

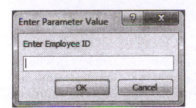

FIGURE B-47   Enter Parameter Value window

Enter your own employee ID. Your query output should resemble the one in Figure B-48.

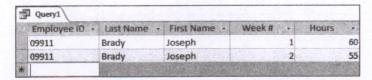

Employee ID	Last Name	First Name	Week #	Hours
09911	Brady	Joseph	1	60
09911	Brady	Joseph	2	55

FIGURE B-48   Output of a Parameter query

MAKING SEVEN PRACTICE QUERIES

This portion of the tutorial gives you additional practice in creating queries. Before making these queries, you must create the specified tables and enter the records shown in the "Creating Tables" section of this tutorial. The output shown for the practice queries is based on those inputs.

AT THE KEYBOARD

For each query that follows, you are given a problem statement and a "scratch area." You also are shown what the query output should look like. Set up each query in Access and then run the query. When you are satisfied with the results, save the query and continue with the next one. Note that you will work with the Employee, Hours Worked, and Wage Data tables.

1. Create a query that shows the employee ID, last name, state, and date hired for employees who live in Delaware *and* were hired after 12/31/99. Perform an ascending sort by employee ID. First

click the Sort cell of the field, and then choose Ascending or Descending. Before creating your query, use the table shown in Figure B-49 to work out your QBE grid on paper.

Field					
Table					
Sort					
Show					
Criteria					
Or:					

FIGURE B-49   QBE grid template

Your output should resemble the one in Figure B-50.

Practice Query 1			
Employee ID ·	Last Name ·	State ·	Date Hired ·
11411	Howard	DE	6/1/2017
22282	Jones	DE	7/15/2004
*			

FIGURE B-50   Number 1 query output

2. Create a query that shows the last name, first name, date hired, and state for employees who live in Delaware *or* were hired after 12/31/99. The primary sort (ascending) is on last name, and the secondary sort (ascending) is on first name. The Primary Sort field must be to the left of the Secondary Sort field in the query setup. Before creating your query, use the table shown in Figure B-51 to work out your QBE grid on paper.

Field					
Table					
Sort					
Show					
Criteria					
Or:					

FIGURE B-51   QBE grid template

If your name were Joseph Brady, your output would look like the one in Figure B-52.

Practice Query 2			
Last Name ·	First Name ·	Date Hired ·	State ·
Brady	Joseph	9/15/2017	MD
Howard	Jane	6/1/2017	DE
Johnson	John	6/1/1996	DE
Jones	Sue	7/15/2004	DE
Smith	Albert	7/15/1987	DE
*			

FIGURE B-52   Number 2 query output

3. Create a query that sums the number of hours worked by U.S. citizens and the number of hours worked by non-U.S. citizens. In other words, create two sums, grouped on citizenship. The heading for total hours worked should be Total Hours Worked. Before creating your query, use the table shown in Figure B-53 to work out your QBE grid on paper.

Field					
Table					
Total					
Sort					
Show					
Criteria					
Or:					

FIGURE B-53   QBE grid template

Your output should resemble the one in Figure B-54.

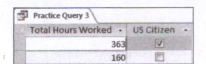

Practice Query 3

Total Hours Worked	US Citizen
363	☑
160	☐

FIGURE B-54   Number 3 query output

4. Create a query that shows the wages owed to hourly workers for Week 1. The heading for the wages owed should be Total Owed. The output headings should be Last Name, Employee ID, Week #, and Total Owed. Before creating your query, use the table shown in Figure B-55 to work out your QBE grid on paper.

Field					
Table					
Sort					
Show					
Criteria					
Or:					

FIGURE B-55   QBE grid template

If your name were Joseph Brady, your output would look like the one in Figure B-56.

Practice Query 4

Last Name	Employee ID	Week #	Total Owed
Howard	11411	1	$420.00
Smith	14890	1	$475.00
Brady	09911	1	$510.00

FIGURE B-56   Number 4 query output

5. Create a query that shows the last name, employee ID, hours worked, and overtime amount owed for hourly employees who earned overtime during Week 2. Overtime is paid at 1.5 times the normal hourly rate for all hours worked over 40. Note that the amount shown in the query should be just the overtime portion of the wages paid. Also, this is not a Totals query—amounts should be shown for individual workers. Before creating your query, use the table shown in Figure B-57 to work out your QBE grid on paper.

Field					
Table					
Sort					
Show					
Criteria					
Or:					

FIGURE B-57 QBE grid template

If your name were Joseph Brady, your output would look like the one in Figure B-58.

Practice Query 5			
Last Name	Employee ID	Hours	OT Pay
Howard	11411	50	$157.50
Brady	09911	55	$191.25

FIGURE B-58 Number 5 query output

6. Create a Parameter query that shows the hours employees have worked. Have the Parameter query prompt for the week number. The output headings should be Last Name, First Name, Week #, and Hours. This query is for nonsalaried workers only. Before creating your query, use the table shown in Figure B-59 to work out your QBE grid on paper.

Field					
Table					
Sort					
Show					
Criteria					
Or:					

FIGURE B-59 QBE grid template

Run the query and enter 2 when prompted for the week number. Your output should look like the one in Figure B-60.

Practice Query 6			
Last Name	First Name	Week #	Hours
Howard	Jane	2	50
Smith	Albert	2	40
Brady	Joseph	2	55

FIGURE B-60 Number 6 query output

7. Create an Update query that gives certain workers a merit raise. First, you must create an additional table, as shown in Figure B-61.

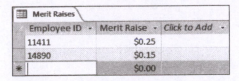

FIGURE B-61   Merit Raises table

Create a query that adds the Merit Raise to the current Wage Rate for employees who will receive a raise. When you run the query, you should be prompted with *You are about to update two rows.* Check the original Wage Data table to confirm the update. Before creating your query, use the table shown in Figure B-62 to work out your QBE grid on paper.

Field					
Table					
Update to					
Criteria					
Or:					

FIGURE B-62   QBE grid template

CREATING REPORTS

Database packages let you make attractive management reports from a table's records or from a query's output. If you are making a report from a table, the Access report generator looks up the data in the table and puts it into report format. If you are making a report from a query's output, Access runs the query in the background (you do not control it or see it happen) and then puts the output in report format.

There are different ways to make a report. One method is to create one from scratch in Design view, but this tedious process is not explained in this tutorial. A simpler way is to select the query or table on which the report is based and then click Report on the Create tab. This streamlined method of creating reports is explained in this tutorial.

Creating a Grouped Report

This tutorial assumes that you already know how to create a basic ungrouped report, so this section teaches you how to make a grouped report. If you do not know how to create an ungrouped report, you can learn by following the first example in the upcoming section.

AT THE KEYBOARD

Suppose you want to create a report from the Hours Worked table. Select the table by clicking it once. Click the Create tab, then click Report in the Reports group. A report appears, as shown in Figure B-63.

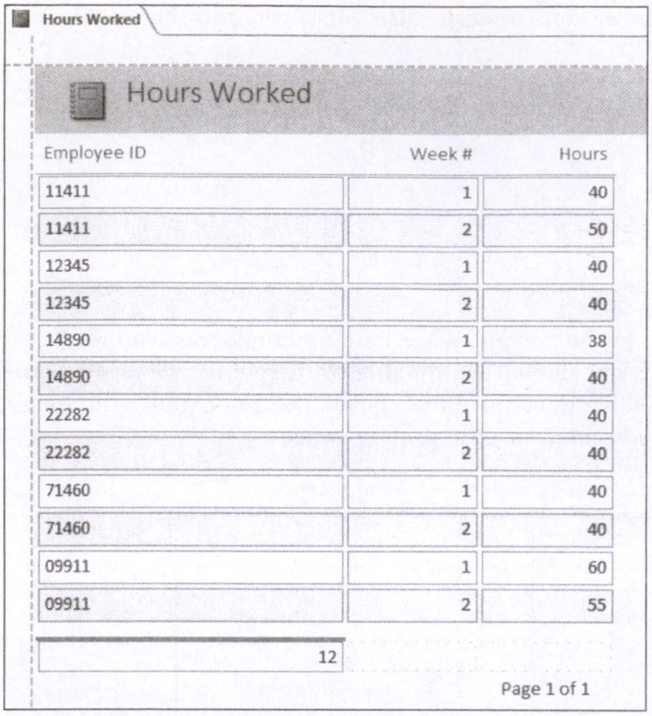

FIGURE B-63   Initial report based on a table

On the Design tab, select the Group & Sort button in the Grouping & Totals group. Your report will have an additional selection at the bottom, as shown in Figure B-64.

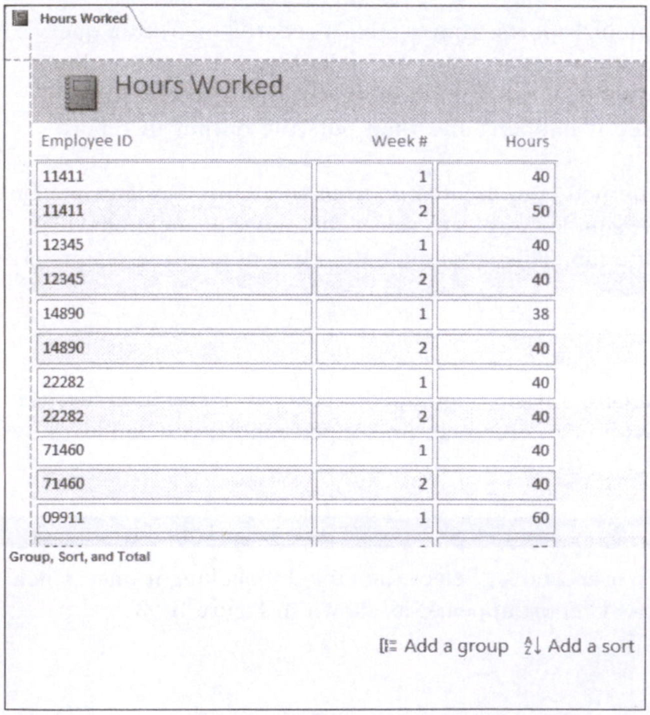

FIGURE B-64   Report with grouping and sorting options

Click the Add a group button at the bottom of the report, and then select Employee ID. Your report will be grouped as shown in Figure B-65.

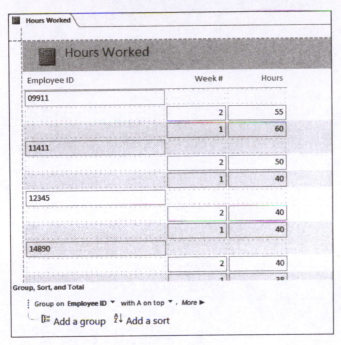

FIGURE B-65 Grouped report

To complete this report, you need to total the hours for each employee by selecting the Hours column heading. Your report will show that the entire column is selected. On the Design tab, click the Totals button in the Grouping & Totals group, and then choose Sum from the menu, as shown in Figure B-66.

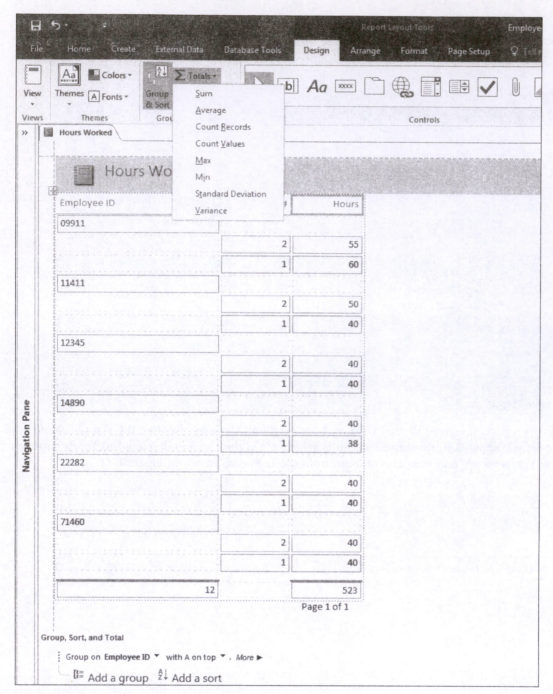

FIGURE B-66   Totaling the hours

Your report will look like the one in Figure B-67.

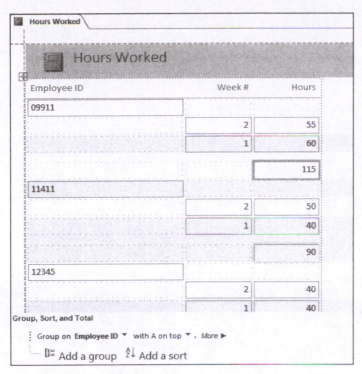

FIGURE B-67   Completed report

Your report is currently in Layout view. To see how the final report looks when printed, click the Design tab and select Report View from the Views group. Your report looks like the one in Figure B-68, although only a portion is shown in the figure.

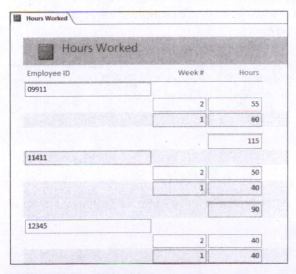

FIGURE B-68   Report in Report view

N O T E

To change the picture or logo in the upper-left corner of the report when in Layout view, click the notebook symbol and press the Delete key. You can insert a logo in place of the notebook by clicking the Design tab and then clicking the Insert Image button in the Controls group.

Moving Fields in Layout View

If you group records based on more than one field in a report, the report will have an odd "staircase" look or display repeated data, or it will have both problems. Next, you will learn how to overcome these problems in Layout view.

Suppose you make a query that shows an employee's last name, first name, week number, and hours worked, and then you make a report from that query, grouping on last name only. See Figure B-69.

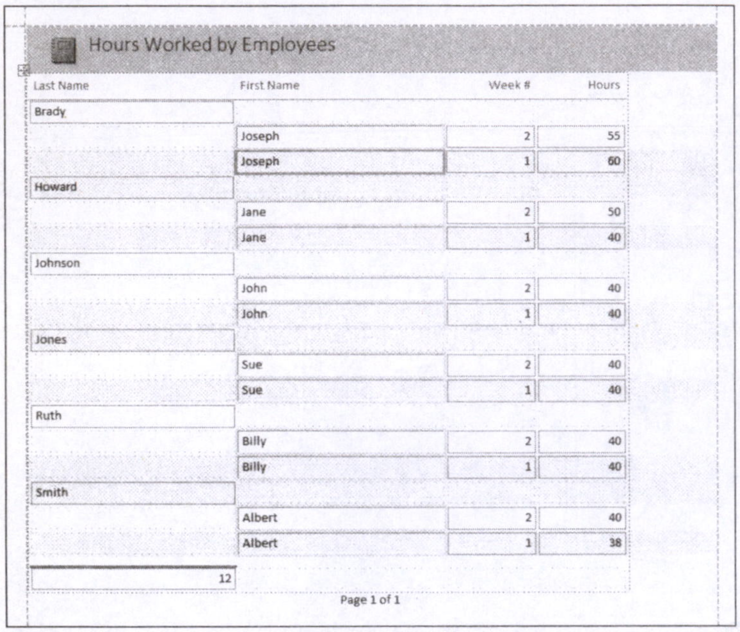

FIGURE B-69   Query-based report grouped on last name

As you preview the report, notice the repeating data from the First Name field. In the report shown in Figure B-69, notice that the first name repeats for each week worked—hence, the staircase effect. The Week # and Hours fields are shown as subordinate to Last Name, as desired.

Suppose you want the last name and first name to appear on the same line. If so, take the report into Layout view for editing. Click the first record for the First Name (in this case, Joseph) and drag the name up to the same line as the Last Name (in this case, Brady). Your report will now show the First Name on the same line as Last Name, thereby eliminating the staircase look, as shown in Figure B-70.

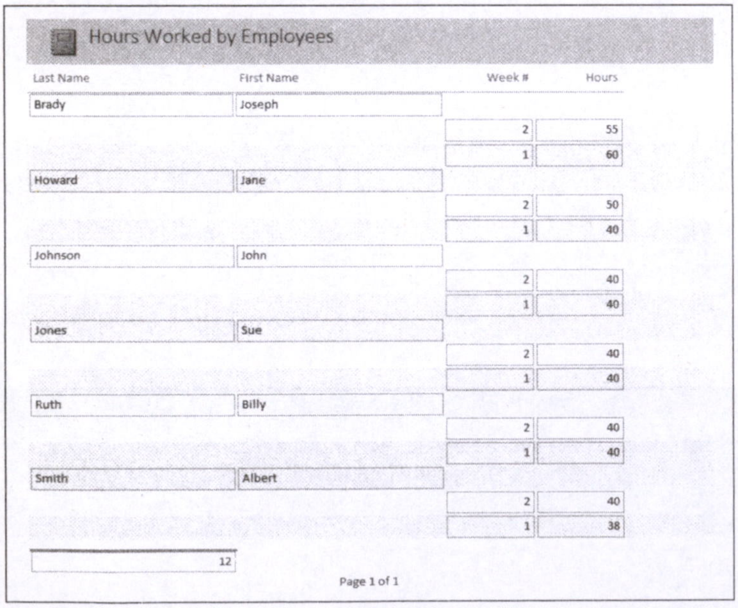

FIGURE B-70   Report in Layout view with Last Name and First Name on the same line

You can now add the sum of Hours for each group. Also, if you want to add more fields to your report, such as Street Address and Zip, you can repeat the preceding procedure.

IMPORTING DATA

Text or spreadsheet data is easy to import into Access. In business, it is often necessary to import data because companies use disparate systems. For example, assume that your healthcare coverage data is on the human resources manager's computer in a Microsoft Excel spreadsheet. Open the Excel application and then create a spreadsheet using the data shown in Figure B-71.

	A	B	C
1	Employee ID	Provider	Level
2	11411	BlueCross	family
3	12345	BlueCross	family
4	14890	Coventry	spouse
5	22282	None	none
6	71460	Coventry	single
7	Your ID	BlueCross	single

FIGURE B-71   Excel data

Save the file and then close it. Now you can easily import the spreadsheet data into a new table in Access. With your Employee database open, click the External Data tab, then click Excel in the Import & Link group. Browse to find the Excel file you just created, and make sure the first radio button is selected to import the source data into a new table in the current database (see Figure B-72). Click OK.

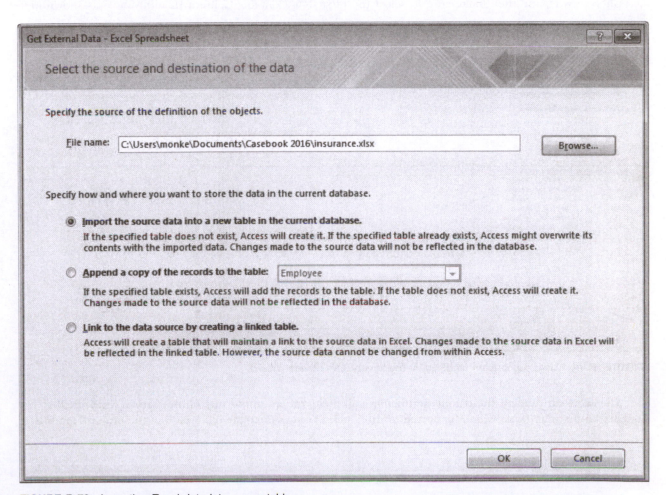

FIGURE B-72   Importing Excel data into a new table

Choose the correct worksheet. Your next screen should look like the one in Figure B-73.

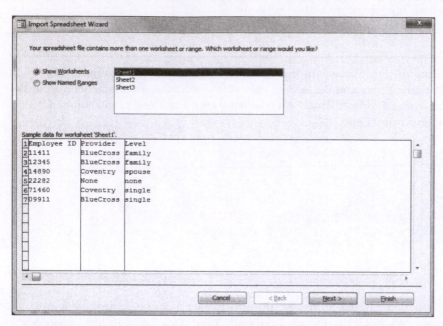

FIGURE B-73   First screen in the Import Spreadsheet Wizard

Choose Next, and then make sure to select the First Row Contains Column Headings box, as shown in Figure B-74.

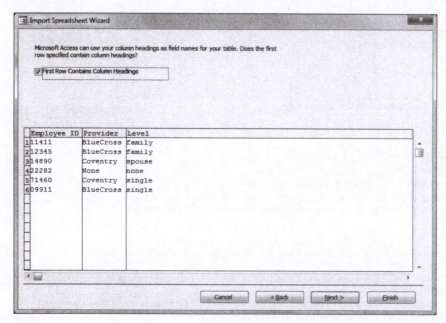

FIGURE B-74   Choosing column headings in the Import Spreadsheet Wizard

Choose Next. Accept the default setting for each field you are importing on the screen. Each field is assigned a text data type, which is correct for this table. Your screen should look like the one in Figure B-75.

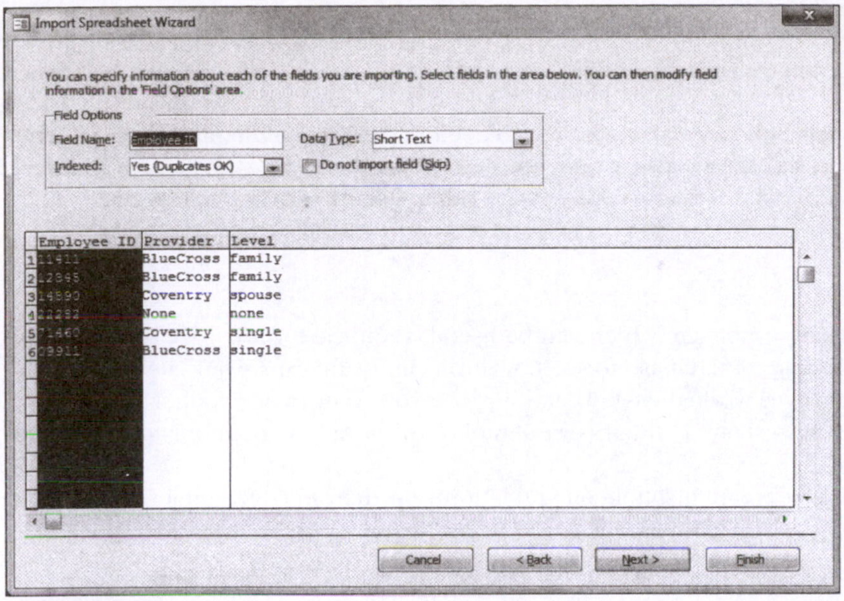

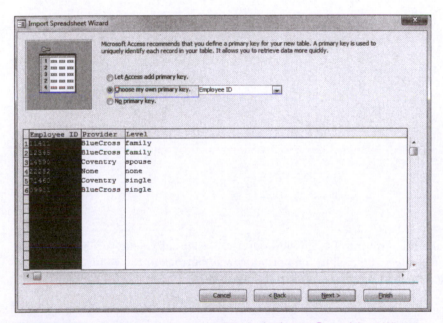

FIGURE B-75 Choosing the data type for each field in the Import Spreadsheet Wizard

Choose Next. In the next screen of the wizard, you will be prompted to create an index—that is, to define a primary key. Because you will store your data in a new table, choose your own primary key (Employee ID), as shown in Figure B-76.

FIGURE B-76 Choosing a primary key field in the Import Spreadsheet Wizard

Continue through the wizard, giving your table an appropriate name. After importing the table, take a look at its design by right-clicking the table and choosing Design View. Note that each field is very wide. Adjust the field properties as needed.

MAKING FORMS

Forms simplify the process of adding new records to a table. Creating forms is easy, and they can be applied to one or more tables.

When you base a form on one table, you simply select the table, click the Create tab, and then select Form from the Forms group. The form will then contain only the fields from that table. When data is entered into the form, a complete new record is automatically added to the table. Forms with two tables are discussed next.

Making Forms with Subforms

You also can create a form that contains a subform, which can be useful when the form is based on two or more tables. Return to the example Employee database to see how forms and subforms would be useful for viewing all of the hours that each employee worked each week. Suppose you want to show all of the fields from the Employee table; you also want to show the hours each employee worked by including all fields from the Hours Worked table as well.

To create the form and subform, first create a simple one-table form on the Employee table. Follow these steps:

1.   Click once to select the Employee table. Click the Create tab, then click Form in the Forms group. After the main form is complete, it should resemble the one in Figure B-77.

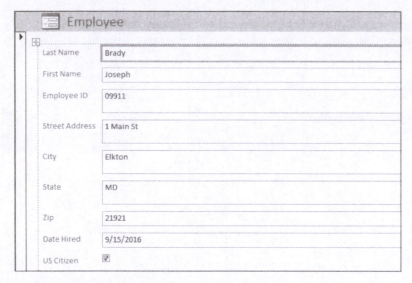

FIGURE B-77   The Employee form

2.   To add the subform, take the form into Design view. On the Design tab, make sure that the Use Control Wizards option is selected, scroll to the bottom row of buttons in the Controls group, and click the Subform/Subreport button, as shown in Figure B-78.

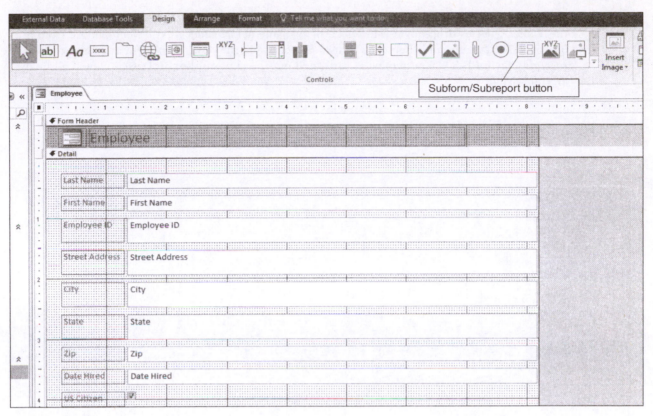

FIGURE B-78 The Subform/Subreport button

3.   Use your cursor to stretch out the box under your main form. You might need to expand the area beneath the main form. The window shown in Figure B-79 appears.

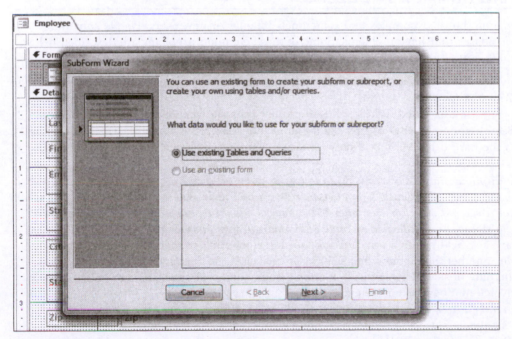

FIGURE B-79 Adding a subform

4. Select Use existing Tables and Queries, click Next, and then select Table: Hours Worked from the Tables/Queries drop-down list. Select all available fields. Click Next, select Choose from a list, click Next again, and then click Finish. Select the Form view. Your form and subform should resemble Figure B-80. You may need to stretch out the subform box in Design view if all fields are not visible.

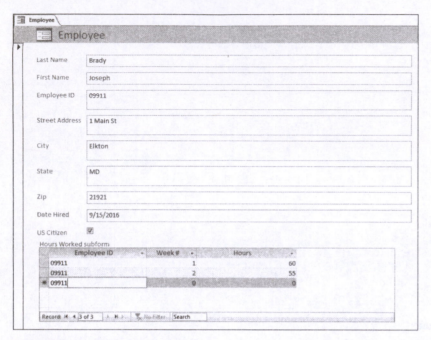

FIGURE B-80   Form with subform

TROUBLESHOOTING COMMON PROBLEMS

Access is a powerful program, but it is complex and sometimes difficult for new users. People sometimes unintentionally create databases that have problems. Some of these common problems are described below, along with their causes and corrections.

1. *"I saved my database file, but I can't find it on my computer or my external secondary storage medium! Where is it?"*
   You saved your file to a fixed disk or a location other than the Documents folder. Use the Windows Search option to find all files ending in .accdb (search for *.accdb). If you saved the file, it is on the hard drive (C:\) or a network drive. Your site assistant can tell you the drive designators.

2. *"What is a 'duplicate key field value'? I'm trying to enter records into my Sales table. The first record was for a sale of product X to customer 101, and I was able to enter that one. But when I try to enter a second sale for customer #101, Access tells me I already have a record with that key field value. Am I allowed to enter only one sale per customer?"*
   Your primary key field needs work. You may need a compound primary key—a combination of the customer number and some other field(s). In this case, the customer number, product number, and date of sale might provide a unique combination of values, or you might consider using an invoice number field as a key.

3. *"My query reads 'Enter Parameter Value' when I run it. What is that?"*
   This problem almost always indicates that you have misspelled a field name in an expression in a Criteria field or calculated field. Access is very fussy about spelling; for example, it is case sensitive. Access is also "space sensitive," meaning that when you insert a space in a field name when defining a table, you must also include a space in the field name when you reference it in a query expression. Fix the typo in the query expression.

4. *"I'm getting an enormous number of rows in my query output—many times more than I need. Most of the rows are duplicates!"*

   This problem is usually caused by a failure to link all of the tables you brought into the top half of the query generator. The solution is to use the manual click-and-drag method to link the common fields between tables. The spelling of the field names is irrelevant because the link fields need not have the same spelling.

5. *"For the most part, my query output is what I expected, but I am getting one or two duplicate rows or not enough rows."*

   You may have linked too many fields between tables. Usually, only a single link is needed between two tables. It is unnecessary to link each common field in all combinations of tables; it is usually sufficient to link the primary keys. A simplistic explanation for why overlinking causes problems is that it causes Access to "overthink" and repeat itself in its answer.

   On the other hand, you might be using too many tables in the query design. For example, you brought in a table, linked it on a common field with some other table, but then did not use the table. In other words, you brought down none of its fields, and/or you used none of its fields in query expressions. In this case, if you got rid of the table, the query would still work. Click the unneeded table's header at the top of the QBE area and press the Delete key to see if you can make the few duplicate rows disappear.

6. *"I expected six rows in my query output, but I got only five. What happened to the other one?"*

   Usually, this problem indicates a data entry error in your tables. When you link the proper tables and fields to make the query, remember that the linking operation joins records from the tables *on common values* (*equal* values in the two tables). For example, if a primary key in one table has the value "123," the primary key or the linking field in the other table should be the same to allow linking. Note that the text string "123" is not the same as the text string " 123"—the space in the second string is considered a character too. Access does not see unequal values as an error. Instead, Access moves on to consider the rest of the records in the table for linking. The solution is to examine the values entered into the linked fields in each table and fix any data entry errors.

7. *"I linked fields correctly in a query, but I'm getting the empty set in the output. All I get are the field name headings!"*

   You probably have zero common (equal) values in the linked fields. For example, suppose you are linking on Part Number, which you declared as text. In one field, you have part numbers "001," "002," and "003"; in the other table, you have part numbers "0001," "0002," and "0003." Your tables have no common values, which means that no records are selected for output. You must change the values in one of the tables.

8. *"I'm trying to count the number of today's sales orders. A Totals query is called for. Sales are denoted by an invoice number, and I made that a text field in the table design. However, when I ask the Totals query to 'Sum' the number of invoice numbers, Access tells me I cannot add them up! What is the problem?"*

   Text variables are words! You cannot add words, but you can count them. Use the Count Totals operator (not the Sum operator) to count the number of sales, each being denoted by an invoice number.

9. *"I'm doing time arithmetic in a calculated field expression. I subtracted the Time In from the Time Out and got a decimal number! I expected eight hours, and I got the number .33333. Why?"*

   [Time Out] – [Time In] yields the decimal percentage of a 24-hour day. In your case, eight hours is one-third of a day. You must complete the expression by multiplying by 24:
   ([Time Out] – [Time In]) * 24. Don't forget the parentheses.

10. *"I formatted a calculated field for Currency in the query generator, and the values did show as currency in the query output; however, the report based on the query output does not show the dollar sign in its output. What happened?"*

    Go to the report Design view. A box in one of the panels represents the calculated field's value. Click the box and drag to widen it. That should give Access enough room to show the dollar sign as well as the number in the output.

11. *"I told the Report Wizard to fit all of my output to one page. It does print to one page, but some of the data is missing. What happened?"*

    Access fits all the output on one page by leaving data out. If you can tolerate having the output on more than one page, deselect the Fit to a Page option in the wizard. One way to tighten output is to enter Design view and remove space from each box that represents output values and labels. Access usually provides more space than needed.

12. *"I grouped three fields in the Report Wizard, and the wizard prints the output in a staircase fashion. I want the grouping fields to be on one line. How can I do that?"*

    Make adjustments in Design view and Layout view. See the "Creating Reports" section of this tutorial for instructions on making these adjustments.

13. *"When I create an Update query, Access tells me that zero rows are updating or more rows are updating than I want. What is wrong?"*

    If your Update query is not set up correctly (for example, if the tables are not joined properly), Access will either try not to update anything, or it will update all of the records. Check the query, make corrections, and run it again.

14. *"I made a Totals query with a Sum in the Group By row and saved the query. Now when I go back to it, the Sum field reads 'Expression,' and 'Sum' is entered in the field name box. Is that wrong?"*

    Access sometimes changes the Sum field when the query is saved. The data remains the same, and you can be assured your query is correct.

15. *"I cannot run my Update query, but I know it is set up correctly. What is wrong?"*

    Check that you have clicked the Enable Content button on the Security Warning message bar.

PRELIMINARY CASE: FELINE NOVELTIES

Setting Up a Relational Database to Create Tables, Forms, Queries, and Reports

PREVIEW

In this case, you will create a relational database for a start-up company that sells toys, treats, and other items for cats. First, you will create four tables and populate them with data. Next, you will create a form and subform for recording orders for monthly boxes of cat items and other cat-oriented supplies. You will create five queries: a select query, a parameter query, an update query, a totals query, and a query used as the basis for a report. Finally, you will create the report from the fifth query.

PREPARATION

- Before attempting this case, you should have some experience using Microsoft Access.
- Complete any part of Tutorial B that your instructor assigns, or refer to the tutorial as necessary.

BACKGROUND

Your friend, Michelle, has approached you about a start-up business she has created. Michelle has always been a cat lover and knows that many of her friends share her love of felines. She has always wanted to be her own boss and has begun to sell specialty cat toys and treats on a monthly basis to her friends locally. The initial reaction to her business has been strong, and she has enlisted your help to computerize her ordering system.

Here is how the business works: Customers sign up for monthly boxes that contain cat toys, treats, and other goodies geared toward cats. Customers pay a monthly fee that is debited to their credit cards and automatically receive a box of goodies. Cats have fickle natures, so the new toys and treats are a delight to them and hence to their owners. Currently, Michelle uses a third party that takes care of credit card payments. She wants you to concentrate on the ordering side of the business. You suggest creating an Access database to track and record all orders for her small business. You have experience using the program from your information systems coursework.

Your first tasks are to design the database, create the tables, and populate them with current data. You have decided to begin in a simple fashion, so your database design includes only four tables, as shown in Figures 1-1, 1-2, 1-3, and 1-4:

- Customers, which maintains records for each customer, including their email address, delivery address, gender, and credit card number.
- Items, which includes item names, descriptions of the monthly boxes and other monthly and single items, their price, and whether they are sent on a monthly basis.
- Orders, which maintains records for each customer's ID number, the date each order was placed, and the date it was delivered.
- Order Line Item, which shows the items in each order and their quantity.

After the database tables are complete and populated with data, you want to computerize several common tasks. First, you need a streamlined way to place each order and the contents of each order. You recognize that a form and subform would be ideal for recording information about orders.

Michelle knows that some of the cats' toys are geared toward a female owner. She is curious to know who her male customers are, so she can buy appropriate items to fill the monthly boxes. A query will easily answer that question.

Michelle began the business with the idea of selling only boxes of toys and treats, but now she is expanding to sell other items. She would like to know how many monthly items have been purchased so far because she suspects these items are still the bulk of her business. You are confident that a totals query will allow Michelle to see the data she needs to plan for the future of her business.

Michelle anticipates that the price of the cat condos she purchases will increase in the near future because she received a low introductory deal. You know you can easily increase prices in the database with an update query. Because you will need this capability soon, you want to practice creating an update query now.

As a business major, you suggest to Michelle that customers eventually would like to search her database to find out what products fit their needs. You can create a query that allows the user to search for particular keywords in products and see what is available for sale. You think this query would be a perfect tool for answering customers' questions.

Finally, Michelle would like a comprehensive order report that lists each customer, what they ordered, and how much money they paid for all items so far. You decide that the best solution is to use a query that feeds into the report.

ASSIGNMENT 1: CREATING TABLES

Use Microsoft Access to create tables that contain the fields shown in Figures 1-1 through 1-4; you learned about these tables in the Background section. Populate the database tables as shown. Add your name to the Customers table with a fictitious ID number; complete the entry by adding your email address, home address, gender, and a fictitious number for a credit card. Order yourself a monthly cat box and one other item.

This database contains the following four tables:

Customer ID	First Name	Last Name	Email Address	Street Address	City	State	Zip	Gender	Credit Card Number
500	Ava	Kerr	ava.kerr@google.com	35A Cherry Orchard	Denver	CO	80201	F	122635211541
501	Victoria	Bailey	victoria.bailey@google.com	5 The Springs	Denver	CO	80201	F	254136597462
502	Hannah	Mitchell	hannah.mitchell@google.com	79 Rydal Ave	Denver	CO	80201	F	852462169841
503	Trevor	Lee	trevor.lee@google.com	101 Winchester Rd	Denver	CO	80201	M	952144520145
504	Phil	Mackay	phil.mackay@google.com	12 Hylton Pl	Denver	CO	80201	M	951447512655
505	Abigail	Russell	abigail.russell@google.com	3 Ash Cl	Denver	CO	80201	F	857141058412
506	Keith	Hill	keith.hill@google.com	28 Trewarton Rd	Denver	CO	80201	M	957410255412
507	Neil	Underwood	neil.underwood@google.com	111 Clarence Rd	Denver	CO	80201	M	944100547725
508	Sonia	Wright	sonia.wright@google.com	43 Emerson Ave	Denver	CO	80201	F	784512684524
509	Carl	Jones	carl.jones@google.com	10 Brynawelon Dr	Denver	CO	80201	M	954125874126
510	Bernadette	Chapman	bernadette.chapman@google.com	1 Central Circle	Denver	CO	80201	F	954711558742

FIGURE 1-1   The Customers table

Item ID	Item Name	Description	Price	Monthly?	
901	Single Cat Monthly	Monthly box of cat toys and treats	$19.99	☑	
902	Multiple Cats Monthly	Monthly box of cat toys and treats f⦙	$35.99	☑	
903	Toy of the month	Monthly unique cat toy	$9.99	☑	
904	Treat of the month	Monthly mouth-watering cat treats	$4.59	☑	
905	Organic litter	Totally organic and fragrance free li⦙	$25.00	☐	
906	Cat Condo	6 foot tall condo with 3 platforms	$219.99	☐	
907	Cat bowls	Multi-colored bowls with cat faces	$18.99	☐	
908	Cat brush	Two sided cat brush	$12.50	☐	
909	Flea comb	Fine-toothed comb for flea control	$5.99	☐	
*			$0.00	☐	

FIGURE 1-2   The Items table

Order ID	Customer ID	Date Ordered	Date Delivered
470	501	1/5/2018	1/15/2018
471	502	1/5/2018	1/15/2018
472	503	1/5/2018	1/15/2018
473	504	1/5/2018	1/15/2018
474	505	1/5/2018	1/15/2018
475	506	1/5/2018	1/15/2018
476	507	1/5/2018	1/15/2018
477	508	1/5/2018	1/15/2018
478	509	1/5/2018	1/15/2018
480	501	2/1/2018	4/1/2018
481	502	3/15/2018	4/3/2018
482	503	2/26/2018	4/10/2018
483	504	3/18/2018	4/3/2018
484	505	3/31/2018	4/20/2018
485	506	2/10/2018	3/31/2018
486	507	2/3/2018	4/3/2018
487	508	3/2/2018	4/10/2018
488	509	1/31/2018	3/30/2018
489	510	3/1/2018	4/16/2018
*			

FIGURE 1-3   The Orders table

Order Line Item		
Order ID	Item ID	Quantity
470	901	1
471	902	2
472	901	1
473	902	3
474	903	2
475	904	3
476	901	1
477	902	4
478	903	2
480	905	2
480	908	1
480	909	1
481	906	2
481	907	2
481	908	1
482	905	2
482	908	1
482	909	1
483	906	2
483	908	1
483	909	1
484	906	1
484	907	1
484	908	1
484	909	1
485	907	2
485	908	1
486	908	1
486	909	1
487	905	2
487	908	1
487	909	1
488	905	1
488	907	3
488	908	1
488	909	1
489	906	1
489	907	1
489	908	1
489	909	1

FIGURE 1-4   The Order Line Item table

ASSIGNMENT 2: CREATING A FORM, QUERIES, AND A REPORT

Assignment 2A: Creating a Form

Create a form for easy recording of orders and the specific items within those orders. The main form should be based on the Orders table, and the subform should include the fields from the Order Line Item table. Save the form as Orders. View one record; if required by your instructor, print the record. Your output should resemble that shown in Figure 1-5.

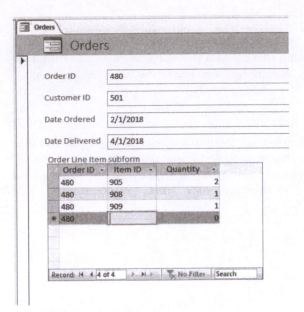

FIGURE 1-5 The Orders form with subform

Assignment 2B: Creating a Select Query

Create a query to list all male customers. Include columns that display the Last Name, First Name, Street Address, City, State, and Zip. Save the query as Male Customers. Your output should resemble that shown in Figure 1-6, but the data may vary. Print the output if desired.

FIGURE 1-6 Male Customers query

Assignment 2C: Creating a Totals Query

Create a totals query that lists the items ordered on a monthly basis and totals up the number of items purchased. In the output, display columns for Item Name and Total Purchased. Sort the list of items from most ordered to least. Note that Total Purchased is a change in column heading from the default setting in the query generator. Save your query as Monthly Items Ordered Summary. Your output should resemble that shown in Figure 1-7. Print the output if desired.

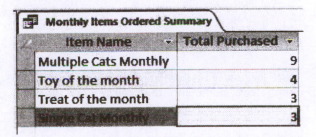

FIGURE 1-7 Monthly Items Ordered Summary query

Assignment 2D: Creating an Update Query

Create a query that updates any item that lists a cat condo by increasing its price by 10 percent. Consider using a wildcard that looks for entries in the Item Name column that contain the word "condo." Click the Run button to test the query. When prompted to change the records, answer "Yes." Save the query as Increased Prices.

Assignment 2E: Creating a Parameter Query

Create a parameter query that prompts for a keyword and then lists all the items whose descriptions hold that keyword. The query should include columns for Item Name, Description, and Price. (Hint: The parameter syntax for this query, including the wildcard, is *Like "*" & [Enter your search term] & "*"*.) Save the query as Search for keywords. Your output should resemble Figure 1-8 after you enter "treat" at the prompt.

Item Name	Description	Price
Single Cat Monthly	Monthly box of cat toys and treats	$19.99
Multiple Cats Monthly	Monthly box of cat toys and treats for multiple cats	$35.99
Treat of the month	Monthly mouth-watering cat treats	$4.59
*		$0.00

FIGURE 1-8   Search for keywords query

Assignment 2F: Generating a Report

Generate a report based on a query that summarizes customers' orders. The query should display columns for Last Name, Street Address, City, Item Name, Quantity, and the Total Price of all ordered items. Save the query as Order Report. From that query, create a report that groups each customer's order and calculates the amount paid. Make any needed adjustments to the output to avoid repeating names and to ensure that all fields and data are visible. Ensure that "Order Report" appears as the title at the top of the report, and save the report under the same name. Your report output should resemble that shown in Figure 1-9, although only a portion of the report appears in the figure.

Order Report

Last Name	Street Address	City	Item Name	Quantity	Total Price
Bailey	5 The Springs	Denver			
			Flea comb	1	$5.99
			Cat brush	1	$12.50
			Organic litter	2	$50.00
			Single Cat Monthly	1	$19.99
					$88.48
Chapman	1 Central Circle	Denver			
			Cat bowls	1	$18.99
			Cat Condo	1	$219.99
			Flea comb	1	$5.99
			Cat brush	1	$12.50
					$257.47

FIGURE 1-9   Order Report

If you are working with a portable storage disk or USB thumb drive, make sure that you remove it *after* closing the database file.

DELIVERABLES

Assemble the following deliverables for your instructor, either electronically or in printed form:

1. Four tables
2. Form and subform: Orders
3. Query 1: Male Customers
4. Query 2: Monthly Items Ordered Summary
5. Query 3: Increased Prices
6. Query 4: Search for keywords
7. Query 5: Order Report
8. Report: Order report
9. Any other required printouts or electronic media

Staple all the pages together. Write your name and class number at the top of each page. If required, make sure that your electronic media are labeled.

THE TRAVEL LIGHT DATABASE

Designing a Relational Database to Create Tables, Forms, Queries, and Reports

PREVIEW

In this case, you will design a relational database for a business that stores, packs, and ships baggage for business travelers. After your design is complete and correct, you will create database tables and populate them with data. Then you will produce one form, five queries, and two reports. The queries will address the following questions or tasks: Which customers have a credit card on file that will soon expire? Which customers travel the greatest number of days? Which customers take the most trips? What are the details of a specified trip? Which trips need to be canceled? Your reports will summarize the inventory of each customer's bag and the trip itinerary for each customer.

PREPARATION

- Before attempting this case, you should have some experience in database design and in using Microsoft Access.
- Complete any part of Tutorial A that your instructor assigns.
- Complete any part of Tutorial B that your instructor assigns, or refer to the tutorial as necessary.
- Refer to Tutorial F as necessary.

BACKGROUND

You love to travel and hope someday to have a job that allows you to do so. You probably caught the travel bug from your grandmother, Ellen, who traveled for years as a top executive for a large consulting firm. Ellen retired in her early 60s and now is beginning a new venture called Travel Light to assist business travelers. The company stores, cleans, and launders the contents of travelers' bags, then packs and ships their suitcases to specified destinations. In other words, frequent travelers can send their business attire to Travel Light. When they need their garments and other effects, Travel Light packs the bags and ships them to the assigned destinations. When travelers return from the trip, Travel Light receives the bags, dry cleans the clothes, and stores them for the next trip. Given the cost and hassle of checking bags these days, Ellen thinks the business model is strong.

At a recent family reunion, you began chatting with Ellen about your information systems course. She found out that you are proficient in designing and implementing databases, so she hired you for the summer to create a prototype system for her new business. The Access database will be a model for Travel Light's future Web site.

On your first day of work, you sit down with Ellen to learn as much as you can about the business. She describes the information she needs to keep for each customer. Aside from recording customers' full names, including their courtesy titles (Dr., Mrs., Ms., or Mr.), she needs a list of their full addresses, email addresses, telephone numbers, and credit card details. Ellen anticipates that the business will grow, and she mentions that some of her customers might eventually have the same name. You suggest that an identification number would be appropriate to uniquely identify each customer.

When customers sign up with Travel Light, they send their business garments and other effects to be stored at a warehouse. Each item is logged with a unique number, the customer's name, the category of garment, and its color. The categories include trousers, blouses, and ties, for example. When customers anticipate that they will be traveling soon, they fill out a form that specifies their destination and travel dates. Travel Light takes care of shipping the customers' baggage to the destination in time to meet the traveling customer. In the destination city, Travel Light contracts with a local firm to deliver the bag to a specified hotel.

You and Ellen discuss how the company's Web site might work. When customers book trips, they need to specify their destination city and the beginning and ending dates of their journey. You suggest that a form would be an excellent solution for this requirement.

Your grandmother's business partner, Alex, takes care of all the financial transactions. He has asked you to develop a good way to identify customers whose credit cards are expiring soon. He can then notify them of the problem and eliminate any potential for interrupted services. You realize that this issue can be easily addressed by a query.

Ellen is curious to know who her best customers are. Because the business charges by each shipment, she would like to know which customers take the most trips. She also thinks it would be useful to know which customers have the most travel days. In the future, she may be able to market directly to customers who make repeated or extended trips to a particular destination. Perhaps she could send them a fresh set of clothing, for example. You are confident that both questions can be handled by queries.

When Travel Light employees receive a request to pack and ship business attire, they want to be able to confirm that all garments are properly packed and shipped. They want to be able to examine the database quickly and make this confirmation. You explain that it is easy to create a query that accepts input and displays the required information—in this case, the destination, dates, and items to pack.

Another request has been submitted by the customer service agent, Sheila. Customers often call and ask her to remove trips that have been canceled, so Sheila wants to be able to quickly delete a trip from the database based on the destination and travel date. You know that a query will handle this request.

Finally, Ellen requests two summary reports that will be useful for review purposes. One report should list all the items, by customer, that have been handed over to Travel Light for shipment. The other report should summarize each customer's trips. You assure Ellen that these straightforward reports will be generated by the database.

ASSIGNMENT 1: CREATING THE DATABASE DESIGN

In this assignment, you design your database tables using a word-processing program. Pay close attention to the logic and structure of the tables. Do not start developing your Access database in Assignment 2 before getting feedback from your instructor on Assignment 1. Keep in mind that you need to examine the requirements in Assignment 2 to design your fields and tables properly. It is good programming practice to look at the required outputs before beginning your design. When designing the database, observe the following guidelines:

- First, determine the tables you will need by listing the name of each table and the fields it should contain. Avoid data redundancy. Do not create a field if it can be created by a calculated field in a query.
- You will need a transaction table. Think about the business event that occurs with each customer's actions. Keep in mind that some customers travel extensively. Avoid duplicating data.
- Document your tables using the table feature of your word processor. Your tables should resemble the format shown in Figure 2-1.
- You must mark the appropriate key field(s) by entering an asterisk (*) next to the field name. Keep in mind that some tables might need a compound primary key to uniquely identify a record within a table.
- Print the database design.

Table Name	
Field Name	Data Type (text, numeric, currency, etc.)
...	...
...	...

FIGURE 2-1   Table design

ASSIGNMENT 2: CREATING THE DATABASE, QUERIES, AND REPORTS

In this assignment, you first create database tables in Access and populate them with data. Next, you create a form, five queries, and two reports.

Assignment 2A: Creating Tables in Access

In this part of the assignment, you create your tables in Access. Use the following guidelines:

- Enter at least 20 customer records that include customers' addresses, email addresses, and credit card information. Add yourself as a customer. Consider using a fake name and address generator on the Web to eliminate typing.
- For simplicity, assume there are 10 different categories of items that could be packed in a customer's bag: trousers, skirts, blouses, shirts, dresses, shoes, belts, bags, scarves, and ties.
- Populate a table that lists the contents of each customer's bag. Each bag must contain at least one item.
- Create entries for at least 50 trips.
- Appropriately limit the size of the text fields; for example, a telephone number does not need the default length of 255 characters.
- Print all tables if your instructor requires it.

Assignment 2B: Creating Forms, Queries, and Reports

You must generate one form, five queries, and two reports, as outlined in the Background section of this case.

Form

Create a form based on your Trips table (or whatever you named the table). Save the form as Trips. Your form should resemble the one in Figure 2-2.

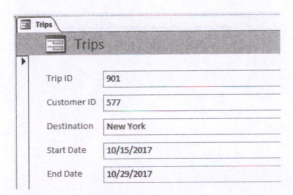

FIGURE 2-2 Trips form

Query 1

Create a select query called Customers with Expiring Credit Cards that lists all customers whose credit cards expire by a specified date. In the output, display columns for the customer's Title, First Name, Middle Initial, Last Name, Address, City, State, and Zip. Your output should resemble that in Figure 2-3, although your data will be different.

Customers with Expiring Credit Cards

Title	First Name	Middle Initial	Last Name	Address	City	State	Zip
Mrs.	Gladys	R	Robinson	4506 Hillside Street	Phoenix	AZ	85034
Mrs.	Ana	W	Bainbridge	3518 Glendale Avenue	Woodland Hills	CA	91303
Ms.	Dorothy	P	Westra	801 Cedarstone Drive	Tiffin	OH	44883
Ms.	Sheila	G	Garcia	2038 Conaway Street	Merom	IN	47861
Mr.	Chris	B	Austin	294 Gorby Lane	Jackson	MS	39201
Mr.	Arthur	G	Love	571 Larry Street	Milwaukee	WI	53233
Dr.	Luis	J	Simon	3080 Mesa Drive	Las Vegas	NV	89102
Mrs.	Denise	D	Chew	677 Pride Avenue	New York	NY	10005
Mr.	Neil	A	Springer	4691 Meadowview Drive	Hot Springs	VA	24445
Mr.	Eric	J	Salazar	4866 Tator Patch Road	Hickory Hills	IL	60457
Mr.	Ronald	C	Blanch	406 Roosevelt Road	Mound Valley	KS	67354
Mr.	Bruce	S	McIntyre	3799 Cimmaron Road	Santa Ana	CA	92704
Dr.	Geraldine	J	Arnett	1858 Vernon Street	California	CA	21102
Mr.	Wayne	S	Reid	814 Chandler Hollow Road	Pittsburgh	PA	15212
Mr.	Randy	H	Stevens	2088 Shobe Lane	Sterling	CO	80751
Ms.	Olive	D	Pena	16 Ridenour Street	Miami	FL	33131
Ms.	Shirley	K	Ortiz	2135 Orphan Road	Eau Claire	WI	54701
Ms.	Nicole	J	Torres	3451 Ritter Street	Huntsville	AL	35816
Mr.	Jesse	S	Polson	217 Felosa Drive	Irvine	CA	92614
Ms.	Annie	E	Ali	480 Bottom Lane	Medina	NY	14103
Mrs.	Emily	K	Smith	1938 Kelly Street	Charlotte	NC	28206
Ms.	Andrea	R	Holley	1536 Private Lane	Albany	GA	31701
Mr.	Ronald	R	Whiting	4543 Counts Lane	Hartford	CT	61036
Mr.	Steven	M	Wilson	199 Pritchard Court	Marshall	MN	56258
Mr.	Ron	S	Bliss	141 Romrog Way	Burwell	NE	68823

FIGURE 2-3 Customers with Expiring Credit Cards query

Query 2

Create a query called Top Traveler that calculates the number of days each customer has traveled and then displays columns with each customer's Title, First Name, Middle Initial, Last Name, and Days Traveled. Sort the output so that the customer who has traveled the greatest number of days is shown at the top of the list. Note the column heading change from the default setting provided by the query generator. Your output should look like that in Figure 2-4, although your data will be different.

Top Traveler

Title	First Name	Middle Initial	Last Name	Days Traveled
Mr.	Warren	C	Manning	35
Mr.	Douglas	T	Jackson	34
Mr.	George	D	Bustamante	25
Ms.	Susan	O	Warren	17
Ms.	Jennie	S	Sheffer	17
Ms.	Maria	F	Stroman	10
Mr.	Clifford	M	Felix	10
Mr.	William	D	Colby	10
Mr.	Richard	S	Welsh	5
Mr.	Randy	H	Stevens	5

FIGURE 2-4 Top Traveler query

Query 3

Create a query similar to that of Query 2. This query, called Number of Trips, calculates the number of trips each customer has taken and is booked to take. The query should include columns for Title, First Name, Middle Initial, Last Name, and Number of Trips. Sort the output so that the customer with the greatest number of trips is shown at the top of the list. Note the column heading change from the default setting provided by the query generator. Your output should resemble the format shown in Figure 2-5, but the data will be different.

Number of Trips

Title	First Name	Middle Initial	Last Name	Number of Trips
Mr.	Warren	C	Manning	7
Ms.	Jennie	S	Sheffer	6
Mr.	George	D	Bustamante	5
Ms.	Susan	O	Warren	4
Mr.	Douglas	T	Jackson	4
Ms.	Maria	F	Stroman	2
Mr.	Clifford	M	Felix	2
Mr.	William	D	Colby	2
Mr.	Richard	S	Welsh	1
Mr.	Randy	H	Stevens	1

FIGURE 2-5 Number of Trips query

Query 4

Create a query called Trip Details that prompts for a trip ID and then displays the packing details for the specified trip. The query should include columns for Start Date, End Date, Destination, Category Name of the packed item, and its Color. Your output should resemble the format shown in Figure 2-6, but the data will be different.

Trip Details

Start Date	End Date	Destination	Category Name	Color
11/2/2017	11/7/2017	San Jose	blouse	green
11/2/2017	11/7/2017	San Jose	skirt	White
11/2/2017	11/7/2017	San Jose	trousers	White
11/2/2017	11/7/2017	San Jose	scarf	green

FIGURE 2-6 Trip Details query

Query 5

Create a query that deletes a trip record based on a prompt for a destination city and starting date. Test the query by running it. Save your query as Cancel a Trip.

Report 1

Create a report named Bag Inventory that summarizes the contents of each customer's bag. The report's output should display headings for Last Name, First Name, Category Name, and Color. You need to create a query first to bring the fields from different tables together. Group the report on the customer's Last Name. Adjust your output so that the Last Name and First Name columns are on the same line and all fields are formatted and visible. Depending on your data, the output should resemble that in Figure 2-7. Note that only a portion of the report appears in the figure.

Bag Inventory

Bag Inventory

Last Name	First Name	Category Name	Color
Ali	Annie		
		trousers	red
		dress	green
		skirt	pink
		belt	pink
Arnett	Geraldine		
		blouse	green
		scarf	green
		trousers	White
		skirt	White

FIGURE 2-7 Bag Inventory report

Report 2

Create a report named Trip Itinerary that summarizes each customer's trips. The report's output should show headings for the customer's full name, destination, start date of the trip, and end date. You need to create a query first to bring the fields from different tables together. Group the report on the customer's Last Name. Adjust your output so that the name columns are on the same line and all fields are formatted and visible. Depending on your data, the output should resemble that in Figure 2-8. Note that only a portion of the report appears in the figure.

Last Name	Title	First Name	Middle Initial	Destination	Start Date	End Date
Ali	Ms.	Annie	E			
				Richmond	12/16/2017	12/21/2017
Arnett	Dr.	Geraldine	J			
				San Jose	11/2/2017	11/7/2017
Burrows	Ms.	Martina	R			
				Arlington	1/21/2018	1/26/2018
Bustamante	Mr.	George	D			
				Pittsburgh	2/12/2018	2/17/2018
				St. Louis	2/6/2018	2/11/2018
				Salt Lake City	1/29/2018	2/3/2018
				Orlando	12/28/2017	1/2/2018
				Las Vegas	12/14/2017	12/19/2017

FIGURE 2-8 Trip Itinerary report

ASSIGNMENT 3: ANALYZING THE DATA AND MAKING A PRESENTATION

Data analytics evaluates data in order to help people make interpretations about it. A Microsoft Access database is an excellent tool for data analytics. Databases are easily scalable—that is, data can easily be added to a database, and all generated queries, forms, and reports will display the additional data, unlike a spreadsheet. For example, if the customer table includes new records, they will be displayed in any existing query that uses customer data.

The head of marketing at Travel Light, Marcus, is interested in growing the business. He would like to see a report that details the top customers—the ones who travel the most days and take the most trips. With this information, he can tailor his marketing campaigns. Your second and third queries answer these questions. Write a brief memo to Marcus explaining your results; include details from your queries' outputs. For details on writing a memo, see Tutorial E.

Create a presentation that you will use to explain the database to your grandmother and any clerical staff she might hire. Include the design of your database tables and instructions for using the database. Discuss future improvements to the database, such as customers' ability to edit the database in order to add contents to their bag. Your presentation should take less than 10 minutes, including a brief question-and-answer period.

DELIVERABLES

Assemble the following deliverables for your instructor, either electronically or in printed form:

1. Word-processed design of tables
2. Tables created in Access
3. Form: Trips
4. Query 1: Customers with Expiring Credit Cards
5. Query 2: Top Traveler
6. Query 3: Number of Trips
7. Query 4: Trip Details
8. Query 5: Cancel a Trip
9. Query for Report 1

10. Report 1: Bag Inventory
11. Query for Report 2
12. Report 2: Trip Itinerary
13. Memo
14. Presentation materials
15. Any other required printouts or electronic media

Staple all the pages together. Write your name and class number at the top of each page. Make sure that your electronic media are labeled, if required.

THE PERSONAL TRAINER DATABASE

Designing a Relational Database to Create Tables,
Forms, Queries, and Reports

PREVIEW

In this case, you will design a relational database for a personal trainer who tracks fitness information about his clients. After your design is complete and correct, you will create database tables and populate them with data. Then you will produce two forms with subforms, six queries, and one report. The queries will show which clients are over 60 years old, list today's appointments for the trainer, list the top 5 percent of clients who can do the most push-ups, display clients' training hours, and display clients' weight loss. You will also produce a report that tracks the fitness assessments of clients.

PREPARATION

- Before attempting this case, you should have some experience in database design and in using Microsoft Access.
- Complete any part of Tutorial A that your instructor assigns.
- Complete any part of Tutorial B that your instructor assigns, or refer to the tutorial as necessary.
- Refer to Tutorial F as necessary.

BACKGROUND

Your high school friend, Sheldon, is a personal trainer. You ran into Sheldon at a Fourth of July fireworks celebration in your hometown and began talking about his personal training business. He has become so popular that he can't keep up with all the paperwork needed to track his clients. Because you are studying database design and Access, you know that the software is a perfect fit for the small database system Sheldon needs to keep his records straight. You offer to help him in exchange for some free personal training sessions.

You agree to meet for lunch the next day to discuss the business. Sheldon explains that he has a large number of clients. Client information is recorded on index cards and includes their name, address, email address, telephone number, birth date, and height. On the back of each card, Sheldon has written the date of the client's first training session and noted the baseline data collected on that day.

To assess a client's fitness, Sheldon uses a classic set of exercises. To measure strength and endurance, he uses push-ups and crunches. To measure aerobic fitness, he uses a step test and a walking test. On the first day of training, Sheldon weighs the client, puts him or her through the battery of exercises, and records all the results. He measures how many push-ups and crunches the client can do in one minute. The step test measures the client's heartbeat after three minutes of stepping up and down. Finally, the walk test times how long it takes the client to walk one mile.

For some clients, Sheldon has provided assessments on a bimonthly basis and recorded their weights each time as well as the results of the four fitness tests, which enables him to track progress and then tweak clients' fitness routines to improve results. Sheldon has this assessment information saved on his computer in an Excel spreadsheet. Each client has a coded number so he doesn't have to enter their names.

In addition, Sheldon has a large calendar on his wall in which he records his daily appointments for personal training sessions. He would love to be able to transfer this information into electronic form for ease of making additions and deletions.

Once the database tables are created and populated, you suggest some forms to help Sheldon streamline his operations. A form for recording clients' baseline fitness data would be helpful as he interacts with new clients, and a form for recording the bimonthly appointments and assessments of his clients would be useful as well.

Sheldon has some requests for organizing information that he has not been able to accomplish with a paper-based system. First, he would like to be able to identify his clients who are over 60 years old so he can encourage them to remain active and schedule appointments with him. He would also like an easy way to view his daily appointments. You assure him that both tasks can be easily accomplished using queries.

The world of fitness can be quite competitive, and Sheldon likes to challenge some of his clients to improve by competing against each other. You suggest creating a list of the top 5 percent of clients who can do the most push-ups. Sheldon thinks that is a great idea and adds a request to be able to list all clients' training hours for other competitive incentives. Both of these requests fit nicely into Access queries.

Sheldon also requests that the database be able to calculate weight changes in his clients from a series of training sessions. After discussions with him, you realize that you can create a series of two queries that can calculate weight changes.

Finally, Sheldon would like a report that summarizes the bimonthly fitness assessments of his clients. This report will give him a "snapshot" of how clients are responding to his tailored training regime.

ASSIGNMENT 1: CREATING THE DATABASE DESIGN

In this assignment, you design your database tables using a word-processing program. Pay close attention to the logic and structure of the tables. Do not start developing your Access database in Assignment 2 before getting feedback from your instructor on Assignment 1. Keep in mind that you need to examine the requirements in Assignment 2 to design your fields and tables properly. It is good programming practice to look at the required outputs before beginning your design. When designing the database, observe the following guidelines:

- First, determine the tables you will need by listing the name of each table and the fields it should contain. Avoid data redundancy. Do not create a field if it can be created by a calculated field in a query.
- You will need some transaction tables. Think about the business events that occur when clients book their training sessions. Also, think about how Sheldon records his bimonthly assessment figures. Avoid duplicating data.
- Document your tables using the table feature of your word processor. Your tables should resemble the format shown in Figure 3-1.
- You must mark the appropriate key field(s) by entering an asterisk (*) next to the field name. Keep in mind that some tables might need a compound primary key to uniquely identify a record within a table.
- Print the database design, if required.

Table Name	
Field Name	**Data Type (text, numeric, currency, etc.)**
...	...
...	...

FIGURE 3-1 Table design

NOTE

Have your design approved before beginning Assignment 2; otherwise, you may need to redo Assignment 2.

ASSIGNMENT 2: CREATING THE DATABASE, QUERIES, AND REPORTS

In this assignment, you first create database tables in Access and populate them with data. Next, you create two forms, six queries, and a report.

Assignment 2A: Creating Tables in Access

In this part of the assignment, you create your tables in Access. Use the following guidelines:

- Enter data for at least 10 clients, as outlined in the Background section of this case. Use your name as one of the clients. Enter home addresses, telephone numbers, email addresses, birthdates, and heights. Create initial baseline health data for clients, such as their weights, and how they score on the four fitness tests.
- Create at least two bookings for personal training sessions for each client. Create at least two bimonthly health assessments for each client.
- Appropriately limit the size of the text fields; for example, a phone number does not need the default length of 255 characters.
- Print all tables if your instructor requires it.

Assignment 2B: Creating Forms, Queries, and Reports

You will generate two forms with subforms, six queries, and a report, as outlined in the Background section of this case.

Form 1

Create a form and subform based on your Clients table and the Baseline table (or whatever you named the tables). Save the form as Baseline. Your form should resemble the one in Figure 3-2.

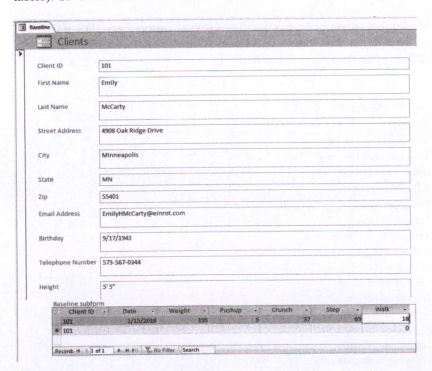

FIGURE 3-2   Baseline form and subform

Form 2

Create a form and subform based on your Clients table and your Appointments table (or whatever you named the tables). Save the form as Appointments. Your form should resemble the one in Figure 3-3.

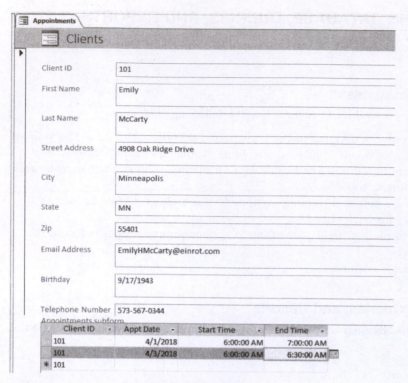

FIGURE 3-3 Appointments form and subform

Query 1

Create a select query called Clients over 60 that lists all clients who are over 60 years of age. The query should display columns for the clients' First Name, Last Name, and Email Address. Your output should resemble that shown in Figure 3-4, although your data will be different.

First Name	Last Name	Email Address
Emily	McCarty	EmilyHMcCarty@einrot.com
Donald	Woodruff	DonaldCWoodruff@cuvox.de
Mary	Heiman	MaryJHeiman@jourrapide.com
Tyrone	Mendoza	TyroneFMendoza@superrito.com
Joanie	Slater	JoanieJSlater@dayrep.com
Mary	Wilson	MarySWilson@teleworm.us
James	Moses	JamesEMoses@rhyta.com
Patricia	Palermo	PatriciaEPalermo@jourrapide.com
Elizabeth	Woodward	ElizabethJWoodward@armyspy.com
Eric	Davidson	EricSDavidson@rhyta.com
Henry	Brantley	HenryPBrantley@rhyta.com
Megan	Ott	MeganAOtt@superrito.com
Clyde	Buckman	ClydeNBuckman@jourrapide.com
Larry	Beale	LarryABeale@jourrapide.com
Joseph	Lloyd	JosephJLloyd@dayrep.com
Hannah	Ritter	HannahMRitter@jourrapide.com
Stephanie	Williams	StephaniePWilliams@fleckens.hu
Victoria	Snow	VictoriaNSnow@rhyta.com
Andrew	Sharp	AndrewASharp@rhyta.com
Roxanne	Courtney	RoxanneWCourtney@einrot.com
Donald	Petersen	DonaldNPetersen@einrot.com
Susan	Rivera	SusanHRivera@dayrep.com
Donna	Caines	DonnaRCaines@dayrep.com

FIGURE 3-4 Clients over 60 query

Query 2

Create a parameter query called Today's Appointments that shows the appointments Sheldon has scheduled for a specified date. The query prompts the user to enter a date and then displays headings for Appt (appointment) Date, First Name, Last Name, Start Time, and End Time. When you enter the date April 1, 2018, the output should resemble that shown in Figure 3-5, although your data will be different.

Appt Date	First Name	Last Name	Start Time	End Time
4/1/2018	Emily	McCarty	6:00:00 AM	7:00:00 AM
4/1/2018	Kathy	Johnson	7:00:00 AM	8:00:00 AM
4/1/2018	Tina	Bangs	8:00:00 AM	9:00:00 AM
4/1/2018	Kevin	Prater	10:00:00 AM	11:00:00 AM
4/1/2018	Pat	Pearce	12:00:00 PM	1:00:00 PM
4/1/2018	Albert	Downey	4:00:00 PM	5:00:00 PM
4/1/2018	Marietta	Dolloff	5:00:00 PM	6:00:00 PM
4/1/2018	Sonya	Clark	6:00:00 PM	7:00:00 PM
4/1/2018	Lela	Decker	7:00:00 PM	8:00:00 PM
4/1/2018	Ray	Moody	8:00:00 PM	9:00:00 PM

FIGURE 3-5 Today's Appointments query

Query 3

Create a query that lists the top 5 percent of clients who did the most push-ups in one minute during their baseline assessment. Display columns for each client's Last Name, First Name, and number of push-ups. Sort the output so that clients who did the most push-ups are shown at the top of the list. (Hint: Under the Design tab, in the Query Setup group, enter "5%" in the Return field.) Save the query as Top 5 Percent. Your data will differ, but the output should look similar to that shown in Figure 3-6.

Last Name	First Name	Pushup
Calton	Esmeralda	40
Brown	Jeffrey	40
Lee	Raul	40
Perkins	Christopher	40
Sweeney	Danny	40
Willis	Robert	40
Hatton	Robert	40
Coleman	Tiffany	40
Sowers	Mack	39
Mitchell	Jessica	39
Ritter	Hannah	39
Forney	Robert	39
Williamson	Arnulfo	38
Cook	Lorie	38
Smith	Helen	38
Condrey	Loretta	38
Johnson	Claudia	38

FIGURE 3-6 Top 5 Percent query

Query 4

Create a query called Training Hours that lists the number of hours each client has trained within a specific range of dates. Display columns for the Client ID, First Name, and Last Name, and calculate values for the Training Hours column. Make sure your output is formatted correctly, as shown in Figure 3-7. Your output should resemble the format shown in Figure 3-7, but the data will be different.

Training Hours

Client ID	First Name	Last Name	Training Hours
101	Emily	McCarty	1.50
102	Kathy	Johnson	1.75
103	Tina	Bangs	2.00
104	Kevin	Prater	1.50
105	Pat	Pearce	1.75
201	Albert	Downey	1.00
202	Marietta	Dolloff	2.00
203	Sonya	Clark	1.00
204	Lela	Decker	1.00
205	Ray	Moody	1.00

FIGURE 3-7 Training Hours query

Query 5

Create a query called Weight Loss that displays columns for each client's Last Name, First Name, Street Address, and Height and calculates values in the Weight Loss column. To calculate weight loss, you must first create a query that lists each client's most recent weight from the bimonthly assessment. Using that query, calculate the difference in weight in a new query. Ensure that your calculated field is properly formatted. Your output should resemble the format shown in Figure 3-8, but the data will be different.

Weight Loss

Last Name	First Name	Street Address	Height	Weight Loss
Pearce	Pat	1203 Green Avenue	5' 10"	9
Downey	Albert	1565 Fleming Street	6' 0"	8
Prater	Kevin	1514 Irving Road	5' 10"	8
Johnson	Kathy	176 Walkers Ridge Way	5' 7"	8
Bangs	Tina	2688 Private Lane	5' 3"	5
Moody	Ray	1394 Quiet Valley Lane	5' 11"	4
Clark	Sonya	2548 University Street	5' 3"	3
Dolloff	Marietta	985 Ridenour Street	5' 1"	3
Decker	Lela	2833 Fincham Road	5' 2"	2
McCarty	Emily	4908 Oak Ridge Drive	5' 5"	1

FIGURE 3-8 Weight Loss query

Report

Create a report called Assessment Summary that helps clients track their bimonthly assessment details. First, you need to create a query to amass the required data. The report should include headings for First Name, Last Name, Street Address, Email Address, the date of the assessment, and its fitness results. Make sure all headings are visible and that the data is formatted correctly, as shown. Depending on your data, the output should resemble that shown in Figure 3-9.

Assessment Summary

Assessment Summary

First Name	Last Name	Street Address	Email Address	Assessment Date	Pushup	Crunch	Step	Walk
Albert	Downey	1565 Fleming Street	AlbertMDowney@fleckens.hu					
				3/1/2018	34	47	104	12
				6/12/2018	32	48	106	12
				4/30/2018	26	54	112	12
Emily	McCarty	4908 Oak Ridge Drive	EmilyHMcCarty@einrot.com					
				4/30/2018	6	40	69	16
				6/12/2018	7	45	68	16
				3/1/2018	10	43	65	16
Kathy	Johnson	176 Walkers Ridge Way	KathyJJohnson@fleckens.hu					
				6/12/2018	21	23	59	16
				3/1/2018	19	25	61	16
				4/30/2018	16	25	64	16

FIGURE 3-9 Assessment Summary report

ASSIGNMENT 3: ANALYZING THE DATA AND MAKING A PRESENTATION

Sheldon can track each client's fitness progression, but he doesn't know how his clients stack up to existing fitness standards. Are Sheldon's clients seeing adequate improvements in their fitness? Explore standards of fitness tests on the Internet and compare the data from your database with the data online. Consider organizing the clients into various age groups and comparing their results with published survey results of fit people in those age brackets. Write a brief memo to Sheldon explaining your results. Include details from your queries' outputs and consider including some graphs from Excel to further explain your results. For details on writing a memo, see Tutorial E.

Create a presentation that explains the database to Sheldon and demonstrates how it is used. Discuss future improvements to the database, such as moving the system online or to Sheldon's mobile device. Your presentation should take less than 10 minutes, including a question-and-answer period.

DELIVERABLES

Assemble the following deliverables for your instructor, either electronically or in printed form:

1. Word-processed design of tables
2. Tables created in Access
3. Form and subform: Baseline
4. Form and subform: Appointments
5. Query 1: Clients over 60
6. Query 2: Today's Appointments
7. Query 3: Top 5 Percent
8. Query 4: Training Hours
9. Query 5: Weight Loss
10. Subquery for Weight Loss query (latest weight)
11. Query for report
12. Report: Assessment Summary
13. Data analytics memo
14. Presentation materials
15. Any other required printouts or electronic media

Staple all the pages together. Include your name and class number at the top of each page. Make sure that your electronic media are labeled, if required.

THE RENT UR CAR DATABASE

*Designing a Relational Database to Create Tables,
Forms, Queries, and Reports*

PREVIEW

In this case, you will design a relational database for a new business that links private vehicle owners with customers who want to rent those vehicles. After your design is complete and correct, you will create database tables and populate them with data. Then you will produce one form with a subform, eight queries, and two reports. Two queries will display lists of high-end cars that are available for rental. Other queries will list the number of days each vehicle has been rented, the total amount of money each customer has spent on rentals, and the number of times each vehicle has been rented. Two more queries will display lists of the top-grossing vehicles and cars that have never been rented. You will also produce two reports based on queries that summarize customer rentals and rental income for vehicle owners.

PREPARATION

- Before attempting this case, you should have some experience in database design and in using Microsoft Access.
- Complete any part of Tutorial A that your instructor assigns.
- Complete any part of Tutorial B that your instructor assigns, or refer to the tutorial as necessary.
- Refer to Tutorial F as necessary.

BACKGROUND

The sharing economy is all the rage now, and many people are turning to alternatives for travel. For example, Airbnb now hosts many travelers who traditionally booked hotel rooms in the past. Car rental is undergoing a transformation as well; private vehicle owners now rent their cars to others when the vehicles are not in use. For example, if you commute to work using public transportation, your car is idle all day. Why not turn your vehicle into a source of extra income? Your cousin, Penny, did just that. She rarely uses her car because she lives in Chicago and takes public transportation everywhere, so she started to let her friends use her car for a daily fee. They made sure to return the car with the same amount of gasoline it contained when they borrowed it. Penny's friends liked the arrangement so much that they encouraged her to start a business for like-minded people who want to rent their cars. The business, called Rent Ur Car, also known as RUC, has taken off. Penny has been keeping records in Microsoft Excel spreadsheets and on paper, but she realizes that the business has outgrown her substandard record-keeping. Because you have been studying databases, she enlists your help over the summer to create a prototype database that will eventually be ported online and have its front end developed into an app.

On the first day of your summer job, you meet with Penny to understand how the business works. She describes its simple model: Owners register with RUC, submit their cars' details, and set a daily rental price. Customers also register with RUC and can book a rental car after browsing the types of vehicles available. Penny takes a small percentage of each transaction to pay herself, her team of workers (including you), and the insurance that covers each car rental. For this project, Penny wants you to focus on the rental aspect of her business and ignore the money she makes from each transaction.

Next, you examine her paper and spreadsheet records to better understand how to design your database. Penny has a listing of all the owners who have registered their cars for rental. The list is a stack of index cards; each contains an owner's name, address, phone number, and email address. The stack is alphabetized and organized in a box. In a separate box, Penny keeps a stack of cards that summarize the vehicles available for rent. Each vehicle's description is written on a card, including the price per day desired and a code that matches up with the owner. In an Excel spreadsheet, Penny has listed each vehicle, customer, and the start and end dates rented.

Although the database design appears fairly straightforward, Penny assures you that there are plenty of tasks to accomplish and questions to answer.

Eventually, you envision the app working this way: Customers can book a vehicle by choosing its ID number after perusing the table of vehicles and indicating their rental start and end dates. Because this app is a prototype built with Microsoft Access, you are confident that a form will test the future app's capabilities.

Penny tells you that many customers call and ask if specific vehicles are available. For example, she wants you to create a query that searches for and then displays a list of any Ferraris in the database. She also would like a query that searches for Corvettes available for rental and then lists the cities where the cars are located.

Penny is interested in analyzing data from the business and has a series of questions related to top performers that she wants you to organize in queries. First, she would like to know which vehicles are rented the most number of days. She is also curious to know who the top customers are, as measured by the amount of money each has spent on rentals. In addition, she wants to know how many times each vehicle has been rented, and she thinks that knowing which vehicles are the top-grossing rentals would be helpful for marketing.

Although Penny never turns down any owners who want to rent their vehicles, she knows that some vehicles are never rented. She wonders if you can create a query that can list these vehicles. You are confident that Microsoft Access is capable of this task.

Occasionally, Penny feels that prices need to be adjusted. As an experiment, she wants you to raise the prices of all BMW rentals by 2 percent. You explain to Penny that an update query can perform this task.

Because Penny is interested in tracking all information in the database, you suggest two formal reports that could be of use to her. The first is a Customer Rental Summary report that lists each customer and what vehicles they have rented so far. The second report is an Owners' Income report, which will display how much money the owners are bringing in with their rentals. Penny agrees that these reports will be useful for her analysis.

ASSIGNMENT 1: CREATING THE DATABASE DESIGN

In this assignment, you design your database tables using a word-processing program. Pay close attention to the logic and structure of the tables. Do not start developing your Access database in Assignment 2 before getting feedback from your instructor on Assignment 1. Keep in mind that you need to examine the requirements in Assignment 2 to design your fields and tables properly. It is good programming practice to look at the required outputs before beginning your design. When designing the database, observe the following guidelines:

- First, determine the tables you will need by listing the name of each table and the fields it should contain. Avoid data redundancy. Do not create a field if it can be created by a calculated field in a query.
- You will need a transaction table. Think about the business events that occur with each car rental. Avoid duplicating data.
- Document your tables using the table feature of your word processor. Your tables should resemble the format shown in Figure 4-1.
- You must mark the appropriate key field(s) by entering an asterisk (*) next to the field name. Keep in mind that some tables might need a compound primary key to uniquely identify a record within a table.
- Print the database design, if required.

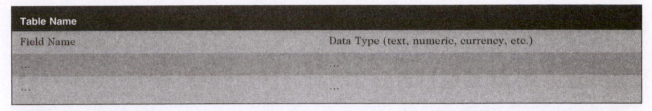

Table Name	
Field Name	Data Type (text, numeric, currency, etc.)
...	...
...	...

FIGURE 4-1   Table design

> **NOTE**
>
> Have your design approved before beginning Assignment 2; otherwise, you may need to redo Assignment 2.

ASSIGNMENT 2: CREATING THE DATABASE, QUERIES, AND REPORTS

In this assignment, you first create database tables in Access and populate them with data. Next, you create a form, eight queries, and two reports.

Assignment 2A: Creating Tables in Access

In this part of the assignment, you create your tables in Access. Use the following guidelines:

- Enter data for at least 10 customers, 10 owners, and 10 vehicles. Consider searching the Internet for name-and-address generators, which will create the necessary details for your data. These generators often create lists in Microsoft Excel. You can then import the Excel spreadsheet into Microsoft Access and adjust for any changes to field types.
- Create records for more than 25 rentals. Consider using Microsoft Excel and the Randbetween function to generate a large amount of data.
- Appropriately limit the size of the text fields; for example, a phone number does not need the default length of 255 characters.
- Print all tables if your instructor requires it.

Assignment 2B: Creating Forms, Queries, and Reports

You will generate one form with a subform, eight queries, and two reports, as outlined in the Background section of this case.

Form

Create a form and subform based on your Cars table and Rentals table (or whatever you named the tables). Save the form as Rental Reservation. Your form should resemble the one in Figure 4-2.

Rental Reservation				

Cars

Owner ID	911
Vehicle ID	12
Vehicle	2005 Land Rover Discovery
Price Per Day	$74.00

Rentals subform

ID	Vehicle ID	Customer ID	Start Date	End Date
12	12	103	9/30/2017	10/2/2017
29	12	142	10/17/2017	10/20/2017
*	12			

Record: 2 of 2   No Filter   Search

FIGURE 4-2   Rental Reservation form and subform

Query 1

Create a select query called Ferraris Available that displays columns for the Vehicle ID, Vehicle, and Price Per Day. Consider using a wildcard because the word *Ferrari* in a field could be embedded with other data. Your output should resemble that shown in Figure 4-3, although your data will be different.

Vehicle ID	Vehicle	Price Per Day
80	1994 Ferrari F333	$315.00
92	2007 Ferrari 612	$370.00

FIGURE 4-3   Ferraris Available query

Query 2

Create a query called Corvettes Available. The query is similar to Query 1 except that it will search for Corvettes. In addition to displaying columns for the Vehicle ID, Vehicle, and Price Per Day, the query will display columns for the City and State where the Corvette is located. The output should resemble that shown in Figure 4-4, although your data will be different.

Vehicle ID	Vehicle	Price Per Da	City	State
65	2007 Chevrolet Corvette	$225.00	Brookline	MA

FIGURE 4-4   Corvettes Available query

Query 3

Create a query that displays the list of rental vehicles and reports how many days each vehicle has been rented. Display columns for Vehicle and Days Rented. Sort the output to view the most rented vehicles at the top. Make sure the column headings are displayed as shown in Figure 4-5. Save the query as Top Days Rented. Your output should resemble the format shown, but the data will be different. Also, note that only a portion of the output is shown in the figure.

Vehicle	Days Rented
2008 Volvo S80	12
2008 Mazda 5	9
2009 SsangYong Actyon	8
1992 Oldsmobile Eighty-Eight	8
2008 Maserati Coupe	8
1996 Alfa Romeo Spider	8
2006 Ford Freestyle	7
2001 Fiat Duna	7
2002 Toyota Avalon	6
2006 Toyota Highlander	6
1998 Saab 9-3	6
1997 Nissan Terrano II	6
1993 Mazda AZ-1	5

FIGURE 4-5   Top Days Rented query

Query 4

Create a query that calculates the total amount of money each customer has spent on car rentals. Display the full names of the customers and their email addresses, and calculate and display the totals spent. Sort the query results to list the best customer first; make sure your output is formatted correctly. Save the query as

Top Customers. Your output should resemble the format shown in Figure 4-6, but the data will be different. Also, note that only a portion of the output is displayed in the figure.

First Name	Last Name	Email Address	Total Spent
Virginia	Valentine	VirginiaTValentine@rhyta.com	$2,698.00
Robert	Jacobs	RobertNJacobs@jourrapide.com	$1,816.00
Henry	Thomas	HenryCThomas@superrito.com	$1,690.00
Theresa	Hernandez	TheresaRHernandez@jourrapide.com	$1,377.00
James	Fender	JamesWFender@dayrep.com	$1,362.00
Mathew	Johnson	MathewEJohnson@fleckens.hu	$1,344.00
Susan	Gibson	SusanBGibson@gustr.com	$1,253.00
Monica	Hamann	MonicaKHamann@dayrep.com	$1,251.00
David	Watts	DavidBWatts@superrito.com	$1,088.00
Michelle	Thomas	MichelleDThomas@jourrapide.com	$1,018.00
Lester	Boettcher	LesterNBoettcher@fleckens.hu	$926.00
Carol	Barnum	CarolSBarnum@jourrapide.com	$901.00
Tessa	Wood	TessaTWood@cuvox.de	$900.00
Joseph	Duran	JosephCDuran@gustr.com	$892.00

FIGURE 4-6 Top Customers query

Query 5

Create a query called Top Times Rented that displays the list of vehicles and reports how many times each car has been rented. Sort the output to show the most rented vehicle at the top of the list. Your output should resemble the format shown in Figure 4-7, but the data will be different. Also, note that only a portion of the output is shown in the figure.

Vehicle	Number of Times Rented
2008 Volvo S80	4
2002 Toyota Avalon	3
1993 Mazda AZ-1	3
1996 Alfa Romeo Spider	3
2008 Maserati Coupe	3
2009 SsangYong Actyon	3
2008 Mazda 5	3
2006 Volkswagen Eos	2
2006 Toyota Highlander	2
2006 Ford Freestyle	2
2005 Dodge Stratus	2
2003 Alfa Romeo 166	2

FIGURE 4-7 Top Times Rented query

Query 6

Create a query called Top Grossing Vehicles that displays each vehicle's name, city, and state and calculates how much money each vehicle's rental has generated. Display the top-grossing vehicle at the top of the list. Your output should resemble the format shown in Figure 4-8, but the data will be different. Also, note that only a portion of the output is shown in the figure.

| Top Grossing Vehicles | | | |
Vehicle	City	State	Gross Income
1996 Alfa Romeo Spider	Buffalo Grove	IL	$1,816.00
1996 Alfa Romeo Spider	Dublin	OH	$1,362.00
1994 Ferrari F333	Johnson City	TN	$1,260.00
1997 Nissan Terrano II	Phoenix	AZ	$1,110.00
2008 Volvo S80	Cincinnati	OH	$900.00
2003 Porsche 996	Atlanta	GA	$892.00
2014 BMW 3 Series Gran Turismo	Johnson City	TN	$832.00
2006 Ford Freestyle	Phoenix	AZ	$824.00
2014 Ford E-Series Wagon	Polk City	FL	$812.00
2001 Fiat Duna	Detroit	MI	$808.00
2009 SsangYong Actyon	Pontiac	MI	$792.00
1994 Opel Astra	Port St Lucie	FL	$784.00
1992 Oldsmobile Eighty-Eight	Oakland	CA	$724.00
1992 Oldsmobile Eighty-Eight	Philadelphia	PA	$724.00
1996 Italdesign Nazca	Toledo	OH	$717.00
2008 Volvo S80	Kent	WA	$675.00

FIGURE 4-8 Top Grossing Vehicles query

Query 7

Create a query called Cars Never Rented that displays a list of vehicle owners' first names, last names, email addresses, vehicles, and rental prices of cars that have never been rented. To correctly complete this query, you must change the join line between the cars table and the rentals table to include all the cars, even if they do not have a match in the rentals table. The criteria for the empty set is "is null." Your output should resemble the format shown in Figure 4-9, but the data will be different. Also, note that only a portion of the output is shown in the figure.

| Cars Never Rented | | | | |
First Name	Last Name	Email Address	Vehicle	Price Per Day
Steven	Weiss	StevenJWeiss@einrot.com	2012 Kia Sportage	$25.00
Joseph	Spring	JosephESpring@dayrep.com	1992 Citroen AX	$223.00
Jeff	Walker	JeffTWalker@rhyta.com	2002 Seat Inca Kombi	$185.00
Ana	Ward	AnaEWard@rhyta.com	1996 Ford Crown Victoria	$202.00
Pauline	Freeman	PaulineRFreeman@gustr.com	2007 GMC Acadia	$93.00
Newton	Witherspoon	NewtonAWitherspoon@superrito.com	2008 Honda Pilot	$175.00
Juan	Fishman	JuanIFishman@fleckens.hu	1992 Subaru Vivio	$112.00
Sally	Frazier	SallyJFrazier@rhyta.com	2001 Tata Aria	$230.00
David	Starks	DavidLStarks@armyspy.com	1997 Mitsubishi Pajero	$236.00
Peggy	Chambliss	PeggyRChambliss@einrot.com	2008 Lexus LS	$219.00
Patricia	Ewell	PatriciaJEwell@jourrapide.com	2008 BMW 328	$154.00
Millard	McElyea	MillardLMcElyea@jourrapide.com	2012 BMW X6	$256.00
Lucy	Treadwell	LucyJTreadwell@superrito.com	2014 Mercedes-Benz GL-Class	$180.00
Lula	Jackson	LulaWJackson@gustr.com	2007 Renault Kangoo	$187.00
Milton	Sisk	MiltonHSisk@fleckens.hu	2011 Mitsubishi Outlander	$122.00
Scott	Hogg	ScottBHogg@rhyta.com	1994 Mazda RX-7	$209.00
Leslie	Numbers	LeslieCNumbers@einrot.com	2010 SsangYong Chairman W	$182.00
Rhonda	Hensley	RhondaJHensley@superrito.com	2010 Suzuki Equator	$57.00

FIGURE 4-9 Cars Never Rented query

Query 8

Create an update query that adds 2 percent to the rental price of all BMWs. Test the query by running it and then examining the vehicles table. Save the query as Increase BMW Price.

Report 1

Create a report called Customer Rental Summary that summarizes all rentals. First, you need to create a query to amass the required data. The report should include headings for First Name and Last Name of each customer, along with headings for their City, State, Vehicle, and Total Price, which is a calculated field. Group the report by the customer's name. Include subtotals that display the total amount of money paid by each customer. Make sure all headings are visible and that the data is formatted correctly, as shown.

Depending on your data, the output should resemble that in Figure 4-10, although only a portion of the output is shown.

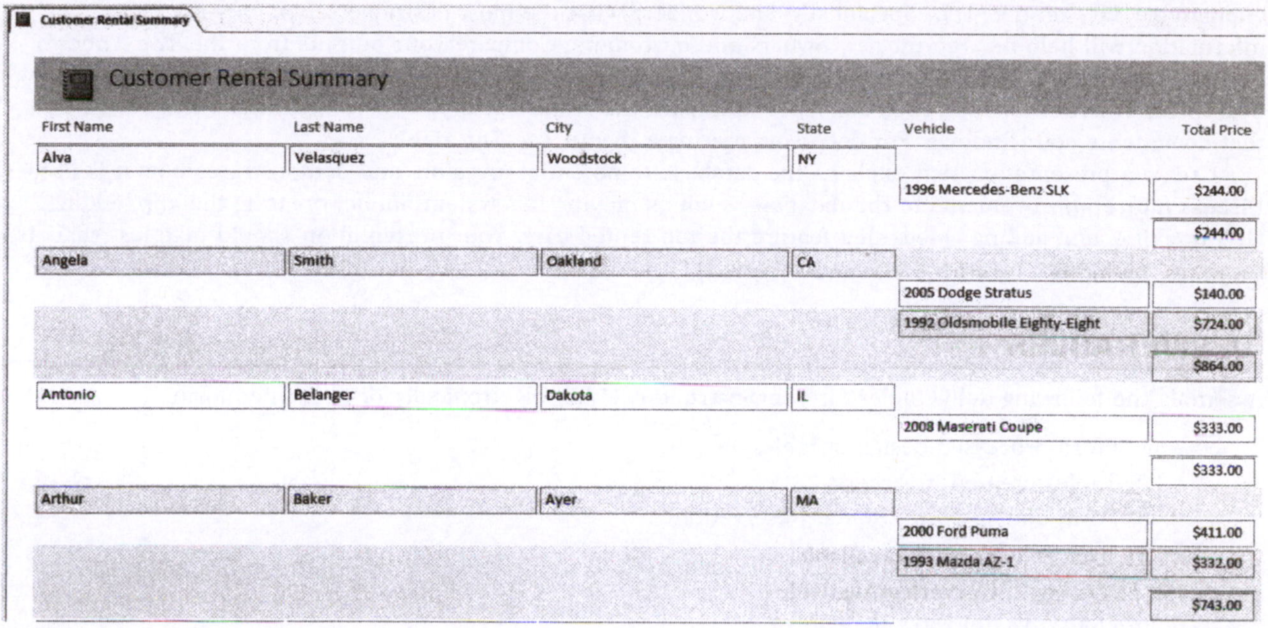

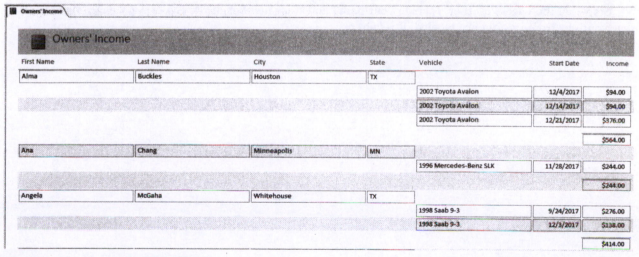

FIGURE 4-10   Customer Rental Summary report

Report 2

Create a report called Owners' Income that summarizes all rental income for vehicle owners. First, you need to create a query to gather the required data. The report should include headings for each owner's First Name, Last Name, City, State, and Vehicle, along with the rental Start Date and the Income from it, which is a calculated field. Group the report by the owner's name. Include subtotals that display the total amount of money generated for each owner. Make sure all headings are visible and that the data is formatted correctly, as shown. Depending on your data, the output should resemble that in Figure 4-11, although only a portion of the output is shown.

FIGURE 4-11   Owners' Income report

ASSIGNMENT 3: ANALYZING THE DATA AND MAKING A PRESENTATION

Penny loves analyzing the data and is curious to know how some of the queries you created differ from comparable data on the Web. Specifically, she wonders what the most desirable rental cars are. This information will help her recruit new owners and customers. Compare your outputs from the Top Times Rented, Top Days Rented, and Top Grossing Vehicles queries with data you find online. Do they differ? How? Search the Internet for top rental car types. Compare the results with your lists and write Penny a memo that documents your findings. For details on writing a memo, see Tutorial E.

Create a presentation that explains the database to potential investors and demonstrates how it is used. Discuss future improvements to the database, such as moving the system online, creating the app, adding GPS tracking, and adding videos that feature the top rented cars. Your presentation should take less than 10 minutes, including a question-and-answer period.

DELIVERABLES

Assemble the following deliverables for your instructor, either electronically or in printed form:

1. Word-processed design of tables
2. Tables created in Access
3. Form and subform: Rental Reservation
4. Query 1: Ferraris Available
5. Query 2: Corvettes Available
6. Query 3: Top Days Rented
7. Query 4: Top Customers
8. Query 5: Top Times Rented
9. Query 6: Top Grossing Vehicles
10. Query 7: Cars Never Rented
11. Query 8: Increase BMW Price
12. Report 1: Customer Rental Summary
13. Report 2: Owners' Income
14. Data analysis memo
15. Presentation materials
16. Any other required printouts or electronic media

Staple all the pages together. Include your name and class number at the top of each page. Make sure that your electronic media are labeled, if required.

THE HOUSEHOLD HELP DATABASE

Designing a Relational Database to Create Tables,
Queries, and Reports

PREVIEW

In this case, you will design a relational database for a prototype online bazaar that matches workers with household jobs. After your tables are designed and created, you will populate the database and create a form with a subform, six queries, and two reports. The form and subform will allow clients to book jobs. The queries will address the following questions: What jobs are scheduled on a specific date? Who are the most frequent clients? Who are the workers, and what are their skills? Which workers earn the most money? Who are the top clients? What are the final customer bills after discounts have been applied? The reports will summarize the customers' final payments and the workers' earnings.

PREPARATION

- Before attempting this case, you should have some experience in database design and in using Microsoft Access.
- Complete any part of Tutorial A that your instructor assigns.
- Complete any part of Tutorial B that your instructor assigns, or refer to the tutorial as necessary.
- Refer to Tutorial F as necessary.

BACKGROUND

People are always looking for good recommendations for help with household jobs and chores, such as handyman work, cleaning, and moving. You and your college roommate recognize the business potential of linking prospective clients with workers who can perform these household jobs and chores. With the popularity of smartphones and apps, you know that a client who needs help can find it quickly with the touch of a finger. You and your roommate have decided to start a company called Household Help, or HHH. The company will solicit workers who want to perform household chores such as cleaning, shopping and delivery, handyman work, and moving. After a thorough background check, these workers will be connected to clients who need their skills. You and your roommate are taking an information systems class and learning about databases and Microsoft Access. The two of you decide to create a prototype system using the software before porting it to an app and smartphones.

You begin by brainstorming about the information that needs to be recorded to run HHH. First, clients need to submit personal information, such as their full name, address, phone number, email address, and credit card information for ease of billing. Workers also need to register after their background checks by providing their full name, home address, and email address.

You envision that HHH will offer four different types of services that clients can request: cleaning, shopping and delivery, handyman jobs, and moving. Each service will be assigned a unique code so you don't have to repeatedly enter the exact name of the task when you populate the database with appointments. In addition, each service will have a specific pay rate per hour. For example, a handyman's services will be more expensive per hour than those of a worker who makes shopping trips and deliveries. To begin, each worker in the database will be associated with one task he or she chooses to perform. In the future, you can see that workers might want to perform more than one task, so you will design your database to allow that possibility.

When clients call or eventually use the app to schedule a task, they will need to specify the worker they want, the date they need the task performed, and the start and end times.

Once your database is designed and implemented, you know that a number of forms, queries, and reports will be useful. Forms will help you enter relevant data into the database. For example, you will create a form that allows clients to book desired jobs.

Next, you will create queries. The first useful query will display the jobs scheduled for a specified date. You will also create a query that lists the most frequent clients. The information from this query can be used to identify clients who might receive coupons or discounts for being faithful customers. You and your roommate want to create a third query that lists workers and their skills. This output could help clients choose their favorite workers to perform tasks they don't want to do themselves.

It is convenient to keep tabs on which workers earn the most money and which clients spend the most money on HHH services. Queries can easily handle both requests. Your roommate also suggests that you can expand the business by offering discounts in areas of the city that are not using HHH yet. By using a query that includes an If statement, you can give discounts to customers who live in a specific zip code.

Finally, you want two professional reports to show to potential investors in your app. One report will summarize the customers' final payments, and the other will display the workers' earnings for each job.

ASSIGNMENT 1: CREATING THE DATABASE DESIGN

In this assignment, you design your database tables using a word-processing program. Pay close attention to the logic and structure of the tables. Do not start developing your Access database in Assignment 2 before getting feedback from your instructor on Assignment 1. Keep in mind that you need to examine the requirements in Assignment 2 to design your fields and tables properly. It is good programming practice to look at the required outputs before beginning your design. When designing the database, observe the following guidelines:

- First, determine the tables you will need by listing the name of each table and the fields it should contain. Avoid data redundancy. Do not create a field if it can be created by a calculated field in a query.
- You will need a transaction table to record all the jobs.
- Document your tables using the table feature of your word processor. Your tables should resemble the format shown in Figure 5-1.
- You must mark the appropriate key field(s) by entering an asterisk (*) next to the field name. Keep in mind that some tables might need a compound primary key to uniquely identify a record within a table.
- Print the database design.

Table Name	
Field Name	Data Type (text, numeric, currency, etc.)
…	…
…	…

FIGURE 5-1   Table design

NOTE

Have your design approved before beginning Assignment 2; otherwise, you may need to redo Assignment 2.

ASSIGNMENT 2: CREATING THE DATABASE, FORMS, QUERIES, AND REPORTS

In this assignment, you first create database tables in Access and populate them with data. Next, you create a form and subform, six queries, and two reports.

Assignment 2A: Creating Tables in Access

In this part of the assignment, you create your tables in Access. Use the following guidelines:

- Create records for clients. You can either enter data that you make up or use a random name generator on the Internet. Make sure you have data for at least 25 clients.
- Create 10 workers' records, with each worker specializing in one service. Make sure your design allows for workers to have more than one specialty in the future.
- Create four tasks that the workers perform: cleaning, shopping and delivery, handyman services, and moving. Each task should have a different pay rate per hour.
- Create at least 25 booked jobs. You can use the Randbetween function in Microsoft Excel to create random data and alleviate typing.
- Appropriately limit the size of the text fields; for example, a client ID number does not need the default length of 255 characters.
- Print all tables if your instructor requires it.

Assignment 2B: Creating Forms, Queries, and Reports

You will create a form and subform, six queries, and two reports, as outlined in the Background section of this case.

Form 1

Create a form and subform based on your Clients table and Jobs table (or whatever you named the tables). Save the form as Clients and Jobs. Your form should look like the one in Figure 5-2.

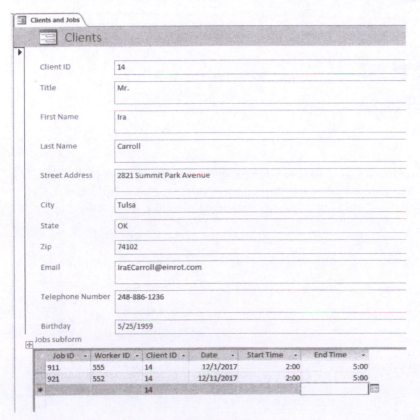

FIGURE 5-2   Clients and Jobs form and subform

Query 1

You want to be able to list which jobs are scheduled for a specified date. Create a query that prompts for a date input and then displays columns for the clients' First Name, Last Name, and Email, as well as the Date and Start Time of jobs on the specified date. Save the query as Jobs on Specific Date. If you enter 12/10/2017, for example, your output should look like that shown in Figure 5-3, although your data will be different.

First Name	Last Name	Email	Date	Start Time
Theresa	Sinclair	TheresaRSinclair@rhyta.com	12/10/2017	8:00
Sue	Bates	SueRBates@teleworm.us	12/10/2017	2:00

FIGURE 5-3   Jobs on Specific Date query

Query 2

You need to determine which clients use HHH the most. Create a query called Most Frequent Clients that displays columns for their First Name, Last Name, Street Address, City, State, and Zip, and that calculates and displays the number of jobs each client has booked. List the clients with the most bookings at the top of the query. Your data will differ, but the layout of the query should look like that shown in Figure 5-4.

First Name	Last Name	Street Address	City	State	Zip	Number of Jobs
Harold	Gaskins	2137 Aspen Court	Tulsa	OK	74102	3
Clint	Byfield	2239 Payne Street	Tulsa	OK	74102	3
Willie	Chumbley	4915 Hickory Lane	Tulsa	OK	74102	3
Aurelio	O'Connor	3267 Havanna Street	Tulsa	OK	74102	2
Galen	Machado	1332 Providence Lane	Tulsa	OK	74102	2
Ira	Carroll	2821 Summit Park Avenue	Tulsa	OK	74102	2
Jay	Thurston	1771 Northwest Boulevard	Tulsa	OK	74102	2
Keith	Diaz	3931 Ottis Street	Tulsa	OK	74102	2
William	Leblanc	2937 Locust View Drive	Tulsa	OK	74102	2
Michael	Lang	2073 Loving Acres Road	Tulsa	OK	74102	1
Patricia	Arnold	3678 Briercliff Road	Tulsa	OK	74102	1
Phil	Grant	123 Timber Ridge Road	Tulsa	OK	74102	1
Ursula	Tindal	607 Cambridge Court	Tulsa	OK	74102	1
Aimee	Robinson	653 Maple Lane	Tulsa	OK	74102	1
Virginia	Hall	2943 Smith Road	Tulsa	OK	74102	1
Dan	Brown	1681 Woodhill Avenue	Tulsa	OK	74102	1
Wesley	Lopez	4180 Reeves Street	Tulsa	OK	74106	1
Clifton	Coleman	3411 Werninger Street	Tulsa	OK	74102	1

FIGURE 5-4   Most Frequent Clients query

Query 3

For advertising purposes, you want to create a list of workers and their skills. Create a query that displays columns for each worker's Task Type, First Name, Last Name, Street Address, City, State, Zip, Email, and Telephone Number. Save the query as Workers and Skills. The results should look like those shown in Figure 5-5.

Task Type	First Name	Last Name	Street Address	City	State	Zip	Email	Telephone Number
Handyman	Stephen	Bishop	906 Bagwell Avenue	Tulsa	OK	74101	StephenRBishop@cuvox.de	352-560-9228
Handyman	Sue	Bates	4775 Davis Avenue	Tulsa	OK	74103	SueRBates@teleworm.us	707-780-9050
Handyman	Russell	Bowser	2744 Rockford Mountain Lane	Tulsa	OK	74101	RussellDBowser@superrito.com	920-223-4343
House Cleaning	Corey	Davis	2016 Calico Drive	Tulsa	OK	74101	CoreyTDavis@einrot.com	509-641-8795
House Cleaning	Joshua	Janson	983 Sigley Road	Tulsa	OK	74101	JoshuaSJanson@einrot.com	785-558-3463
House Cleaning	Margaret	Rittenberry	1927 Front Street	Tulsa	OK	74102	MargaretWRittenberry@armyspy.com	810-378-1385
House Cleaning	Willie	Jackson	1068 Hardman Road	Tulsa	OK	74101	WillieUackson@teleworm.us	802-804-0403
Moving	Theresa	Sinclair	3747 Gnatty Creek Road	Tulsa	OK	74101	TheresaRSinclair@rhyta.com	516-397-4630
Moving	Annetta	Victor	4007 Washburn Street	Tulsa	OK	74101	AnnettaDVictor@rhyta.com	225-292-3986
Shopping and Delivery	Cynthia	Lipsey	3896 Gordon Street	Tulsa	OK	74108	CynthiaCLipsey@gustr.com	909-553-1338
Shopping and Delivery	Shirley	Becnel	2799 Eagles Nest Drive	Tulsa	OK	74101	ShirleyABecnel@rhyta.com	530-677-8910

FIGURE 5-5   Workers and Skills query

Query 4

You and your roommate want to know which workers earn the most money at HHH. Create a query that calculates the total pay each worker has earned. Display columns that list each worker's First Name, Last Name, Email, Task Type, and Total Pay. Sort the output so that the top earners are listed at the top. Save the query as Top Earner. Your output should look like that shown in Figure 5-6, although the data will be different.

Top Earner				
First Name ▾	Last Name ▾	Email ▾	Task Type ▾	Total Pay ▾
Sue	Bates	SueRBates@teleworm.us	Handyman	$540.00
Russell	Bowser	RussellDBowser@superrito.com	Handyman	$495.00
Corey	Davis	CoreyTDavis@einrot.com	House Cleaning	$350.00
Theresa	Sinclair	TheresaRSinclair@rhyta.com	Moving	$270.00
Stephen	Bishop	StephenRBishop@cuvox.de	Handyman	$225.00
Willie	Jackson	WillieJackson@teleworm.us	House Cleaning	$200.00
Shirley	Becnel	ShirleyABecnel@rhyta.com	Shopping and Delivery	$195.00
Joshua	Janson	JoshuaSJanson@einrot.com	House Cleaning	$125.00
Cynthia	Lipsey	CynthiaCLipsey@gustr.com	Shopping and Delivery	$90.00
Annetta	Victor	AnnettaDVictor@rhyta.com	Moving	$54.00

FIGURE 5-6 Top Earner query

Query 5

You also want to know which clients spend the most money at HHH. Create a query called Top Client that calculates the total paid by each client. Display columns that list the clients' First Name, Last Name, and Total Paid. Sort the output so that the top clients are listed at the top. Your output should look like that shown in Figure 5-7, although your data will be different.

Top Client		
First Name ▾	Last Name ▾	Total Paid ▾
Willie	Chumbley	$285.00
Harold	Gaskins	$270.00
Ira	Carroll	$210.00
William	Leblanc	$210.00
Keith	Diaz	$185.00
Jay	Thurston	$180.00
Galen	Machado	$171.00
Aurelio	O'Connor	$150.00
Clint	Byfield	$144.00
Aimee	Robinson	$135.00
Andy	Walter	$90.00
Phil	Grant	$75.00
Patricia	Arnold	$54.00
Virginia	Hall	$54.00
Jack	Reid	$54.00
Michael	Lang	$50.00
Alice	McCabe	$50.00
Clifton	Coleman	$45.00
Ursula	Tindal	$36.00
Carl	Bible	$36.00
Wesley	Lopez	$30.00
Dan	Brown	$30.00

FIGURE 5-7 Top Client query

Query 6

Your roommate wants to offer a 10 percent discount to clients who live in a specified zip code and encourage others in that area to use HHH. Create a query that calculates the total amount of money paid by each client. Then, using an If statement, calculate the 10 percent discount for clients in the specified zip code. Calculate a Final Paid amount after subtracting the discount from the Total Paid amount. Display columns for each customer's Title, First Name, Last Name, Street Address, Zip, Date, Task Type, Total Paid, Discount, and Final Paid. No sorting is necessary. Save your query as Customer Bills. Your output should resemble that shown in Figure 5-8, although the data will be different.

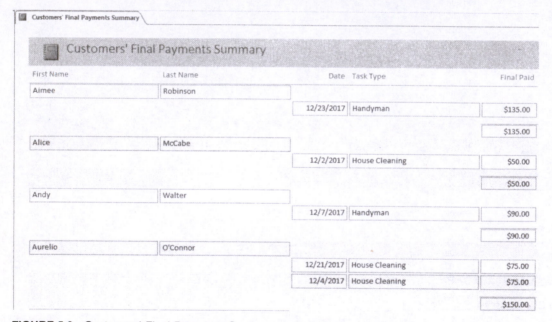

FIGURE 5-8   Customer Bills query

Report 1

Create a report called Customers' Final Payments Summary. First, create a query that will feed into this report. The query should also be named and saved as Customers' Final Payments Summary. This query is based on the Customer Bills query you created in the previous section. Display columns for the customers' First Name, Last Name, Date, Task Type, and Final Paid. Bring the query into the report generator and group the data by First Name and Last Name. Include subtotals for each customer's final paid amount. All headings should be visible, and data should be formatted correctly. Your output should resemble that shown in Figure 5-9, although only the top portion of the report appears in the figure.

FIGURE 5-9   Customers' Final Payments Summary report

Report 2

Create a report called Workers' Earnings. First, create a query that will feed into this report. The query should also be named and saved as Workers' Earnings. Display columns for the workers' First Name, Last Name, Date, Task Type, and Amount Earned. Bring that data into the report generator and group it by First Name and Last Name. Calculate and display subtotals for the amounts of money earned by each worker. All headings should be visible, and data should be formatted correctly. Your output should resemble that shown in Figure 5-10, although only the top portion of the report appears in the figure.

First Name	Last Name	Date	Task Type	Amount Earned
Annetta	Victor			
		12/17/2017	Moving	$54.00
				$54.00
Corey	Davis			
		12/2/2017	House Cleaning	$50.00
		12/1/2017	House Cleaning	$75.00
		12/19/2017	House Cleaning	$75.00
		12/4/2017	House Cleaning	$75.00
		12/9/2017	House Cleaning	$75.00
				$350.00
Cynthia	Lipsey			
		12/3/2017	Shopping and Delivery	$45.00
		12/14/2017	Shopping and Delivery	$45.00
				$90.00

FIGURE 5-10   Workers' Earnings report

ASSIGNMENT 3: ANALYZING THE DATA AND MAKING A PRESENTATION

Government Web sites contain a treasure trove of data available for public use. Consult the site at the Bureau of Labor Statistics (*www.bls.gov*) within the U.S. Department of Labor, look for employment data that supports the benefits of freelance work, and then use that data to make a case for the success of the HHH app. Write a memo to the top clients of HHH that explains your findings. Be sure to include relevant charts or tables of data from the Bureau of Labor Statistics to support your arguments.

Create a presentation that explains all the useful functions of your database. Consider discussing how your system could be expanded to record reviews of individual workers. Think of other improvements that would be helpful to HHH before the app is developed. Your presentation should take less than 15 minutes, including a brief question-and-answer period.

DELIVERABLES

Assemble the following deliverables for your instructor, either electronically or in printed form:

1. Word-processed design of tables
2. Tables created in Access
3. Form: Clients and Jobs
4. Query 1: Jobs on Specific Date
5. Query 2: Most Frequent Clients
6. Query 3: Workers and Skills
7. Query 4: Top Earner
8. Query 5: Top Client
9. Query 6: Customer Bills
10. Report 1: Customers' Final Payments Summary (includes a query)
11. Report 2: Workers' Earnings (includes a query)
12. Memo
13. Presentation materials
14. Any required electronic files

Staple all the pages together. Include your name and class number at the top of each page. Make sure that your electronic media are labeled, if required.

PART 2

DECISION SUPPORT CASES USING MICROSOFT EXCEL SCENARIO MANAGER

BUILDING A DECISION SUPPORT SYSTEM IN EXCEL

A **decision support system (DSS)** is a computer program that can represent a problem a user needs to solve. Such a representation is in effect a model of a problem.

Here's how a DSS program works: The program accepts input from the user or accesses data in the system's files and then runs the input and any other necessary data through the model. The program's output is the information the user needs to solve a problem. Some DSS programs recommend a solution to a problem.

A DSS can be written in any programming language that lets a programmer represent a problem. For example, a DSS can be built in a third-generation language such as Visual Basic or in a database package such as Access. A DSS can also be written in a spreadsheet package such as Excel.

Excel has standard, built-in arithmetic functions as well as many statistical and financial functions. Thus, many kinds of problems—such as those in accounting, operations, and finance—can be modeled in Excel.

This tutorial is organized into four sections as follows:

- **Spreadsheet and DSS Basics**—In this section, you'll learn how to create a DSS program in Excel. Your program will be in the form of a cash flow model. This section will give you practice in spreadsheet design and in building a DSS program.
- **Using Scenario Manager**—In this section, you'll learn how to use an Excel tool called Scenario Manager. With any DSS package, one problem with playing "what if" is deciding where to physically record the results from running each set of data. A user could write the inputs and related results on a sheet of paper. Then, the user might have to enter the data *back* into a spreadsheet for further analysis. Scenario Manager solves this problem. It can be set up to capture inputs and related results as "scenarios," which are then summarized on a separate sheet in the Excel workbook.
- **Practicing with Scenario Manager**—You will work on a new case problem using Scenario Manager.
- **Reviewing Excel Basics**—This section reviews additional information you may need to do the spreadsheet cases that follow this tutorial.

SPREADSHEET AND DSS BASICS

Assume it is late in Year 1 of a three-year period, and you are trying to build a model of a company's net income (profit) and cash flow for Years 2 and 3. The problem is to forecast net income and cash flow in those years. The company is likely to use the forecasts to make decisions, so the estimates should be as accurate as you can make them. After researching the problem, you decide that the estimates should be based on three factors: (1) Year 1 results, (2) estimates of the underlying economic variables, and (3) the cost of products the company sells.

Your model will use an income statement and cash flow framework. The user can enter values for two possible states of the economy in Years 2 and 3: an O for an optimistic outlook or a P for a pessimistic outlook. The state of the economy is expected to affect the number of units the company can sell as well as each unit's selling price. In a good (optimistic) economy, more units can be sold at a higher price. The user can also enter values into your model to see two possible trends in the cost of goods sold: U for up or D for down. A U means that the cost of an item sold will be higher than it was in Year 1; a D means that the cost will be less.

Presumably, the company will do better in a good economy and with lower input costs—but how much better? The user can play "what if" with the input variables and note the effect on net income and year-end cash levels. For example, a user can ask these questions: What if the economy is good and costs go up? What will net income and cash flow be in that case? What will happen if the economy is down and costs go down? What will be the company's net income and cash flow in that case? With an Excel software model, the answers to such questions can be quantified.

Organization of the DSS Model

Your spreadsheets should have the following sections:

- Constants
- Inputs
- Summary of Key Results
- Calculations of values that will be used in the Income and Cash Flow statements
- Income and Cash Flow statements

Here, as an extended illustration, a DSS model is built for the forecasting problem described. Next, you'll look at each spreadsheet section. Figures C-1 and C-2 show how to set up the spreadsheet. (You can also use the spreadsheet skeleton if you prefer; this will save you time. Select Tutorial C in your data files, and then select **TutC.xlsx**.)

	A	B	C	D
1	**TUTORIAL EXERCISE**			
2				
3	**Constants**	**Year 1**	**Year 2**	**Year 3**
4	Tax Rate	NA	0.33	0.35
5	Number of Business Days	NA	300	300
6				
7	**Inputs**	**Year 1**	**Year 2**	**Year 3**
8	Economic Outlook (O=Optimistic, P=Pessimistic)	NA		NA
9	Purchase Price Outlook (U=Up, D=Down)	NA		NA
10				
11	**Summary of Key Results**	**Year 1**	**Year 2**	**Year 3**
12	Net Income After Taxes	NA		
13	End-of-Year Cash On Hand	NA		
14				
15	**Calculations**	**Year 1**	**Year 2**	**Year 3**
16	Number of units sold in a day	1000		
17	Selling price per unit	$7.00		
18	Cost of goods sold per unit	$3.00		
19	Number of units sold in a year	NA		

FIGURE C-1 Tutorial skeleton 1

	A	B	C	D
21	**Income Statement and Cash Flow Statement**	**Year 1**	**Year 2**	**Year 3**
22	Beginning-of-year cash on hand	NA		
23	Sales (Revenue)	NA		
24	Cost of goods sold	NA		
25	Income before taxes	NA		
26	Income tax expense	NA		
27	Net income after taxes	NA		
28	End-of-year cash on hand	$10,000		

FIGURE C-2 Tutorial skeleton 2

Each spreadsheet section is discussed next.

Constants Section

This section of Figure C-1 records values that are used in spreadsheet calculations. In a sense, the constants are input values used by the model, except that they do not change. In this tutorial, the constants are Tax Rate and the Number of Business Days.

Inputs Section

The inputs shown in Figure C-1 are for the Economic Outlook and Purchase Price Outlook (the outlook for manufacturing input costs). Inputs could conceivably be entered for *each year* the model is covered (here, Year 2 and Year 3), which would let you enter an O for Year 2's economy in one cell and a P for Year 3's economy in another cell. Alternatively, one input for the two-year period could be entered in one cell. For simplicity, the latter approach is used in this example.

Summary of Key Results Section

This section of the spreadsheet captures Year 2 and Year 3 Net Income After Taxes (profit) and End-of-Year Cash On Hand, which you should assume are the two relevant outputs of this model. The summary merely repeats results in one easy-to-see location; otherwise, these results could appear in various places in the spreadsheet. Collecting key results in one place also makes for easier charting.

Calculations Section

This area is used to compute the following data:

- The Number of units sold in a day, which is a function of the Year 1 value and the economic outlook input value
- The Selling price per unit, which is similarly derived
- The Cost of goods sold per unit, which is a function of the Year 1 value and the purchase-price outlook value
- The Number of units sold in a year, which equals the number of units sold in a day multiplied by the number of business days in a year

The formulas could be embedded in the Income Statement and Cash Flow Statement section of the spreadsheet, which will be described shortly. Doing that, however, would result in expressions that are complex and difficult to understand. Putting the intermediate calculations into a separate Calculations section breaks up the work into modules. This is good form because it simplifies your programming.

Income Statement and Cash Flow Statement Section

This section is the "body" of the spreadsheet. It shows the following:

- Beginning-of-year cash on hand, which equals cash at the end of the *prior* year.
- Sales (Revenue), which equals the units sold during the year multiplied by the unit selling price.
- Cost of goods sold, which is units sold during the year multiplied by the price paid to acquire or make the unit sold.
- Income before taxes, which equals sales minus cost of goods sold.
- Income tax expense, which is zero when there are losses; otherwise, it is the income before taxes multiplied by the tax rate.
- Net income after taxes, which equals income before taxes minus income tax expense.
- End-of-year cash on hand, which is beginning-of-year cash on hand plus net income.

In the real world, cash flow estimates must also account for changes in other accounts, such as receivables and payables. In this case, assume that sales are collected immediately—that is, there are no receivables or bad debts. Also assume that suppliers are paid immediately—that is, there are no payables.

Constructing the Spreadsheet Model

Next, you will work through the following three steps to build your spreadsheet model:

- Make a "skeleton" of the spreadsheet.
- Fill in the "easy" cell formulas.
- Enter the "hard" spreadsheet formulas.

Making a Skeleton

Your first step is to set up a skeleton worksheet. Alternatively, you can use the skeleton file, as previously noted. The worksheet should have headings, text string labels, and constants—but no formulas yet.

To set up the skeleton, you must first grasp the problem conceptually. The best way to do that is to work backward from what the "body" of the spreadsheet will look like. Here, the body is the Income Statement and Cash Flow Statement section. Set up the body in your mind or on paper, and then do the following:

- Decide what amounts should be in the Calculations section. In the income statement of this tutorial's model, Sales (Revenue) will be Number of units sold in a day multiplied by Selling price per unit. You will calculate the intermediate amounts (Number of units sold in a year and Selling price per unit) in the Calculations section.
- Set up the Summary of Key Results section by deciding what *outputs* are needed to solve the problem.
- The Inputs section should be reserved for amounts that can change: the controlling variables, which here are the Economic Outlook and the Purchase Price Outlook.
- Use the Constants section for values you will need to use but that are not in doubt; that is, you will not have to input them or calculate them. The Tax Rate is a good example of such a value.
- Type in the Excel skeleton shown in Figures C-1 and C-2.

NOTE

A designation of NA means that a cell will not be used in any formula in the worksheet. The Year 1 values are needed only for certain calculations, so for the most part, the Year 1 column's cells show NA. (Recall that the forecast is for Years 2 and 3.) Also be aware that you can "break" a text string in a cell by pressing the Alt and Enter keys at the same time at the break point, which makes the cell "taller." To show centered data and create borders in cells, see "Formatting Cells" later in this tutorial.

Entering the "Easy" Formulas

You can enter formulas in any order you choose. We recommend entering the conceptually easier formulas first and then moving on to more difficult ones. Thus, the next step is to enter the "easy" formulas, starting with those in the Summary of Key Results section. To prepare, you should format the section's cells as currency with zero decimals. (For details, see "Formatting Cells" later in this tutorial.) As previously mentioned, the Summary of Key Results section (see Figure C-3) simply echoes results shown in other places. Consider Figures C-1 and C-2, and note that cell C27 in Figure C-2 holds the Year 2 Net income after taxes. You need to echo that amount to cell C12, so the formula in C12 is simply =C27. The simple logic is: "Copy what is in C27 into C12."

NOTE

With the insertion point in C12, the cell's contents—in this case, the formula =C27—appear in the editing window above the lettered column indicators, as shown in Figure C-3.

	A	B	C	D
11	**Summary of Key Results**	Year 1	Year 2	Year 3
12	Net Income After Taxes	NA	$0	
13	End-of-Year Cash On Hand	NA		

FIGURE C-3 Echoing Year 2 Net Income After Taxes to Summary of Key Results section

At this point, cell C27 has a zero value, but that does not prevent you from copying the formula in the cell. Copy cell C12's formula to the right, to cell D12. Copying puts =D27 into D12, which is what you want. (Year 3's Net income after taxes is in D27.)

To perform the copy operation, you can use the following steps:

1. Click in the cell or range of cells that you want to copy.
2. Hold down the Control key and press C (Ctrl+C).
3. Select the destination cell. If a range of cells is the destination, select the upper-left cell of the destination range.
4. Hold down the Control key and press V (Ctrl+V).
5. Press the Escape key to deactivate the copied cell or range.

You can also take the following steps to copy cell contents:

1. Select the Home tab.
2. Click in the cell or range of cells that you want to copy.
3. In the Clipboard group, select Copy.
4. Select the destination cell. If a range of cells is the destination, select the upper-left cell of the destination range.
5. In the Clipboard group, select Paste.
6. Press the Escape key to deactivate the copied cell or range.

As you can see in Figure C-4, End-of-Year Cash On Hand for Year 2 cash is echoed to cell C13. Echo the cash results in cell C28 to cell C13. (Enter the formula =C28 in cell C13, as shown in Figure C-4.)

C13	▾	:	✕ ✓ *fx*	=C28		

	A	B	C	D
11	Summary of Key Results	Year 1	Year 2	Year 3
12	Net Income After Taxes	NA	$0	$0
13	End-of-Year Cash On Hand	NA	$0	

FIGURE C-4 Echoing Year 2 End-of-Year Cash On Hand to Summary of Key Results section

Copy the formula from C13 to D13.

At this point, the Calculations section formulas will not be entered because they are not all "easy" formulas. We will move on to the easier formulas in the Income and Cash Flow Statements section, as if the Calculations section formulas were already done. Again, the fact that the Calculations section cells are empty does not stop you from referencing the cells in other formulas. You should format the cells in the Income Statement and Cash Flow Statement section for currency with zero decimals.

As you can see in Figure C-5, Beginning-of-year cash on hand is the cash on hand at the end of the *prior* year. Cell B28 has the End-of-year cash on hand for Year 1. In cell C22 for Year 2, type =B28, as shown in Figure C-5.

C22	▾	:	✕ ✓ *fx*	=B28		

	A	B	C	D
21	Income Statement and Cash Flow Statement	Year 1	Year 2	Year 3
22	Beginning-of-year cash on hand	NA	$10,000	
23	Sales (Revenue)	NA		
24	Cost of goods sold	NA		
25	Income before taxes	NA		
26	Income tax expense	NA		
27	Net income after taxes	NA		
28	End-of-year cash on hand	$10,000		

FIGURE C-5 Echo of Year 1 End-of-year cash on hand to Year 2 Beginning-of-year cash on hand

Your next step is to copy the formula in cell C22 to the right.

Sales (Revenue) is the Number of units sold in a year multiplied by Selling price per unit. In cell C23, enter =C17*C19, as shown in Figure C-6.

FIGURE C-6   Entering the formula to compute Year 2 sales

The formula =C17*C19 multiplies the unit selling price by the units sold for the year. (Cells C17 and C19 are empty now, which is why Sales shows a zero after the formula is entered.) Copy the formula to the right, to cell D23.

The Cost of goods sold is handled similarly. In C24, enter =C18 * C19, which equals Cost of goods sold per unit multiplied by Number of units sold in a year. Copy the formula to the right.

In cell C25, the formula for Income before taxes is =C23–C24. Enter the formula and copy it to the right.

Income taxes are paid only on positive income before taxes. In cell C26, the Income tax expense is zero when the Income before taxes is zero or less; otherwise, Income tax expense equals the Tax Rate multiplied by income before taxes. The Tax Rate is a constant (in cell C4). An IF statement is needed to express this logic:

IF(Income before taxes is <= 0,

    then put zero tax in C26,

        else, in C26, put a number equal to multiplying the Tax Rate by the income before taxes)

C25 stands for Income before taxes, and C4 stands for Tax Rate. In Excel, substitute those cell addresses:

=IF(C25 <= 0, 0, C4 * C25)

Copy the income tax expense formula to the right.

In cell C27, Net income after taxes is Income before taxes minus Income tax expense: =C25–C26. Enter the formula and then copy it to the right.

The End-of-year cash on hand is the Beginning-of-year cash on hand plus Net income after taxes. In cell C28, enter =C22+C27. Copy the formula to the right. The Income Statement and Cash Flow Statement section at this point is shown in Figure C-7.

FIGURE C-7   Status of Income Statement and Cash Flow Statement

Entering the "Hard" Formulas

The next step is to finish the spreadsheet by filling in the "hard" formulas. In our example, formulas that use Inputs section values are considered the "hard" ones.

In cell C8, enter an O for Optimistic, and in C9, enter a U for Up. There is nothing special about these values—they just give the worksheet formulas input values to process. Recall that the inputs will cover both Year 2 and Year 3. Enter NA in cells D8 and D9 to remind yourself that those cells will not be used for input or be referenced by other worksheet formulas. Your Inputs section should look like the one shown in Figure C-8.

	A	B	C	D
		Year 1	Year 2	Year 3
7	**Inputs**			
8	Economic Outlook (O=Optimistic, P=Pessimistic)	NA	O	NA
9	Purchase Price Outlook (U=Up, D=Down)	NA	U	NA

FIGURE C-8 Entering two input values

Recall that cell addresses in the Calculations section are already referred to in formulas in the Income Statement and Cash Flow Statement section. The next step is to enter formulas for those calculations. Before doing that, format the Number of units sold in a day and Number of units sold in a year for zero decimals, and format the Selling price per unit and Cost of goods sold per unit for currency with two decimals.

The easiest formula in the Calculations section is the Number of units sold in a year, which is the Number of Business Days (in C5) multiplied by the Number of units sold in a day, as shown in cell C16. In C19, enter =C5*C16, as shown in Figure C-9.

C19		X ✓ *fx*	=C5*C16	

	A	B	C	D
3	**Constants**	Year 1	Year 2	Year 3
4	Tax Rate	NA	0.33	0.35
5	Number of Business Days	NA	300	300
6				
7	**Inputs**	Year 1	Year 2	Year 3
8	Economic Outlook (O=Optimistic, P=Pessimistic)	NA	O	NA
9	Purchase Price Outlook (U=Up, D=Down)	NA	U	NA
10				
11	**Summary of Key Results**	Year 1	Year 2	Year 3
12	Net Income After Taxes	NA	$0	$0
13	End-of-Year Cash On Hand	NA	$10,000	$10,000
14				
15	**Calculations**	Year 1	Year 2	Year 3
16	Number of units sold in a day	1000		
17	Selling price per unit	$7.00		
18	Cost of goods sold per unit	$3.00		
19	Number of units sold in a year	NA	0	

FIGURE C-9 Entering the formula to compute Year 2 Number of units sold in a year

Copy the formula to cell D19 for Year 3.

Assume that if the Economic Outlook is Optimistic, the Year 2 Number of units sold in a day will be 6 percent more than in Year 1; in Year 3, they will be 6 percent more than in Year 2. Also assume that if the Economic Outlook is Pessimistic, the Number of units sold in a day in Year 2 will be 1 percent less than those sold in Year 1; in Year 3, they will be 1 percent less than those sold in Year 2. An IF statement is needed in cell C16 to express this logic:

IF(economy variable = Optimistic,

   Then Number of units sold in a day will go UP 6%,

   Else Number of units sold in a day will go DOWN 1%)

Substituting cell addresses:

=IF($C$8 = "O", B16 * 1.06, B16 * .99)

NOTE

In Excel, quotation marks denote text. The input is one letter of text, so quotation marks are needed around the O. Also note that multiplying by 1.06 results in a 6 percent increase, whereas multiplying by 0.99 results in a 1 percent decrease.

Enter the entire IF formula into cell C16, as shown in Figure C-10. Absolute addressing is needed when referring to the input value ($C$8), because the address is in a formula that gets copied *and* you do not want the cell reference to change (to D8, which has the value NA) when you copy the formula to the right. Absolute addressing maintains the $C$8 reference when the formula is copied.

C16	fx	=IF($C$8="O",B16*1.06,B16*0.99)	

	A	B	C	D
15	**Calculations**	**Year 1**	**Year 2**	**Year 3**
16	Number of units sold in a day	1000	1,060	
17	Selling price per unit	$7.00		
18	Cost of goods sold per unit	$3.00		

FIGURE C-10 Entering the formula to compute Year 2 Number of units sold in a day

Copy the formula in C16 to D16 for Year 3.

The Selling price per unit is also a function of the Economic Outlook. Assume that the two-part rule is as follows:

- If the Economic Outlook is Optimistic, the Selling price per unit in Year 2 will be 1.07 times that of Year 1; in Year 3, it will be 1.07 times that of Year 2.
- On the other hand, if the Economic Outlook is Pessimistic, the Selling price per unit in Year 2 and Year 3 will equal the per-unit price in Year 1; that is, the price will not change.

Test your understanding of the selling price calculation by figuring out the formula for cell C17. Enter the formula and copy it to the right. (Hint: You will need to use absolute addressing properly.)

The Cost of goods sold per unit is a function of the Purchase Price Outlook. Assume that the two-part rule is as follows:

- If the Purchase Price Outlook is Up (U), Cost of goods sold per unit in Year 2 will be 1.25 times that of Year 1; in Year 3, it will be 1.25 times that of Year 2.
- On the other hand, if the Purchase Price Outlook is Down (D), the multiplier in years 2 and 3 will be 1.01.

Again, to test your understanding, figure out the formula for cell C18. Enter and copy the formula to the right. Again, you will need to use absolute addressing.

Your formulas for selling price and cost of goods sold, given Optimistic and Up input values, should yield the calculated values shown in Figure C-11.

	A	B	C	D
15	**Calculations**	**Year 1**	**Year 2**	**Year 3**
16	Number of units sold in a day	1000	1,060	1,124
17	Selling price per unit	$7.00	$7.49	$8.01
18	Cost of goods sold per unit	$3.00	$3.75	$4.69
19	Number of units sold in a year	NA	318,000	337,080

FIGURE C-11 Calculated values given Optimistic and Up input values

Assume that you change the input values to Pessimistic and Down. Your formulas should yield the calculated values shown in Figure C-12.

	A	B	C	D
15	**Calculations**	**Year 1**	**Year 2**	**Year 3**
16	Number of units sold in a day	1000	990	980
17	Selling price per unit	$7.00	$7.00	$7.00
18	Cost of goods sold per unit	$3.00	$3.03	$3.06
19	Number of units sold in a year	NA	297,000	294,030

FIGURE C-12 Calculated values given Pessimistic and Down input values

That completes the body of your spreadsheet. The values in the Calculations section ripple through the Income Statement and Cash Flow Statement section because the income statement formulas reference the calculations. Assuming inputs of Optimistic and Up, the income and cash flow numbers should look like those in Figure C-13.

	A	B	C	D
21	**Income Statement and Cash Flow Statement**	**Year 1**	**Year 2**	**Year 3**
22	Beginning-of-year cash on hand	NA	$10,000	$806,844
23	Sales (Revenue)	NA	$2,381,820	$2,701,460
24	Cost of goods sold	NA	$1,192,500	$1,580,063
25	Income before taxes	NA	$1,189,320	$1,121,398
26	Income tax expense	NA	$392,476	$392,489
27	Net income after taxes	NA	$796,844	$728,909
28	End-of-year cash on hand	$10,000	$806,844	$1,535,753

FIGURE C-13 Completed Income Statement and Cash Flow Statement section

USING SCENARIO MANAGER

You are now ready to use Excel's Scenario Manager to capture inputs and results as you play "what if" with the spreadsheet.

There are four possible combinations of input values: O-U (Optimistic-Up), O-D (Optimistic-Down), P-U (Pessimistic-Up), and P-D (Pessimistic-Down). Financial results for each combination will be different. Each combination of input values can be referred to as a scenario. Scenario Manager records the results of each combination of input values as a separate scenario and then shows a summary of all scenarios in a separate worksheet. Those summary worksheet values can be used as a raw table of numbers and then printed or copied into a Microsoft Word document. The table of data can then be the basis for an Excel chart, which can also be printed or inserted into a document.

The four sets of input values produce different financial results. When you use Scenario Manager, you define the four scenarios; then you have Excel (1) sequentially run the input values "behind the scenes" and (2) put the results for each input scenario in a summary sheet.

When you define a scenario in Scenario Manager, you give it a name and identify the input cells and input values. Then you identify the output cells so Excel can capture the output values in a summary sheet.

To start, select the Data tab. In the Forecast group, click the drop-down arrow on the What-If Analysis icon, and then click the Scenario Manager option. Initially, no scenarios are defined, as you can see in Figure C-14.

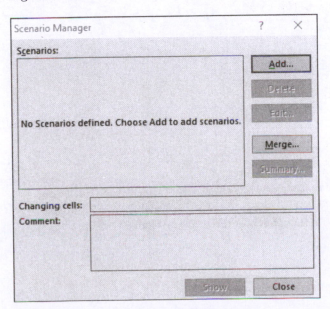

FIGURE C-14 Initial Scenario Manager window

You can use this window to add, delete, or edit scenarios. Toward the end of the process, you create the summary sheet.

NOTE

When working with this window and its successors, do not press the Enter key to navigate. Use mouse clicks to move from one step to the next.

To start defining a scenario, click the Add button. In the resulting Add Scenario window, name the first scenario Opt-Up. Then type the input cells in the Changing cells field—here, they are C8:C9. (Note that C8 and C9 are contiguous input cells. Noncontiguous input cell ranges are separated by a comma.) Excel may add dollar signs to the cell address, but do not be concerned about that. The window should look like the one shown in Figure C-15.

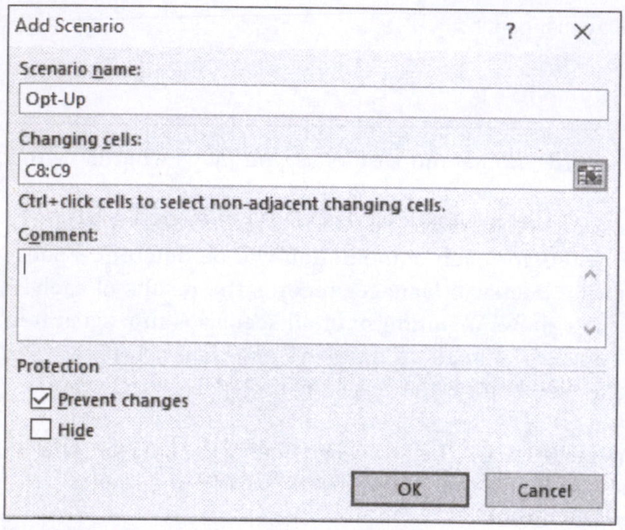

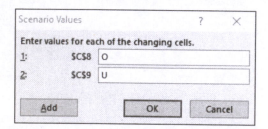

FIGURE C-15 Entering Opt-Up as a scenario

Now click OK, which moves you to the Scenario Values window. Here you indicate what the input *values* will be for the scenario. The values in the *current* spreadsheet cells will be displayed. They might or might not be correct for your scenario. For the Opt-Up scenario, you need to enter an O and a U, if not the current values. Enter those values if needed, as shown in Figure C-16.

FIGURE C-16 Entering Opt-Up scenario input values

Click OK, which takes you back to the Scenario Manager window. Enter the other three Opt-Down, Pess-Up, and Pess-Down scenarios, including the related input values. When you finish, you should see that the names and changing cells for the four scenarios have been entered, as in Figure C-17.

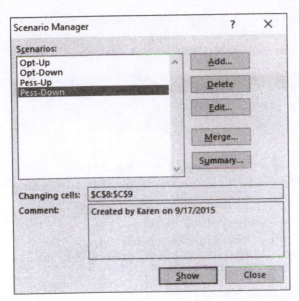

FIGURE C-17 Scenario Manager window with all scenarios entered

You can now create a summary sheet that shows the results of running the four scenarios. Click the Summary button to open the Scenario Summary window. You must provide Excel with the output cell addresses—they will be the same for all four scenarios. (The output *values* in those output cells change as input values are changed, but the *addresses* of the output cells do not change.)

Assume that you are interested primarily in the results that have accrued at the end of the two-year period. These results are your two Year 3 Summary of Key Results section cells for Net Income After Taxes and End-of-Year Cash On Hand (D12 and D13). Type those addresses in the window's input area, as shown in Figure C-18. (Note that if the Result cells are noncontiguous, the address ranges can be entered and separated by a comma.)

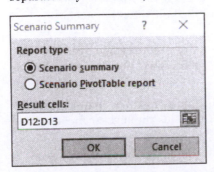

FIGURE C-18 Entering Result cell addresses in Scenario Summary window

Then click OK. Excel runs each set of inputs "behind the scenes" and collects results as it goes. (You do not see this happening on the screen.) Excel creates a new sheet called the Scenario Summary (denoted by the sheet's lower tab) and takes you there, as shown in Figure C-19.

		Current Values:	Opt-Up	Opt-Down	Pess-Up	Pess-Down
Scenario Summary						
Changing Cells:						
	$C$8	O	O	O	P	P
	$C$9	U	U	D	U	D
Result Cells:						
	$D$12	$728,909	$728,909	$1,085,431	$441,964	$752,953
	$D$13	$1,535,753	$1,535,753	$2,045,679	$1,098,681	$1,552,944

Notes: Current Values column represents values of changing cells at time Scenario Summary Report was created. Changing cells for each scenario are highlighted in gray.

FIGURE C-19 Scenario Summary sheet created by Scenario Manager

One slightly annoying visual element is that the Current Values in the spreadsheet are given an output column that duplicates one of the four defined scenarios. To delete the extra column, select it, select the Home tab, select the Delete icon's drop-down arrow within the Cells group, and select Delete Sheet Columns.

NOTE

To delete a sheet's row, follow the steps in the preceding sentence, but select Delete Sheet Rows instead of Delete Sheet Columns.

Another annoyance is that column A goes unused. You can click and delete it as you've been doing to move everything to the left. That should make columns of data easier to see on the screen without scrolling. Other ways to make the worksheet easier to read include:

- Entering text in column A to describe the input and output cells
- Centering cell values by using the Center icon in the Home tab's Alignment group
- Showing data in Currency format by using the Number Format drop-down menu within the Home tab's Number group

When you finish, your summary sheet could resemble the one shown in Figure C-20.

	A	B	C	D	E	F
1	Scenario Summary					
2			Opt-Up	Opt-Down	Pess-Up	Pess-Down
4	Changing Cells:					
5	Economic Outlook	$C$8	O	O	P	P
6	Purchase Price Outlook	$C$9	U	D	U	D
7	Result Cells:					
8	Net Income After Taxes -- Year 3	$D$12	$728,909	$1,085,431	$441,964	$752,953
9	End-of-year Cash on Hand -- Year 3	$D$13	$1,535,753	$2,045,679	$1,098,681	$1,552,944

FIGURE C-20 Scenario Summary sheet after formatting

Note that column C shows the Optimistic-Up case. The Net Income After Taxes in that scenario is $728,909, and End-of-Year Cash On Hand is $1,535,753. Columns D, E, and F show the other scenario results.

As an important postscript to this exercise, note that DSS spreadsheets are used to guide decision making, which means that the spreadsheet's results must be interpreted in some way. Here are two practice questions based on the results in Figure C-20:

- What combination of Year 3 Net Income After Taxes and End-of-Year Cash On Hand would be best? Clearly, Optimistic-Down (O-D) is the best result, right? It yields the highest income and highest cash.
- What is the worst combination? Pessimistic-Up (P-U), right? It yields the lowest income and lowest cash.

Results are not always that easy to interpret, but the analytical method is the same. You have a situation that you cannot understand very easily without software assistance. You build a model of the situation in the spreadsheet, enter the inputs, collect the results, and then interpret the results to help with decision making.

Using Summary Sheets

When you complete Scenario Manager case studies, you'll need to manipulate summary sheets and their data. Next, you will look at some of those operations.

Rerunning Scenario Manager

The Scenario Summary sheet does not update itself when the spreadsheet formulas or inputs change. To see an updated Scenario Summary sheet, you must rerun Scenario Manager by clicking the Summary button in the Scenario Manager dialog box and then clicking OK. Another summary sheet is created; it does not overwrite a prior one.

Deleting Unwanted Scenario Manager Summary Sheets

Suppose you want to delete a summary sheet. With the summary sheet on the screen, follow this procedure:

1. Select the Home tab.
2. Within the Cells group, select the Delete icon's drop-down arrow.
3. Select Delete Sheet. When asked if you really want to delete the sheet, click Delete.

You can also delete a sheet by right-clicking its tab at the bottom of the screen. In the resulting menu, select Delete. Click Delete again when asked if you really want to delete the sheet.

Charting Summary Sheet Data

The summary sheet results can be conveniently charted using the Chart Wizard, as discussed in Tutorial F.

Copying Summary Sheet Data to the Clipboard

If you want to put the summary sheet data into the Clipboard to use in a Microsoft Word document, follow these steps:

1. Select the data range.
2. Copy the data range into the Clipboard by following the copying operation described earlier in this tutorial.
3. Open your Microsoft Word document.
4. Click the cursor where you want the upper-left part of the data to be positioned.
5. Paste the data into the document by selecting Paste in the Home tab's Clipboard group.

PRACTICING WITH SCENARIO MANAGER

Suppose you have an uncle who works for a large company. He has a good job and makes a decent salary (currently, $80,000 a year). At age 65, which will be in three more years, he must retire from his company and start drawing his pension.

However, the company has an early-out plan in which employees are paid to quit early. The company pays all employees in the plan a bonus in the year they retire and each year thereafter, before the official retirement date. (After the official retirement date, employees start to receive their actual pension—in your uncle's case, after three more years of work.) If your uncle left the company early, he could find a part-time hourly job to make ends meet in the years before taking his normal pension.

The opportunity to leave early is open for three years after the end of the current year, which is now ending. That means your uncle could leave the company any year in the next three years, getting the early-out bonuses in the years he is retired early. Thus, if he works another year, he would lose the bonus for that year. If he works two more years, he would lose two years of early-out bonuses, and so forth until he must retire.

Another factor in your uncle's thinking is whether to continue his country club membership. He likes the club, but it is a cash drain. The retirement decision can be revisited each year, but the decision about the country club membership must be made now. If your uncle does not withdraw now, he says he will remain a member (and incur costs) indefinitely.

Your uncle has called you in to make a spreadsheet model of his situation in Scenario Manager. Your spreadsheet would let him play "what if" with the preretirement and country club possibilities and see his various projected personal finances for each of the next three years. With each scenario, your uncle wants to know what "cash on hand" will be available for each year in the period.

Complete the spreadsheet for your uncle. Your Summary of Key Results, Calculations, and Income Statement and Cash Flow Statement section cells must show values *by cell formula*. In other words, do not hard-code amounts in those sections. Also do not use the address of a cell if its contents are NA in any of your formulas. Set up your spreadsheet skeleton as shown in the figures that follow. Name your spreadsheet **UNCLE.xlsx**. You can also use the spreadsheet skeleton named UNCLE.xlsx from your data files.

Constants Section

Your spreadsheet should have the constants shown in Figure C-21. An explanation of line items follows the figure.

	A	B	C	D	E
1	**YOUR UNCLE'S EARLY RETIREMENT DECISION**				
2	**Constants**	**Year 0**	**Year 1**	**Year 2**	**Year 3**
3	Salary increase factor	NA	0.03	0.03	0.02
4	Part-time wages expected (retired)	NA	$10,000	$10,200	$10,500
5	Buyout amount	NA	$45,000	$30,000	$10,000
6	Cost of living (not retired)	NA	$41,000	$42,000	$43,000
7	Country club dues	NA	$12,000	$13,000	$14,000

FIGURE C-21 Constants section values

- Salary increase factor—Your uncle's salary as of the current working year just ended (Year 0) is $80,000. As you can see, raises are expected each year; for example, a 3 percent raise is expected in the upcoming year (Year 1). If your uncle does not retire in a year, he will get his salary (including a raise) for the year.

- Part-time wages expected—For the next three years, your uncle has estimated his part-time wages in a year that he is retired from the company and working part-time (Years 1 to 3). For example, he thinks he could earn $10,000 in part-time wages in Year 1 if he retired.

- Buyout amount—The amounts for the company's preretirement buyout plan are shown. For example, if your uncle retires now (and does not work for the company in Years 1 through 3), he gets $45,000, $30,000, and $10,000 in Year 1 through Year 3. If he works another year, then leaves before Year 2 starts, he will give up the $45,000 payment for Year 1 but will get $30,000 and $10,000 in Year 2 and Year 3.

- Cost of living (not retired)—Your uncle has estimated how much cash he needs to meet his living expenses, assuming he continues to work for the company. His cost of living would be $41,000 in Year 1, increasing each year thereafter.

- Country club dues—Country club dues will be $12,000 for Year 1. Dues increase each year thereafter, as shown.

Inputs Section

Your spreadsheet should have the inputs shown in Figure C-22. An explanation of line items follows the figure.

	A	B	C	D	E
9	**Inputs**	**Year 0**	**Year 1**	**Year 2**	**Year 3**
10	Retired [R] or Working [W]	NA			
11	Stay in club? [Y] or [N]	NA		NA	NA

FIGURE C-22 Inputs section

- Retired or Working—Enter an R if your uncle would be retired in the year or a W if he would still be working. If he is working the next three years, you should enter the pattern WWW. If he plans to retire now (that is, not work Year 1), you would enter the pattern RRR. If he works for one year and then retires, you should enter the pattern WRR.

- Stay in club?—If your uncle stays in the club, you should enter a Y. If your uncle leaves the club now, you should enter an N. The decision applies to all years.

Summary of Key Results Section

Your spreadsheet should show the results in Figure C-23.

	A	B	C	D	E
13	**Summary of Key Results**	**Year 0**	**Year 1**	**Year 2**	**Year 3**
14	End-of-year cash on hand	NA			

FIGURE C-23 Summary of Key Results section

Each year's End-of-year cash on hand value is echoed from cells in the spreadsheet body.

Calculations Section

Your spreadsheet should calculate, by formula, the values shown in Figure C-24. Calculated amounts are used later in the spreadsheet. An explanation of line items follows the figure.

	A	B	C	D	E
16	**Calculations**	**Year 0**	**Year 1**	**Year 2**	**Year 3**
17	Tax rate	NA			
18	Cost of living	NA			
19	Yearly salary or part-time wages	$80,000			
20	Country club dues paid	NA			

FIGURE C-24 Calculations section

- Tax rate—Your uncle's tax rate depends on whether he is retired. Retired people have lower overall tax rates. If he is retired in a year, your uncle's rate is expected to be 15 percent of income before taxes. In a year in which he works full time, the rate will be 30 percent.
- Cost of living—In any year that your uncle continues to work for the company, his cost of living is the amount shown in the Cost of living (not retired) field of the Constants section in Figure C-21. But, if he chooses to retire, his cost of living will be $15,000 less than the amount shown in Figure C-21.
- Yearly salary or part-time wages—If your uncle keeps working, his salary increases each year. The yearly percentage increases are shown in the Constants section. Thus, salary earned in Year 1 would be 3 percent more than that earned in Year 0, salary earned in Year 2 would be 3 percent more than that earned in Year 1, and salary earned in Year 3 would be 2 percent more than that earned in Year 2. If your uncle retires in a certain year, he will make the part-time wages shown in the Constants section.
- Country club dues paid—If your uncle leaves the club, the dues are zero each year; otherwise, the dues are as shown in the Constants section.

Income Statement and Cash Flow Statement Section

This section begins with the cash on hand at the beginning of the year, followed by the income statement, and concluding with the calculation of cash on hand at the end of the year. The format is shown in Figure C-25. An explanation of line items follows the figure.

	Income Statement and Cash Flow Statement	Year 0	Year 1	Year 2	Year 3
22					
23	Beginning-of-year cash on hand	NA			
24					
25	Salary or wages	NA			
26	Buyout income	NA			
27	Total cash inflow	NA			
28	Country club dues paid	NA			
29	Cost of living	NA			
30	Total costs	NA			
31	Income before taxes	NA			
32	Income tax expense	NA			
33	Net income after taxes	NA			
34					
35	End-of-year cash on hand	$30,000			

FIGURE C-25 Income Statement and Cash Flow Statement section

- Beginning-of-year cash on hand—This amount is the cash on hand at the end of the prior year. Note that cash on hand at the end of the current year is $30,000.
- Salary or wages—This amount is a yearly calculation, which can be echoed here.
- Buyout income—This amount is the year's buyout amount if your uncle is retired that year. Buyout amounts are shown in the Constants section.
- Total cash inflow—This amount is the sum of salary or part-time wages and the buyout amount.

- Country club dues paid—This amount is a calculation, which can be echoed here.
- Cost of living—This amount is a calculation, which can be echoed here.
- Total costs—This amount is the sum of the Cost of living and Country club dues paid.
- Income before taxes—This amount is the Total cash inflow minus Total costs.
- Income tax expense—This amount is zero when Income before taxes is zero or less; otherwise, the calculated tax rate is applied to the Income before taxes.
- Net income after taxes—This amount is Income before taxes minus Income tax expense.
- End-of-year cash on hand—This amount is the Beginning-of-year cash on hand plus the year's Net income after taxes.

Scenario Manager Analysis

Set up Scenario Manager and create a Scenario Summary sheet. Your uncle wants to look at the following four possibilities:

- Retire now, staying in the club ("Loaf-In").
- Retire now, leaving the club ("Loaf-Out").
- Work three more years (that is, do not take any buyout bonuses), staying in the club ("Delay-In").
- Work three more years, leaving the club ("Delay-Out").

You should enter the noncontiguous input cell ranges as follows: C10:E10, C11. The only output cell should be the Year 3 End-of-year cash on hand cell in the Summary of Key Results section.

Your uncle will choose the option that yields the highest Year 3 End-of-year cash on hand. You must look at your Scenario Summary sheet to see which strategy yields the highest amount.

To check your work, you should attain the values shown in Figure C-26. You should format the Summary sheet appropriately; for example, see Figure C-26.

	A	B	C	D	E	F
1	Scenario Summary					
2			Loaf-In	Loaf-Out	Delay-In	Delay-Out
4	Changing Cells:					
5	Retired or Working, Year 1	$C$10	R	R	W	W
6	Retired or Working, Year 2	$D$10	R	R	W	W
7	Retired or Working, Year 3	$E$10	R	R	W	W
8	Stay in Club?	$C$11	Y	N	Y	N
9	Result Cells:					
10	End-of-year cash, Year 3	$E$14	$23,120	$58,370	$92,189	$119,489

FIGURE C-26 Scenario Summary

REVIEWING EXCEL BASICS

In this section, you'll begin by reviewing how to perform some basic operations. Then you'll work through more cash flow calculations. Working through this section will help you complete the spreadsheet cases in this book.

Basic Operations

You'll review the following topics: formatting cells, showing Excel cell formulas, understanding circular references, using the AND and OR functions in IF statements, and using nested IF statements.

Formatting Cells

You may have noticed that some data in this tutorial's first spreadsheet was centered in the cells. Follow these steps to center data in cells:

1. Highlight the cell range to format.
2. Select the Home tab.
3. In the Alignment group, select the Middle Align icon to change the vertical alignment.
4. In the Alignment group, select the Center icon to change the horizontal alignment.

You can also put a border around cells, which might be desirable for highlighting cells in the Inputs section. Follow these steps:

1. Highlight the cell that needs a border.
2. Select the Home tab.
3. In the Font group, select the drop-down arrow of the Borders icon.
4. Choose the desired border from the menu.

You can format numerical values for Currency by following these steps:

1. Highlight the cell or range of cells that should be formatted.
2. Select the Home tab.
3. In the Number group, use the Number Format drop-down arrow to select Currency and the number of decimals, and then click OK.

You can format numerical values for decimal places using this procedure:

1. Highlight the cell or range of cells that should be formatted.
2. Select the Home tab.
3. In the Number group, click the Increase Decimal icon once to add one decimal value. Click the Decrease Decimal icon to eliminate a decimal value.

You can use the available automatic styles to change the appearance of the text:

1. Highlight the cell or range of cells that you want to change.
2. Select the Home tab.
3. Within the Styles group, click the Cell Styles drop-down arrow, and then choose the style you want to apply, such as Heading 1 or Title in the Titles and Headings group.

You can increase or decrease the indentation used for your row headings, which makes the text under each section much easier to see:

1. Highlight the cell or range of cells that you want to change.
2. Select the Home tab.
3. In the Alignment group, click the Increase Indent button (or Decrease Indent, as the case may be).

You can copy all the format properties of a certain cell to other cells using the Format Painter:

1. Select the cell whose format you want to transfer elsewhere.
2. Click the Format Painter button (the paintbrush icon) in the Home tab's Clipboard group. When you click the button, the mouse pointer turns into a paintbrush.
3. Select the cells that you want to format.
4. To turn off the Format Painter, click its button again or press the Esc key.

Showing Excel Cell Formulas

If you want to see Excel cell formulas, follow these steps:

1. Press the Ctrl key and the back quote key (') at the same time. The back quote faces the opposite direction from a normal quotation mark; on most keyboards, it shares the key with the tilde (~) mark.
2. To restore, press the Ctrl and back quote keys again.

Understanding a Circular Reference

A formula has a circular reference when it *refers to itself either directly or indirectly.* In this book's cases, Excel cannot properly evaluate such a formula. The problem is best described by an example. Suppose the formula in cell C18 is =C18−C17. Excel is trying to compute a value for cell C18, so it must evaluate the formula, then put the result on the screen in C18. Excel tries to subtract the contents of C17 from the contents of C18, but nothing is in C18. Can you see the circularity? To establish a value for C18, Excel must know what is in C18. However, that value is what you are trying to compute in the first place. The process is circular—hence, the term "circular reference." As another simple example, consider a formula in one cell that refers to a formula in a second cell, and the formula in the second cell that refers to the formula in the first cell. For example, cell C7 has the formula =C6, and cell C6 is =C7.

To be sure that Excel will point out circular references, you should do the following:

1. Click the File tab.
2. Click Options in the left column menu.
3. Click Formulas in the left column of the Excel Options window.
4. In the Calculation Options section, deselect the "Enable iterative calculation" check box, and then click OK.

Now when you enter a formula that has a circular reference, you will receive a warning message. You can close the message, but that will not fix the problem. You *must* fix the formula that has the circular reference if you want the spreadsheet to give you accurate results.

Using the AND Function and the OR Function in IF Statements

An IF statement has the following syntax:

IF(test condition, result if test is True, result if test is False)

The test conditions in this tutorial's IF statements tested only one cell's value, but a test condition can test more than one value of a cell.

Here is an example from this tutorial's first spreadsheet, in which selling price was a function of the economy. Assume for the sake of illustration that Year 2's selling price per unit depends on the economy *and* on the purchase-price outlook. There are two possibilities: (1) If the economic outlook is optimistic *and* the company's purchase-price outlook is down, the selling price will be 110% times the prior year's price. (2) In all other cases, the selling price will be 103% times the prior year's price. The first possibility's test requires two things to be true *at the same time*: C8 = "O" *AND* C9 = "D." To implement the test, the AND() function is needed. The code in cell C17 would be as follows:

=IF(AND($C$8 = "O", $C$9 = "D"), B17 * 1.10, B17 * 1.03)

When the test that uses the AND() function evaluates to True, the result is B17 * 1.10. When the test evaluates to False, the result is the second possibility's outcome: B17 * 1.03.

Now suppose the first possibility is as follows: If the economic outlook is optimistic *or* the purchase-price outlook is down, the selling price will be 110% times the prior year's price. Assume in all other cases that the selling price will be 103% times the prior year's price. Now the test requires *only one of* two things to be true: C8 = "O" *OR* C9 = "D." To implement that test, the OR() function is needed. The code in cell C17 would be:

=IF(OR($C$8 = "O", $C$9 = "D"), B17 * 1.10, B17 * 1.03)

Using IF Statements Inside IF Statements ("Nesting IFs")

Recall from the previous section that an IF statement has this syntax:

IF(test condition, result if test is True, result if test is False)

In the examples shown thus far, only two courses of action were possible, so only one test was needed in the IF statement. However, there can be more than two courses of action; if so, the "result if test is False" clause needs to show further testing. Look at the following example.

Assume again that the Year 2 selling price per unit depends on the economy and the purchase-price outlook. Here is the logic: (1) If the economic outlook is optimistic *and* the purchase-price outlook is down, the selling price will be 110% times the prior year's price. (2) If the economic outlook is optimistic *and* the purchase-price outlook is up, the selling price will be 107% times the prior year's price. (3) In all other cases, the selling price will be 103% times the prior year's price. The code in cell C17 would be as follows:

=IF(AND($C$8 = "O", $C$9 = "D"), B17 * 1.10,

IF(AND($C$8 = "O", $C$9 = "U"), B17 * 1.07, B17 * 1.03))

The first IF statement tests to see if the economic outlook is optimistic and the purchase-price outlook is down. If not, further testing is needed to see whether the economic outlook is optimistic and the purchase-price outlook is up, or whether some other situation prevails.

NOTE

The line is broken in the previous example because the page is not wide enough, but in Excel, the formula would appear on one line. The embedded "IF" is not preceded by an equal sign.

Cash Flow Calculations: Borrowing and Repayments

The Scenario Manager cases in this book may require you to account for money that the company borrows or repays. Possible borrowing and repayment calculations are discussed next. At times, you will be asked to think about a question and fill in the answer. Correct responses are found at the end of this section.

Assume two things about a company's borrowing and repayment of debt. First, assume that the company wants to have a certain minimum cash level at the end of a year, and thus at the start of the next year. Second, assume that a bank will provide a loan to make up the shortfall if year-end cash falls short of the desired minimum cash level.

Here are some examples to test your understanding. Assume that NCP stands for "net cash position" and that NCP equals beginning-of-year cash plus net income after taxes for the year. In other words, the NCP is the cash available at year's end before any borrowing or repayment. For the three examples in Figure C-27, compute the amounts the company needs to borrow to reach its minimum year-end cash level.

Example	NCP	Minimum Cash Required	Amount to Borrow
1	$50,000	$10,000	?
2	$8,000	$10,000	?
3	−$20,000	$10,000	?

FIGURE C-27   Examples of borrowing

One additional assumption you can make is that the company will use its excess cash at year's end to pay off as much debt as possible without going below the minimum-cash threshold. Excess cash is the NCP *minus* the minimum cash required on hand—amounts over the minimum are available to repay any debt.

In the examples shown in Figure C-28, compute excess cash and then compute the amount to repay. To aid your understanding, you may also want to compute ending cash after repayments.

Example	NCP	Minimum Cash Required	Beginning-of-year Debt	Repay?	Ending Cash
1	$12,000	$10,000	$4,000	?	?
2	$12,000	$10,000	$10,000	?	?
3	$20,000	$10,000	$10,000	?	?
4	$20,000	$10,000	$0	?	?
5	$60,000	$10,000	$40,000	?	?
6	−$20,000	$10,000	$10,000	?	?

FIGURE C-28   Examples of repayment

In the Scenario Manager cases, your spreadsheet will need two bank financing sections beneath the Income and Cash Flow Statements section. The first section will calculate any needed borrowing or repayment at year's end to compute year-end cash. The second section will calculate the amount of debt owed at the end of the year, after borrowing or repayment of debt.

The first new section, in effect, extends the end-of-year cash calculation, which was shown in Figure C-13. Previously, the amount equaled cash at the beginning of the year plus the year's net income. Now the calculation will include cash obtained by borrowing and cash repaid. Figure C-29 shows the structure of the calculation.

	A	B	C	D
28				
29	Net Cash Position (NCP) = Beginning-of-year cash on hand plus Net income after taxes	NA		
30	Add: Borrowing from bank	NA		
31	Less: Repayment to bank	NA		
32	End-of-year cash on hand	$10,000		

FIGURE C-29   Calculation of end-of-year cash on hand

The heading in cell A28 was previously End-of-year cash on hand (see Figure C-13). However, borrowing increases cash and repayment of debt decreases cash. So, End-of-year cash on hand is now computed two rows down (in C32 for Year 2, in the example). The value in row 29 must be a subtotal for the Beginning-of-year cash on hand plus the year's Net income after taxes. That subtotal is the NCP. Note that the formula in cell C22 for Beginning-of-year cash on hand would now be =B32.

The second new section computes end-of-year debt and is called Debt Owed, as shown in Figure C-30.

	A	B	C	D
34	**Debt Owed**	**Year 1**	**Year 2**	**Year 3**
35	Beginning-of-year debt owed	NA		
36	Add: Borrowing from bank	NA		
37	Less: Repayment to bank	NA		
38	End-of-year cash debt owed	$15,000		

FIGURE C-30 Debt Owed section

As you can see in Figure C-30, $15,000 was owed at the end of Year 1. The End-of-year debt owed equals the Beginning-of-year debt owed plus any new Borrowing from bank (which increases debt owed), minus any Repayment to bank (which reduces it). So, in the example, the formula in cell C38 would be:

=C35+C36–C37

Assume that the amounts for Borrowing from bank and Repayment to bank are calculated in the first new section. Thus, the formula in cell C36 would be =C30. The formula in cell C37 would be =C31. Beginning-of-year debt owed is equal to the debt owed at the end of the prior year, of course. The formula in cell C35 for Beginning-of-year debt owed would be an echoed formula. Can you see what it would be?

Now that you have seen how the borrowing and repayment data are shown, we can discuss the logic of the borrowing and repayment formulas.

Calculation of Borrowing from Bank

The logic of this calculation in English is:

> If (cash on hand before financing transactions is greater than the minimum cash required,
>> then borrowing is not needed;
>> else, borrow enough to get to the minimum cash).

Or (a little more precisely):

> If (NCP is greater than the minimum cash required,
>> then Borrowing from bank = 0;
>> else, borrow enough to get to the minimum cash).

Suppose the desired minimum cash at year's end is $10,000, which is a constant in your spreadsheet's cell C6. Assume that the NCP is shown in your spreadsheet's cell C29. The logic of the borrowing formula (assumed to be in cell C30) would be as follows:

IF(NCP > Minimum Cash, 0; otherwise, borrow enough to get to the minimum).

You have cell addresses that stand for NCP (cell C29) and Minimum Cash (C6). To develop the formula for cell C30, substitute the cell addresses for NCP and Minimum Cash. The harder logic is for the "else" clause. At this point, you could look ahead to the Borrowing answers in Figure C-31. In Example 2, $2,000 was borrowed. Which cell was subtracted from which other cell to calculate that amount? Substitute cell addresses in the Excel formula for Year 2's borrowing formula in cell C31:

=IF(>= ,   0,   -   )

The answer is at the end of this section in Figure C-33.

Calculation of Repayment to Bank

The logic of this calculation in English is:

IF(beginning of year debt = 0, repay 0 because nothing is owed, but

IF(NCP is less than the minimum, repay zero, because you must *borrow*, but

IF(extra cash available equals or exceeds the debt, repay the whole debt,

ELSE(to stay above the minimum cash, repay only the extra cash available))))

Look at the following formula skeleton. Assume that the repayment will be in cell C31. Assume also that debt owed at the beginning of the year is in cell C35 and minimum cash is in cell C6. "Extra cash" is the excess of NCP over the minimum cash needed. Substitute cell addresses for concepts to complete the formula for Year 2 repayment. (Clauses appear on different lines because of page width limitations.)

=IF(= 0, 0,
    IF(<= , 0,
        IF((–) >= , ____,
            (–))))

The answer is shown at the end of this section in Figure C-34.

Answers to Questions about Borrowing and Repayment Calculations

Figures C-31 and C-32 answer the questions about borrowing and repayment calculations.

Example	NCP	Minimum Cash Required	Amount to Borrow	Comments
1	$50,000	$10,000	$0	NCP > Minimum, no need to borrow
2	$8,000	$10,000	$2,000	Need $2K to get to Minimum ($10K–$8K)
3	–$20,000	$10,000	$30,000	Need $30K to get to Minimum ($10K–(–$20K))

FIGURE C-31 Answers to examples of borrowing

Example	NCP	Minimum Cash Required	Beginning-of-year Debt	Repay?	Ending Cash
1	$12,000	$10,000	$4,000	$2,000	$10,000
2	$12,000	$10,000	$10,000	$2,000	$10,000
3	$20,000	$10,000	$10,000	$10,000	$10,000
4	$20,000	$10,000	$0	$0	$20,000
5	$60,000	$10,000	$40,000	$40,000	$20,000
6	–$20,000	$10,000	$10,000	$0	NA

FIGURE C-32 Answers to examples of repayment

Note the following points about the repayment calculations shown in Figure C-32.

- In Examples 1 and 2, only $2,000 "extra" cash is available for debt repayment (12,000 – 10,000) to avoid going below the minimum cash.
- In Example 3, extra cash available for repayment is $10,000 (20,000 – 10,000), so all beginning debt can be repaid, leaving the minimum cash.
- In Example 4, no debt is owed, so no debt need be repaid.
- In Example 5, cash available for repayment is $50,000 (60,000 – 10,000), so all of the $40,000 beginning debt can be repaid, leaving more than the minimum cash.
- In Example 6, no cash is available for repayment. The company must borrow.

Figures C-33 and C-34 show the formulas to calculate borrowing and repayment of debt.

=IF(C29 >= C6, 0, C6−C29)

FIGURE C-33 Calculation of borrowing

=IF(C35 = 0, 0, IF(C29 <= C6, 0, IF ((C29−C6) >= C35, C35, C29−C6)))

FIGURE C-34 Calculation of repayment

CASE **6**

PHILLY LANDSCAPING

Decision Support Using Microsoft Excel

PREVIEW

Your father-in-law, Steve, owns and operates a small but successful landscaping company in the suburbs of Philadelphia. However, the continuing success of the company strongly depends on his ability to do a lot of the day-to-day work. Steve recently turned 50, and the thought of continued intense labor is not very appealing to him. He is faced with a choice: invest money in the company to build it to a point that all he has to do is manage it from a distance, or sell the company. Steve has come to you to help him model the outcome of his choices and provide recommendations. You will use Microsoft Excel to provide Steve a look into the future.

PREPARATION

- Review spreadsheet concepts discussed in class and in your textbook.
- Complete any exercises that your instructor assigns.
- Complete any part of Tutorial C that your instructor assigns. You may need to review the use of If statements and the section called "Cash Flow Calculations: Borrowing and Repayments."
- Review file-saving procedures for Windows programs.
- Refer to Tutorials E and F as necessary.

BACKGROUND

Philly Landscaping, your father-in-law's company, has been in business for 25 years, and during this time it has earned many loyal customers. The customers like the up-front pricing, attention to detail, and job follow-through that Steve provides. Steve is now 50 and is taking a hard look at his retirement plans (better late than never). He was recently offered $3 million by a competitor to buy him out and acquire his clientele. Steve's financial advisor has estimated that the proceeds from the sale could yield an annual income of $100,000. Steve loves his company and would like to continue working with his loyal customers for many years to come. However, he is also tempted by the thought of an early retirement and moving to his summer house in Long Beach Island, New Jersey. So, he finds himself at a crossroads—he can sell the company, invest the proceeds of the sale, and let the stock market provide him a steady income, or he can take out a loan to build the company to the point that he can stop working and still make a reasonable living.

That's where you come in! Steve knows of your Excel and finance skills and has asked you to help him model the outcome of each decision. If he wants to take out a loan, the bank will need to see forecasted profits to make its decision. Steve has given you a full briefing of Philly Landscaping's business model, pricing schedules, and assumptions he is willing to make about the future in order to facilitate your analysis. Your work will create a cash flow forecast for the next 10 years to assist him and the bank in making decisions.

Philly Landscaping offers a variety of services tailored for each of the seasons that focus on the company's most profitable activities:

- Spring yard work and general clean-up. These activities include getting the yard ready for spring and summer, and miscellaneous cleaning around the house:
  - Clean up any fall and winter debris, such as leaves, stones, and sticks.
  - If the growing season has begun, cut the grass short and collect the clippings.

- Dethatch the lawn. Dethatching removes dead roots and grasses that can build up during a growing season. This has a similar effect to brushing a dog to remove the undercoat.
- Aerate the lawn. Aerating breaks up the soil surface and punches holes into the earth, allowing air, water, nutrients, and new seeds to penetrate the soil.
- Clear gutters of any debris that may have accumulated over the winter.
- Power wash patios and siding.
- Summer yard work. During summers the company's work switches to maintenance operations focused primarily on two activities:
  - Lawn mowing and edging.
  - Driveway seal coating. For customers with asphalt driveways, this job is a must every two to three years. The asphalt must be resealed to prevent normal wear and tear from becoming cracks or other types of expensive damage.
- Fall yard clean-up. As you would expect, fall activities focus on cleaning up leaves, although other services are provided as well:
  - Lawn fertilizing with specially formulated winterizing fertilizers that are higher in potassium than regular lawn food. Potassium is the nutrient that makes grasses more winter-hardy.
  - Filling in brown spots with an all-in-one lawn repair mixture that contains grass seed, a special "quick starter" lawn fertilizer, and mulch.
  - Weed control. If broadleaf weeds such as dandelions have taken over the lawn, fall is the time to fight back. Weeds, like most plants, are in energy-absorbing mode during the fall. They drink in everything that comes their way, including weed killers.
- Winter activities, which focus on snow clearing and large tree clean-up.
  - Snow removal and salt treating of driveways and walk paths.
  - Removing deadwood and trimming trees when they are leafless is easier during the winter.

Steve is also comfortable making several assumptions about the business, which you will use as constants or inputs:

- Tax rate
- Annual payments for a loan
- Costs
- Customer base changes
- Annual income required for retirement

Steve understands that your model will provide him with enough guidance to make an informed decision. Now that you are familiar with the company's operations and pricing schedules, you can begin the process of putting together the decision support system (DSS) so you can answer Steve's questions.

Assignment 1 contains information you will need to create the DSS and write formulas for the Calculations section, including formulas for expected work, annual expenses and revenues, and calculated flags. Keep in mind that Steve has at least three options:

- Do nothing.
- Sell the company and invest the proceeds, which would yield an annual income of approximately $100,000.
- Take out a loan to build the company to the point that a general manager could be hired at an annual salary of $50,000 to run operations.

You will use Excel to determine how the different options or scenarios would affect annual cash flows, total net income after 10 years, and the ability to hire a general manager. Your scenarios will focus on the following important questions:

- What will happen if nothing is done?
- Will Steve be able to retire early by investing money into the company?
- Will there be enough money to hire a general manager?
- What will the cash flow look like in the different scenarios?

In summary, your DSS will include the following inputs:

- Customer base change percentage
- Annual repayment of the loan
- Annual income required for retirement

Your DSS model must account for the effects of the preceding inputs on the Calculations section. If you design your model well, it will let you develop "what-if" scenarios with all inputs, see the results, and allow Steve to make a decision about his retirement.

ASSIGNMENT 1: CREATING A SPREADSHEET FOR DECISION SUPPORT

In this assignment, you will produce a spreadsheet that models Philly Landscaping's estimated 2017 revenues, expenses, and profits; provides forecasts of 10 years of cash flows for the company; and allows for the input of other variables to answer Steve's questions. In Assignment 2, you will use your spreadsheet to gather data and then write a memorandum that documents your analysis and findings. In Assignment 3, you will prepare and give an oral presentation of your analysis and conclusions to Steve.

First, you need to create the spreadsheet model based on your conversations with Steve and your understanding of the questions he would like to have answered. The model will cover 11 years—2017 as the base year and 10 subsequent years as requested by the bank to provide estimated cash flows. This section helps you set up each of the following spreadsheet components before entering cell formulas:

- Constants
- Inputs
- Summary of Key Results
- Calculations

A discussion of each section follows. The spreadsheet skeleton for this case is available for you to use; it will save you time. To access the spreadsheet skeleton, go to your data files, select Case 6, and then select **Philly Landscaping.xlsx**.

Constants Section

Your spreadsheet should include the constants, otherwise known as assumptions, shown in Figure 6-1. An explanation of the line items follows the figure.

PHILLY LANDSCAPING		
CONSTANTS		**2017**
Prices		
Rough Yard Work per Square Foot	$	0.003
Gutter Cleaning per Linear Foot	$	0.075
Power Washing per Square Foot	$	0.050
Lawn Mowing and Edging per Square Foot	$	0.001
Driveway Seal Coating per Square Foot	$	0.100
Fall Leaf Clearing per Square Foot	$	0.003
Snow Removal per Square Foot	$	0.025
Costs		
Average Cost of Labor and Materials	$	0.30
Customer Base		
Customers		850
Average Lawn Surface (Sq Ft)		43,560
Average Power Washing Surface (Sq Ft)		5,000
Average Gutter Length (Linear Ft)		150
Average Snow Removal Surface (Sq Ft)		2,500
Average Driveway Seal Coating Surface (Sq Ft)		2,500
Average Fall Leaf Clearing Surface (Sq Ft)		43,560
Economic and Environmental Factors		
Tax Rate		25%

FIGURE 6-1 Constants section

- Prices—These prices are based on averages that Steve provided.

  - Rough Yard Work per Square Foot
  - Gutter Cleaning per Linear Foot
  - Power Washing per Square Foot
  - Lawn Mowing and Edging per Square Foot
  - Driveway Seal Coating per Square Foot
  - Fall Leaf Clearing per Square Foot
  - Snow Removal per Square Foot

- Costs—The average cost of labor and materials is based on averages Steve provided from previous years.
- Customer Base—These values show the company's current number of customers and average lot coverage areas for various company services. Most of these averages are shown in square footage (Sq Ft).

  - Customers—This value shows the number of customers currently served by the company.
  - Average Lawn Surface (Sq Ft)
  - Average Power Washing Surface (Sq Ft)
  - Average Gutter Length (Linear Ft)
  - Average Snow Removal Surface (Sq Ft)
  - Average Driveway Seal Coating Surface (Sq Ft)
  - Average Fall Leaf Clearing Surface (Sq Ft)

- Economic and Environmental Factors—Based on conversations with his accountant, Steve feels comfortable using a 25 percent tax rate for the model.

Inputs Section

As Steve explained earlier, he would like to answer some important questions to determine his best option for retirement. First, the model needs to evaluate the impact of the loan on the customer base's growth. Second, the model needs to evaluate the repayment of the loan if it is approved. Finally, Steve has different ideas on how much money he will need to retire comfortably; he thinks an amount between $75,000 and $100,000 annually would be sufficient. The DSS will determine whether these options are viable.

Your spreadsheet should include the following inputs, as shown in Figure 6-2. Note that the spreadsheet extends to 2027, as explained earlier, but the remaining figures in this case have been cropped to fit the page.

INPUTS						
Year		2017	2018	2019	2020	2021
Customer Base Change %	NA					
Annual Payments For Loan	NA					
Annual Income Required For Retirement	NA					

FIGURE 6-2 Inputs section

- Customer Base Change %—This value is the expected change in the size of the customer portfolio. The value could be positive, negative, or zero starting in 2017.
- Annual Payments For Loan—The bank's loan officer has provided an estimate of an annual total payment of $120,000 for a loan of $1 million with a 3 percent interest rate over 10 years.
- Annual Income Required For Retirement—This value represents what Steve is willing to accept as annual retirement income.

Summary of Key Results Section

Your spreadsheet should include the results shown in Figure 6-3. A general explanation of this section follows the figure.

SUMMARY OF KEY RESULTS						
Year		2017	2018	2019	2020	2021
Annual Income						
Enough Income to Hire Manager?	NA					
Income Over Expected Annuity Earnings?	NA					

FIGURE 6-3 Summary of Key Results section

For each year starting in 2017, this section should include values that are already calculated elsewhere in the spreadsheet. The formulas in the Summary of Key Results section will echo results from throughout your model; no long or complicated formulas need to be used in this section. The purpose of gathering the results together is to make for an easier job when configuring Scenario Manager later.

Calculations Section

To create an accurate decision tool, you should calculate intermediate results that will be used to determine the year-end numbers needed for the model. It is generally a good idea to arrive at these final numbers in a series of steps rather than in one short calculation. Errors are easier to identify if the steps are broken out, and it also makes troubleshooting a breeze. The calculations shown in Figures 6-4, 6-5, and 6-6 are based on 2017 values in the Constants section (Customer Base values and prices); starting in 2018, the calculations take into account the inputs from each scenario. When called for, use absolute referencing properly. Values must be computed by cell formula; hard-code numbers in formulas only when you are told to do so. Cell formulas should not reference a cell with a value of "NA."

An explanation of each item in this section follows the figure in which the item is shown.

CALCULATIONS					
Expected Business	2017	2018	2019	2020	2021
Rough Yard Work					
Lawn Mowing and Edging					
Power Washing					
Gutter Cleaning					
Snow Removal					
Driveway Seal Coating					
Fall Leaf Clearing					

FIGURE 6-4 Expected Business section of calculations

- Rough Yard Work—The product of the average lawn surface and the number of customers. Steve tells you that only 25 percent of customers request this service. Format cells for numbers with zero decimals.
- Lawn Mowing and Edging—The product of the average lawn surface and the number of customers. Steve tells you that only 25 percent of customers request this service. Format cells for numbers with zero decimals.
- Power Washing—The product of the average power washing surface and the number of customers. Format cells for numbers with zero decimals.
- Gutter Cleaning—The product of the average gutter length and the number of customers. Format cells for numbers with zero decimals.
- Snow Removal—The product of the average snow removal surface and the number of customers. Format cells for numbers with zero decimals.
- Driveway Seal Coating—The product of the average driveway seal coating surface and the number of customers. Format cells for numbers with zero decimals.
- Fall Leaf Clearing—The product of the average lawn surface and the number of customers. Steve tells you that 75 percent of customers request this service. Format cells for numbers with zero decimals.

Expected Revenue	2017	2018	2019	2020	2021
Rough Yard Work					
Lawn Mowing and Edging					
Power Washing					
Gutter Cleaning					
Snow Removal					
Driveway Seal Coating					
Fall Leaf Clearing					
Total Revenue					

FIGURE 6-5 Expected Revenue section of calculations

- Rough Yard Work—Total expected revenue multiplied by the unit price in the Constants section. Format cells for currency with zero decimals.
- Lawn Mowing and Edging—Total expected revenue multiplied by the unit price in the Constants section. Format cells for currency with zero decimals.
- Power Washing—Total expected revenue multiplied by the unit price in the Constants section. Format cells for currency with zero decimals.

- Gutter Cleaning—Total expected revenue multiplied by the unit price in the Constants section. Format cells for currency with zero decimals.
- Snow Removal—Total expected revenue multiplied by the unit price in the Constants section. Format cells for currency with zero decimals.
- Driveway Seal Coating—Total expected revenue multiplied by the unit price in the Constants section. Format cells for currency with zero decimals.
- Fall Leaf Clearing—Total expected revenue multiplied by the unit price in the Constants section. Format cells for currency with zero decimals.
- Total Revenue—The sum of all revenues for the year. Format cells for currency with zero decimals.

Expenses	2017	2018	2019	2020	2021
Labor and Materials					
Loan Repayment					
Total Expense					
Income Before Taxes					
Tax Expense					
Net Income					
Enough Income to Hire Manager?	NA				
Income Over Expected Annuity Earnings?	NA				

FIGURE 6-6 Expenses section of calculations

- Labor and Materials—Based on current estimates, the annual expense for labor and materials is $500,000. This number will need to be updated based on customer base changes starting in 2018. Format cells for currency with zero decimals.
- Loan Repayment—Repayment would start in 2018 if the loan offer is approved. Format cells for currency with zero decimals.
- Total Expense—The sum of labor and materials and the loan repayment. Format cells for currency with zero decimals.
- Income Before Taxes—The difference between total revenue and total expense. Format cells for currency with zero decimals.
- Tax Expense—The tax liability based on the tax rate in the Constants section. Format cells for currency with zero decimals.
- Net Income—The difference between net income before taxes and tax expense. Format cells for currency with zero decimals.
- Enough Income to Hire Manager?—Starting in 2018, if the difference between net income and the amount required to retire is over $50,000, enter "Yes." Otherwise, enter "No."
- Income Over Expected Annuity Earnings?—Starting in 2018, if net income is greater than the estimated annuity value ($100,000), enter "Yes." Otherwise, enter "No."

ASSIGNMENT 2: USING THE SPREADSHEET FOR DECISION SUPPORT

Complete the case by (1) using the spreadsheet to answer Steve's questions, (2) thoroughly analyzing your data, and (3) documenting your findings in a memo.

Steve needs to understand the impacts of a few different options he is considering. He wants to determine his available cash flow at the end of each year based on the following scenarios:

1. Do nothing—Assume that no changes will be made and keep all of Steve's assumptions. With this scenario, he anticipates an annual 5 percent decrease in the customer base. Annual income in this scenario is $65,000.
2. Accept the bank loan with low return on investment (ROI)—Steve has met with the bank's loan officer, who estimated that a 10-year loan with 3 percent annual payments would total $120,000. Using the loan for capital expenses and marketing campaigns, Steve expects that the customer base can grow at 6 percent annually starting in 2018. Annual income in this scenario is $100,000.
3. Accept the bank loan with high ROI—Again, the loan officer estimated that a 10-year loan with 3 percent annual payments would total $120,000. Using the loan for capital expenses and

marketing campaigns, Steve expects that the customer base can grow at 13 percent annually starting in 2018.

4. Accept buyout offer—In this scenario, Steve would accept the buyout offer from a competitor, invest it, and start collecting $100,000 annually from the annuity. Note that this scenario would require a one-time change to the customer base, from 850 to 0.

Assignment 2A: Using the Spreadsheet to Gather Data

You have built the spreadsheet to model several possible situations. For each of the four test scenarios, you want to know the annual cash flow, whether Steve will be able to hire a general manager, and whether income from the company surpasses the estimated annuity value.

You will run "what-if" scenarios with the four sets of input values using Scenario Manager. (See Tutorial C for details on using Scenario Manager.) Set up the four scenarios. Your instructor may ask you to use conditional formatting to make sure your input values are proper. Note that in Scenario Manager you can enter noncontiguous cell ranges, such as C19, D19, C20:F20.

The relevant output cells are Annual Income, Enough Income to Hire Manager?, and Income Over Expected Annuity Earnings? from 2018 to 2027. All of these cells are shown in the Summary of Key Results section. Run Scenario Manager to gather the data in a report. When you finish, print the spreadsheet with the input for any of the scenarios, print the Scenario Manager summary sheet, and then save the spreadsheet file a final time.

Assignment 2B: Documenting Your Results in a Memo

Use Microsoft Word to write a brief memo that documents your analysis and results. You can address the memo to Steve, the owner of Philly Landscaping. Observe the following requirements:

- Set up your memo as described in Tutorial E.
- In the first paragraph, briefly state the business situation and the purpose of your analysis.
- Next, describe the scenarios tested.
- State your conclusions.
- Support your statements graphically, as your instructor requires. Your instructor may ask you to return to Excel and copy the results of the Scenario Manager summary sheet into the memo. You should include a summary table built in Word based on the Scenario Manager summary sheet results. (This procedure is described in Tutorial E.)

Your table should have the format shown in Figure 6-7.

	Do Nothing	Loan—Low ROI	Loan—High ROI	Buyout
Sum of cash flow from 2018 to 2027				
Year with enough profit to hire general manager?				
Year with income over expected annuity earnings?				

FIGURE 6-7 Format of table to insert in memo

ASSIGNMENT 3: GIVING AN ORAL PRESENTATION

Your instructor may ask you to explain your analysis and results in an oral presentation. If so, assume that Steve wants the presentation to last 10 minutes or less. Use visual aids or handouts that you think are appropriate. See Tutorial F for tips on preparing and giving an oral presentation.

DELIVERABLES

Your completed case should include the following deliverables for your instructor:

- A printed copy of your memo
- Printouts of your spreadsheet and scenario summary
- Electronic copies of your memo and Excel DSS model

CASE **7**

THE ELECTRIC CAR FINANCIAL ANALYSIS

Decision Support Using Microsoft Excel

PREVIEW

In this case, you will use Microsoft Excel to see if a company named Electric Car has enough cash to get through the next three years without needing external financing.

PREPARATION

- Review spreadsheet concepts discussed in class and in your textbook.
- Complete any exercises that your instructor assigns.
- Complete any part of Tutorial C that your instructor assigns. You may need to review the use of If statements and the section called "Cash Flow Calculations: Borrowing and Repayments."
- Review file-saving procedures for Windows programs.
- Refer to Tutorials E and F as necessary.

BACKGROUND

Fifteen years ago, Fred Smith was the vice president of engineering for one of the country's major automobile manufacturers. Fred was worried about the harmful environmental effects from burning gasoline inside internal combustion engines, and he was convinced that the government would soon ban the engine for environmental reasons. He wanted the company to start making battery-powered vehicles, but after much debate, management decided not to do so.

Frustrated with that decision, Fred struck out on his own. He and a few younger engineers started their own automobile company, which they named Electric Car. Fred and his team were sure they could make an attractive car that would achieve high speeds while running solely on battery power. They were sure they could sell the car to an increasingly affluent and environmentally sensitive public.

Their strategy had three phases. In the first phase, the company would develop an expensive sports car. This car might not be profitable, but it would establish the company's brand name. In the second phase, they would introduce a more affordable family sedan that would have broader appeal. This car would firmly establish Electric Car as a successful automobile company that was in business for the long haul.

The first- and second-phase cars would not burn gasoline. However, their batteries would need to be charged occasionally, which means a power plant somewhere in the country would have to burn hydrocarbons into the open air to create electricity for recharging. This process would be cleaner than burning gasoline inside a car engine, but Fred and his team wanted to be able to say their cars required no burning of hydrocarbons in the open air. So, in the third phase of its strategy, the company would modify the roofs of its cars to generate solar power that would continuously recharge the batteries.

Fred and his team developed an attractive sports car that accelerated as quickly as any competing car. Fred realized that he could sell the car on the Internet, so there was no need to develop an expensive dealership network.

In the early years, Electric Car obtained working capital by selling common stock and by selling notes at a floating interest rate. The company spent a lot of money in its early years. Major expenditures were for these purposes:

- Establishing an automobile manufacturing site
- Research and development (R&D) costs for building a new kind of car and long-lasting batteries
- A network of charging stations using leased land at convenience stores or at interstate rest stops
- Sports car trade-in guarantees

Electric Car's sports car sold well immediately because of its sleek lines, amazing acceleration, and resale option. In the plan, a buyer was guaranteed that the sports car would have a good trade-in value for eight years for any new car. For example, a sports car purchased in 2010 from Electric Car for $65,000 would be guaranteed to be worth $50,000 in 2017, $48,000 in 2018, and $46,000 in 2019. If an owner could not get the guaranteed amount for a trade-in, the company would write a check for the difference.

The program helped overcome buyer reluctance in the company's early years. There were some early claims against Electric Car, but the program has not been a great financial drain on the company in recent years. However, the company's public accountants say that a liability must be recorded for potential claims, which are estimated to be $1 billion at most. Management thinks the program is no longer needed and has discontinued it, but the potential liability for older sales still exists.

Electric Car has reached the end of the first phase of its strategy and is looking forward to the second phase. Two major developments in recent years will require capital expenditures in the foreseeable future:

- Electric Car engineers have designed and learned to build the reasonably priced family sedan, which they plan to start selling next year. As sales increase, the production line will be expanded accordingly.
- Through their R&D, company engineers have learned to make a better battery that will increase travel time between recharges. This gives them a marketing advantage for the future. They have entered into a joint venture with their battery supplier to capitalize on the R&D. They will build their own plant to make next-generation car batteries, which will ensure a stable supply of batteries at more controllable costs.

This is an important transition point for the company. Management hopes that family sedan sales will be adequate to establish profitability within the next three years. If Electric Car can achieve these profits, management thinks the company will be in the car business for the long run. At this point the company has $9 billion in cash, but management knows that much of this money will be exhausted in the next three years. Here is the key financial question for management: What are the chances the company can make it through 2020 without having to raise new capital in the financial markets?

ASSIGNMENT 1: CREATING A SPREADSHEET FOR DECISION SUPPORT

In this assignment, you will produce a spreadsheet that models Electric Car's financial situation. Then, in Assignment 2, you will use the spreadsheet for decision support and write a memorandum that documents your analysis and findings. In Assignment 3, you will prepare and give an oral presentation of your analysis and conclusions to company management.

First, you will create the spreadsheet model of the decision. The model covers the three years from 2018 to 2020. This section helps you set up each of the following spreadsheet components before entering cell formulas:

- Constants
- Inputs
- Summary of Key Results
- Calculations
- Income and Cash Flow statements
- Debt Owed

A discussion of each section follows. The spreadsheet skeleton for this case is available for you to use; it will save you time. To access the spreadsheet skeleton, go to your data files, select Case 7, and then select **ElectricCar.xlsx**.

Constants Section

Your spreadsheet should include the constants shown in Figure 7-1. An explanation of the line items follows the figure.

	A	B	C	D	E
1	**Electric Car Company**				
2					
3	CONSTANTS	2017	2018	2019	2020
4	TAX RATE	NA	20%	20%	20%
5	MINIMUM CASH NEEDED TO START YEAR	NA	$ 1,000,000,000	$ 1,000,000,000	$ 1,000,000,000
6	PROJECTED CAPITAL COSTS	NA	$ 2,000,000,000	$ 2,000,000,000	$ 2,000,000,000
7	RESEARCH AND DEVELOPMENT COSTS	NA	$ 500,000,000	$ 500,000,000	$ 500,000,000
8	FIXED COSTS	NA	$ 500,000,000	$ 500,000,000	$ 500,000,000
9	COST OF OPERATING A CHARGER STATION	NA	$ 100,000	$ 100,000	$ 100,000
10	INTEREST RATE ON DEBT OWED	NA	2%	2%	2%

FIGURE 7-1   Constants section

- Tax Rate—The income tax rate is expected to be 20 percent each year.
- Minimum Cash Needed to Start Year—The company wants to have at least $1 billion in cash at the beginning of each year. Assume that the company could borrow from a friendly banker at the end of a year in order to begin the new year with that amount.
- Projected Capital Costs—The company expects to spend $2 billion a year on the expanded manufacturing line, battery factory, and other projects.
- Research and Development Costs—R&D is ongoing at an expected $500 million a year.
- Fixed Costs—Other expenses for the year, such as sales and administrative costs, are expected to be $500 million a year.
- Cost of Operating a Charger Station—Yearly expenses associated with each charger station average $100,000 a year.
- Interest Rate on Debt Owed—The notes have a floating rate, which currently is 2 percent. Management thinks this rate will persist.

Inputs Section

Your spreadsheet should include the following inputs for the years 2018 to 2020, as shown in Figure 7-2.

	A	B	C	D	E
12	INPUTS	2017	2018	2019	2020
13	COST OF GASOLINE (D/S/U)		NA	NA	NA
14	GUARANTY CLAIM RATE (.XX)	NA			
15	UNIT COST REDUCTION FACTOR	NA			
16	NUMBER OF NEW CHARGER LOCATIONS	NA			
17	UNITS -- MARKET MOMENTUM EFFECT (% PTS)	NA			

FIGURE 7-2   Inputs section

- Cost of Gasoline (D/S/U)—The cost of a gallon of gasoline has an effect on electric car sales and selling prices. When the cost goes up, more electric cars are sold, and for a higher price. When the cost goes down, the effects are the opposite. Thus, Electric Car management hopes for higher gas prices in the coming years. Enter "D" if the price of gasoline is expected to decline, "U" if the price is expected to go up, and "S" if the price is expected to be stable. The entry applies to all years.
- Guaranty Claim Rate (.XX)—What percentage of the possible $1 billion liability will be claimed? If you expect 1 percent in a year, for example, enter ".01."
- Unit Cost Reduction Factor—As the company learns more about making cars and modernizes its plant, the unit cost of a car should decline. If you expect a 1 percent decline in a year, for example, enter ".01."
- Number of New Charger Locations—As a marketing tool, the company needs to keep expanding the number of locations. Enter the number of new locations expected in a year.
- Units—Market Momentum Effect (% PTS)—Management thinks that time is on its side: Over time, buying an electric car will be seen as the progressive thing to do, and car sales will

increase as a result. Management calls this effect the "market momentum effect"—each year the market will move the company's way to a certain extent, regardless of other economic factors. If you expect the number of cars sold to increase by 6 percentage points (% PTS) in a year, for example, enter "6."

Summary of Key Results Section

Your spreadsheet should include the results shown in Figure 7-3.

	A	B	C	D	E
19	SUMMARY OF KEY RESULTS	2017	2018	2019	2020
20	NET INCOME AFTER TAXES	NA			
21	END-OF-THE-YEAR CASH ON HAND	NA			
22	END-OF-THE-YEAR DEBT OWED	NA			

FIGURE 7-3 Summary of Key Results section

For each year, your spreadsheet should compute net income after taxes, cash on hand at the end of the year, and debt owed to noteholders and the bank. These values are computed elsewhere in the spreadsheet and should be echoed here.

Calculations Section

You should calculate intermediate results (see Figure 7-4) that will be used in the income and cash flow statements that follow. When called for, use absolute referencing properly. Values must be computed by cell formula; hard-code numbers in formulas only when you are told to do so. Cell formulas should not reference a cell with a value of "NA," which stands for "not applicable."

An explanation of each item in this section follows the figure.

	A	B	C	D	E
24	CALCULATIONS	2017	2018	2019	2020
25	CHARGER LOCATIONS	600			
26	CHANGE IN UNITS SOLD (% POINTS)	NA			
27	MARKET MOMENTUM EFFECT	NA			
28	GAS PRICE EFFECT	NA			
29	NEW CHARGER LOCATION EFFECT	NA			
30	TOTAL CHANGE	NA			
31	UNITS SOLD – SPORT	53,000			
32	UNITS SOLD – FAMILY	0			
33	CHANGE IN SELLING PRICE (% POINTS)	NA			
34	MARKET MOMENTUM EFFECT	NA	2	2	2
35	GAS PRICE EFFECT	NA			
36	NEW CHARGER LOCATION EFFECT	NA			
37	TOTAL CHANGE	NA			
38	SELLING PRICE – SPORT	$ 75,000			
39	SELLING PRICE – FAMILY	$ -			
40	UNIT COST – SPORT	$ 78,000			
41	UNIT COST – FAMILY	$ -			

FIGURE 7-4 Calculations section

- Charger Locations—There were 600 locations at the end of 2017. The number of locations will increase each year by the related value in the Inputs section.
- Change in Units Sold (% Points)—Three factors will affect the number of sports cars and family sedans sold in a year: the market momentum effect, the cost of gasoline, and the number of new charger locations.
- Market Momentum Effect—This percentage increase is a value from the Inputs section, which can be echoed here.
- Gas Price Effect—The direction of the price of gas is a value from the Inputs section. If the price is expected to decrease, the effect is minus 5 percent (in other words, unit sales will decline by 5 percent in the year). If the price is expected to increase, the effect is plus 5 percent (unit sales will increase by 5 percent in the year). If prices are expected to be stable, there is no effect.

- New Charger Location Effect—If there are more than 100 new charger locations, the expected effect on units sold is plus 5 percent. If there are between 76 and 100 new charger locations, the effect is plus 3 percent. If there are between 26 and 75 new charger locations, the effect is plus 2 percent. Otherwise, there will be no effect.
- Total Change—The total expected percentage change in units sold is the sum of the market, gas price, and charger location effects.
- Units Sold–Sport—The number of units sold in a year is a function of the number sold in the prior year and the total percentage change in units expected. For example, if 53,000 sports cars were sold in 2017 and a 10 percent increase was expected in 2018, the number of units sold would be 1.10 × 53,000, or 58,300.
- Units Sold–Family—No family sedans were sold in 2017. Management thinks 20,000 will be sold in 2018, plus or minus the expected change in units sold. Thus, if a 10 percent increase was expected in 2018, the number of units sold would be 1.10 × 20,000, or 22,000. In succeeding years, the number of units sold will be a function of the number sold in the prior year and the total percentage change in units expected.
- Change in Selling Price (% Points)—Three factors will affect the selling price of sports cars and family sedans sold in a year: the market momentum effect, the cost of gasoline, and the number of new charger locations.
- Market Momentum Effect—A 2 percent increase is expected each year. You can hard-code a "2" in each year.
- Gas Price Effect—If gas prices are expected to rise, sports car and sedan selling prices will increase by 3 percent in the year. Otherwise, there will be no effect on selling prices.
- New Charger Location Effect—If the number of new charger locations exceeds 25, sports car and sedan selling prices will increase by 1 percent in the year. If there are 25 or fewer new charger locations, there will be no effect on selling prices.
- Total Change—The total expected percentage change in sports car and family sedan selling prices is the sum of the market, gas price, and charger location effects.
- Selling Price–Sport—The selling price in a year is a function of the prior year's price and the total percentage change expected. For example, in 2017 the selling price was $75,000. If a 5 percent total change was expected, the 2018 selling price would be 1.05 × $75,000, or $78,750.
- Selling Price–Family—No family sedans were sold in 2017, so there was no 2017 selling price. Management thinks $35,000 should be the selling price in 2018, plus or minus the expected change. Thus, if a 5 percent increase was expected in 2018, the selling price would be 1.05 × $35,000, or $36,750. In succeeding years, the price will be a function of the price in the prior year and the total percentage change expected.
- Unit Cost–Sport—The unit cost of production in a year is a function of the prior year's cost and the cost reduction factor, which is a value from the Inputs section. For example, the unit cost in 2017 was $78,000. If a 2 percent decrease was expected in 2018, the unit cost would be .98 × $78,000, or $76,440.
- Unit Cost–Family—No family sedans were made for sale in 2017. Management estimates a $30,000 unit cost in 2018, minus the effect of any cost reduction factor. Thus, if a 2 percent decrease was expected in 2018, the unit cost would be .98 × $30,000, or $29,400. In succeeding years, the unit cost will be a function of the cost in the prior year and the cost reduction factor expected in the year.

Income and Cash Flow Statements

The forecast for net income and cash flow starts with the cash on hand at the beginning of the year. This value is followed by the income statement and the calculation of cash on hand at year's end. For readability, format cells in this section as currency with zero decimals. Values must be computed by cell formula; hard-code numbers in formulas only if you are told to do so. Cell formulas should not reference a cell with a value of "NA." Your spreadsheets should look like those shown in Figures 7-5 and 7-6. A discussion of each item in the section follows each figure.

	A	B	C	D	E
43	**INCOME STATEMENT AND CASH FLOW STATEMENT**	_2017_	_2018_	_2019_	_2020_
44	BEGINNING-OF-THE-YEAR CASH ON HAND	NA			
45					
46	REVENUE				
47	AUTO SALES – SPORT	NA			
48	AUTO SALES – FAMILY	NA			
49	TOTAL REVENUE	NA			
50	COSTS AND EXPENSES				
51	COST OF SPORT AUTOS SOLD	NA			
52	COST OF FAMILY AUTOS SOLD	NA			
53	RESEARCH AND DEVELOPMENT COSTS	NA			
54	CHARGER LOCATION OPERATING COSTS	NA			
55	PRICE GUARANTY PAYMENTS	NA			
56	FIXED COSTS	NA			
57	TOTAL COSTS AND EXPENSES	NA			
58	INCOME BEFORE INTEREST AND TAXES	NA			
59	INTEREST EXPENSE	NA			
60	INCOME BEFORE TAXES	NA			
61	INCOME TAX EXPENSE	NA			
62	NET INCOME AFTER TAXES	NA			

FIGURE 7-5   Income and Cash Flow statements section

- Beginning-of-the-Year Cash on Hand—This value is the cash on hand at the end of the prior year.
- Revenue—Sports car and family sedan revenues are functions of the units sold and the selling price, which are values from the Calculations section.
- Total Revenue—This value is the sum of sports car and family sedan revenues.
- Cost of Sport and Family Autos Sold—These values are functions of the units sold and the related unit costs, which are taken from the Calculations section.
- Research and Development Costs—This value is a constant, which can be echoed here.
- Charger Location Operating Costs—This amount is a function of the number of charger locations (from the Calculations section) and the charger station operating cost, which is a constant.
- Price Guaranty Payments—In your formula, this amount for 2018 is a function of the guaranty claim rate for the year (from the Inputs section) and the assumed $1 billion liability. You should hard-code $1 billion for 2018. In succeeding years, the amount is a function of the guaranty claim rate for the year and the assumed liability, which is $1 billion minus any claims paid in prior years. For example, if $100 million in claims are paid in 2018, the assumed liability would be reduced to $900 million in 2019.
- Fixed Costs—This value is a constant, which can be echoed here.
- Total Costs and Expenses—This value is the sum of the cost of cars sold, R&D costs, charger location operating costs, price guaranty payments, and fixed costs.
- Income Before Interest and Taxes—This value is the difference between Total Revenue and Total Costs and Expenses.
- Interest Expense—This amount is the product of debt owed at the beginning of the year and the interest rate on debt owed, which is a constant.
- Income Before Taxes—This amount is the difference between income before interest and taxes and interest expense.
- Income Tax Expense—This amount is zero if income before taxes is zero or negative. Otherwise, income tax expense is the product of the year's tax rate (from the Constants section) and income before taxes.
- Net Income After Taxes—This amount is the difference between income before taxes and income tax expense.

Line items for the year-end cash calculation are shown in Figure 7-6. In the figure, column B represents 2017, column C is for 2018, and so on. Year 2017 values are NA except for end-of-year cash on hand, which is $9 billion.

Values must be computed by cell formula; hard-code numbers in formulas only when you are told to do so. Cell formulas should not reference a cell with a value of "NA." An explanation of each item follows the figure.

	A	B	C	D	E
63					
64	SCHEDULED CAPITAL EXPENDITURES	NA			
65	REPAYMENT TO NOTE HOLDERS	NA	$ 600,000,000	$ 600,000,000	$ 600,000,000
66	NET CASH POSITION (NCP) BEFORE BORROWING FROM BANK	NA			
67	ADD: BORROWING FROM BANK	NA			
68	EQUALS: END-OF-THE-YEAR CASH ON HAND	$ 9,000,000,000			

FIGURE 7-6   End-of-year cash on hand section

- Scheduled Capital Expenditures—These outlays are shown in the Constants section. They reduce cash on hand.
- Repayment to Note Holders—$3 billion is owed to noteholders at the end of 2017, with five years remaining on the debt. $600 million must be repaid each year to noteholders. You can hard-code the amount for each year.
- Net Cash Position (NCP) Before Borrowing from Bank—This amount equals cash at the beginning of the year plus the year's net income after income taxes, minus scheduled capital expenditures and minus payments to noteholders.
- Add: Borrowing from Bank—Assume that the company can borrow from a bank at the end of the year to reach the minimum cash needed to start the next year. If the NCP is less than this minimum amount, the company would borrow enough to start the next year with the minimum. Borrowing increases cash on hand, of course. Borrowing would be under a line of credit. Each year the company would need to pay interest on any amounts borrowed under the line of credit, but amounts borrowed would accumulate until a principal repayment schedule was negotiated, which would not happen until 2021.
- Equals: End-of-the-Year Cash on Hand—This amount is the NCP plus any bank borrowing.

Debt Owed Section

This section shows a calculation of debt owed to noteholders and to the bank, as shown in Figure 7-7. Year 2017 values are NA except for end-of-year debt owed, which is $3 billion for the remaining notes payable.

	A	B	C	D	E
70	DEBT OWED	2017	2018	2019	2020
71	BEGINNING-OF-THE-YEAR DEBT OWED	NA			
72	ADD: BORROWING FROM BANK	NA			
73	LESS: REPAYMENT TO NOTEHOLDERS	NA			
74	EQUALS: END-OF-THE-YEAR DEBT OWED	$ 3,000,000,000			

FIGURE 7-7   Debt Owed section

Values must be computed by cell formula; hard-code numbers in formulas only when you are told to do so. Cell formulas should not reference a cell with a value of "NA." An explanation of each item follows the figure.

- Beginning-of-the-Year Debt Owed—Debt owed at the beginning of a year equals the debt owed at the end of the prior year.
- Add: Borrowing from Bank—This amount has been calculated elsewhere and can be echoed to this section. Borrowing increases the amount of debt owed.
- Less: Repayment to Noteholders—This amount has been shown elsewhere and can be echoed to this section. Repayments reduce the amount of debt owed.
- Equals: End-of-the-Year Debt Owed—This is the amount owed at the beginning of a year plus borrowing during the year, minus repayments to noteholders during the year.

ASSIGNMENT 2: USING THE SPREADSHEET FOR DECISION SUPPORT

Complete the case by (1) using the spreadsheet to gather data about possible financial scenarios and (2) documenting your findings in a memo.

Management wants to get through the next three years without incurring significant bank debt and without having to go to the financial markets to sell common stock or issue notes. In three years, the current notes payable will be nearly paid off, and management hopes the company will be profitable enough to start Phase 3 of its master plan.

Management asks you to consider three scenarios for the three-year period from 2018 to 2020: Optimistic, Pessimistic, and So-So. The input values for these scenarios are as follows:

1. Optimistic: The cost of gasoline is Up, the claim rate in each of the three years is 1 percent, the cost reduction factor in each of the three years is 3 percent, there are 30 new charger locations each year, and the momentum effect each year is 7 percent.

2. Pessimistic: The cost of gasoline is Down, the claim rate in each of the three years is 10 percent, the cost reduction factor each year is 1 percent, there are no new charger locations each year, and the momentum effect each year is 2 percent.

3. So-So: The cost of gasoline is Stable, the claim rate in each of the three years is 5 percent, the cost reduction factor each year is 2 percent, there are 20 new charger locations each year, and the momentum effect each year is 4 percent.

The key year is 2020. By then, (1) Management would like to see a positive net income for the year. (2) Management wants to owe nothing to the bank; only $1.2 billion of notes payable would remain. (3) Management wants the company's cash on hand to exceed $1 billion. This outcome would tell management that the grand strategy is still viable.

Failing that outcome, however, management could accept some amount owed to the bank, as long as the company had turned the corner and was making money in 2020. Management would conclude that the company still has a good chance of succeeding.

Assignment 2A: Using the Spreadsheet to Gather Data

You have built the spreadsheet to model the company's financial situation. You will run "what-if" scenarios with the three sets of input values using Scenario Manager. (See Tutorial C for details on using Scenario Manager.) Set up the three scenarios. Your instructor may ask you to use conditional formatting to make sure your input values are proper; conditional formatting is discussed in Tutorial E. Note that in Scenario Manager, you can enter noncontiguous cell ranges, such as C19, D19, C20:F20.

The relevant output cells are 2020 net income, 2020 cash on hand, 2019 total debt owed, and 2020 total debt owed. (A comparison of 2019 and 2020 debt levels will show whether bank debt was needed in 2020.) Run Scenario Manager to gather the data into a report. When you finish, print the spreadsheet with the input for any of the scenarios, print the Scenario Manager summary sheet, and then save the spreadsheet file for the final time.

Assignment 2B: Documenting Your Results in a Memo

Use Microsoft Word to write a brief memo that documents your analysis and results. You can address the memo to Fred Smith. Observe the following requirements:

- Set up your memo as described in Tutorial E.
- In the first paragraph, briefly state the business situation and the purpose of your analysis.
- Next, describe the three scenarios tested and the related results.
- State your conclusions: Are there scenarios that indicate management's strategy will succeed?
- State your opinion and your reasoning: Does it appear that the company can be a long-term success in the car industry?
- Support your statements graphically, as your instructor requires. Your instructor may ask you to return to Excel and copy the Scenario Manager summary sheet results into the memo. You should include a summary table built in Word based on the Scenario Manager summary sheet results. (The process of creating a table in Word is described in Tutorial E.)

Your table should be in the format shown in Figure 7-8.

Scenario	2020 Net Income	2020 Cash	2019 Debt	2020 Debt
Optimistic				
So-So				
Pessimistic				

FIGURE 7-8 Format of table to insert in memo

ASSIGNMENT 3: GIVING AN ORAL PRESENTATION

Your instructor may ask you to explain your analysis and results in an oral presentation. If so, assume that Fred Smith wants you to explain your analysis and results to him and his management team. See Tutorial F for tips on preparing and giving an oral presentation.

DELIVERABLES

Your completed case should include the following deliverables for your instructor:

- A printed copy of your memo
- Printouts of your spreadsheet and scenario summary
- Electronic copies of your memo and Excel DSS model

PART **3**

DATA ANALYSIS CASES IN MICROSOFT ACCESS AND EXCEL

TUTORIAL D

DATA ANALYTICS

Data analytics is a multidisciplinary approach used to analyze data and make predictions with the goal of making better business decisions. Data analytics leverages the insights gathered from data analysis to give direction to business strategy and recommend which actions to take. From a business perspective, analytics refers to the set of methods, rules, or steps used to complete data analysis. This tutorial covers two important aspects of data analytics: an introduction to data cleaning and the differences between analytical and operational data.

Data moves through an information system in the following way:

1. Data is collected.
2. The data is cleaned and processed.
3. The data is used to support daily business operations or a decision-making application.

Data cleaning is discussed in the first part of this tutorial. The differences between analytical and operational data are discussed next; they come into play in the third step of the preceding process.

DATA CLEANING

Data can be collected into a file by a human being or a computer program. Either way, errors can arise. For example, data entry clerks can make typing errors, or data can be corrupted during transmission from its source to storage media. Erroneous input files should not be made available to applications because they can lead to errors in transaction processing or decision-making errors. Because of these possibilities, data should be "cleaned" or "cleansed" before it is introduced into an application for processing.

Data cleaning is not the same thing as data validation, although the two topics are related. In data validation, an entry is checked before it is saved in a data file. We have all seen this step in action with Web forms, which are designed to "trap" obvious mistakes. For example, a Web form rejects numbers entered into fields that instead should contain text, and it prevents users from submitting an incomplete form.

Data validation techniques cannot guarantee that all errors will be trapped, and errors could arise during transmission from the source to a storage medium. Therefore, data cleaning is needed before the data file is actually used.

As you will see in the following sections, a data record can present problems if it is incomplete, a duplicate of another record, or otherwise incorrect in some way. Incomplete records can be dropped from a file, or missing values can be calculated and entered into the record. Duplicate records may be removed from the file. Records with incorrect values can be removed, or incorrect values may be fixed.

A log should be kept to record deletions, corrections, and all other actions taken as a result of data cleaning. The log should contain a copy of all problematic records.

In the real world, many software environments exist for capturing and recording data; these environments may have built-in data cleaning features. The following examples assume that Microsoft Excel has been used to record the data and to deal with any problems it detects. Excel is a good program for introducing the fundamentals of data cleaning in the following sections.

To begin, assume that you have a file of statistics about Little League baseball players on two teams, the Robins and the Penguins. The file is called BaseballStats.xlsx and is available for you to use if you want to work along. To get this file, select Tutorial D from your data files and then select **BaseballStats.xlsx**.

You will work with the contents of this file to learn important data cleaning principles. The file is shown in Figure D-1. An explanation of the data values follows the figure.

	A	B	C	D	E	F	G	H	I
1	Player ID	First Name	Last Name	Team	Gender	Start Date	At Bats	Hits	Average
2	1	Pete	Smith	Robins	M	3/6/2015	147	86	0.585
3	2	Sue	Jones	Penguins	F	4/1/2015	101	68	0.673
4	2	Sue	Jones	Penguins	F	4/1/2015	101	68	0.673
5	3	Al	Longoria	Robins	M	3/15/2015	164	165	1.006
6	4	John	Forsyth	Robins	M	3/6/2015	130	84	0.646
7	5	John	Bogart	Penguins	M	4/1/2015	114	65	0.570
8	6	Jean	Cruize	Penguins	F	4/15/2015	150	79	0.527
9	7	Horace	Dooper	Robins	M	3/15/2015	112	77	0.688
10	8	Alice	Mantle	Robins	F	3/22/2015	1173	54	0.046
11	9	Ajay	Maris	Penguins	M	4/7/2015	120	71	0.592
12	10	Keefer	Berra	Penguins	M	4/1/2015	113	64	0.566
13	11	Bruce	Skowron	Robins	M	4/15/2015	160		0.350
14	12	Jenny	Wentz	Robins	F	3/15/2015	110	63	0.573
15	13	Pat	McAlister	Penguins	M	3/22/2015	120	79	0.658
16	14	Mary	Lombardi	Penguins	F	4/7/2015	180	85	0.472
17	15	Tom	Shaw	Robinz	M	4/7/2015	138	78	0.565

FIGURE D-1   Contents of BaseballStats file

- Player ID—Each player is assigned a unique ID. There should be no duplicate IDs.
- First Name—The player's first name.
- Last Name—The player's last name.
- Team—The name of the player's team.
- Gender—Assume that boys and girls can play on the same team. This column should only include values of M and F.
- Start Date—This date indicates when the player began playing in the league.
- At Bats—This value is the player's number of official at-bats as a hitter.
- Hits—This value is the number of times the player reached base after a hit in an at-bat.
- Average—This value is the ratio of hits to at-bats.

Incomplete Records

A record in Excel is incomplete if one of its cells is empty. Excel has an ISBLANK function to detect empty cells. For example, it could be used with column H, as shown in Figure D-2.

J2			fx	=ISBLANK(H2)						

	A	B	C	D	E	F	G	H	I	J
1	Player ID	First Name	Last Name	Team	Gender	Start Date	At Bats	Hits	Average	
2	1	Pete	Smith	Robins	M	3/6/2015	147	86	0.585	FALSE
3	2	Sue	Jones	Penguins	F	4/1/2015	101	68	0.673	FALSE
4	2	Sue	Jones	Penguins	F	4/1/2015	101	68	0.673	FALSE
5	3	Al	Longoria	Robins	M	3/15/2015	164	165	1.006	FALSE

FIGURE D-2   Testing for empty cells in column H

The ISBLANK function returns TRUE or FALSE—TRUE if the test cell is empty and FALSE if it contains a value. In this example, one cell (H13) is blank, as shown in Figure D-3.

	A	B	C	D	E	F	G	H	I	J
1	Player ID	First Name	Last Name	Team	Gender	Start Date	At Bats	Hits	Average	
2	1 Pete	Smith	Robins	M		3/6/2015	147	86	0.585	FALSE
3	2 Sue	Jones	Penguins	F		4/1/2015	101	68	0.673	FALSE
4	2 Sue	Jones	Penguins	F		4/1/2015	101	68	0.673	FALSE
5	3 Al	Longoria	Robins	M		3/15/2015	164	165	1.006	FALSE
6	4 John	Forsyth	Robins	M		3/6/2015	130	84	0.646	FALSE
7	5 John	Bogart	Penguins	M		4/1/2015	114	65	0.570	FALSE
8	6 Jean	Cruize	Penguins	F		4/15/2015	150	79	0.527	FALSE
9	7 Horace	Dooper	Robins	M		3/15/2015	112	77	0.688	FALSE
10	8 Alice	Mantle	Robins	F		3/22/2015	1173	54	0.046	FALSE
11	9 Ajay	Maris	Penguins	M		4/7/2015	120	71	0.592	FALSE
12	10 Keefer	Berra	Penguins	M		4/1/2015	113	64	0.566	FALSE
13	11 Bruce	Skowron	Robins	M		4/15/2015	160		0.350	TRUE
14	12 Jenny	Wentz	Robins	F		3/15/2015	110	63	0.573	FALSE
15	13 Pat	McAlister	Penguins	M		3/22/2015	120	79	0.658	FALSE
16	14 Mary	Lombardi	Penguins	F		4/7/2015	180	85	0.472	FALSE
17	15 Tom	Shaw	Robinz	M		4/7/2015	138	78	0.565	FALSE

FIGURE D-3　Empty cell H13 revealed by the ISBLANK function

What would happen, you might ask, if there was a space or some other unreadable character in cell H13? Would ISBLANK return TRUE or FALSE? A space is actually a one-character text string, so in this case the cell would not be empty—FALSE would be returned. Note that the ISNUMBER function would identify the inappropriate space in cell H13, as shown in Figure D-4.

J2　　fx　=ISNUMBER(H2)

	A	B	C	D	E	F	G	H	I	J
1	Player ID	First Name	Last Name	Team	Gender	Start Date	At Bats	Hits	Average	
2	1 Pete	Smith	Robins	M		3/6/2015	147	86	0.585	TRUE
3	2 Sue	Jones	Penguins	F		4/1/2015	101	68	0.673	TRUE
4	2 Sue	Jones	Penguins	F		4/1/2015	101	68	0.673	TRUE
5	3 Al	Longoria	Robins	M		3/15/2015	164	165	1.006	TRUE
6	4 John	Forsyth	Robins	M		3/6/2015	130	84	0.646	TRUE
7	5 John	Bogart	Penguins	M		4/1/2015	114	65	0.570	TRUE
8	6 Jean	Cruize	Penguins	F		4/15/2015	150	79	0.527	TRUE
9	7 Horace	Dooper	Robins	M		3/15/2015	112	77	0.688	TRUE
10	8 Alice	Mantle	Robins	F		3/22/2015	1173	54	0.046	TRUE
11	9 Ajay	Maris	Penguins	M		4/7/2015	120	71	0.592	TRUE
12	10 Keefer	Berra	Penguins	M		4/1/2015	113	64	0.566	TRUE
13	11 Bruce	Skowron	Robins	M		4/15/2015	160		0.350	FALSE
14	12 Jenny	Wentz	Robins	F		3/15/2015	110	63	0.573	TRUE
15	13 Pat	McAlister	Penguins	M		3/22/2015	120	79	0.658	TRUE
16	14 Mary	Lombardi	Penguins	F		4/7/2015	180	85	0.472	TRUE
17	15 Tom	Shaw	Robinz	M		4/7/2015	138	78	0.565	TRUE

FIGURE D-4　Space in cell H13 shown not to be a number by the ISNUMBER function

If there is a way to compute the correct missing value—or at least an acceptable value—it might be inserted and the corrected record might be retained. Otherwise, incomplete records can be removed to a log file for later inspection. In any case, the action taken should be logged for later review. In the example Excel file, the log can be kept as another worksheet. Assuming that you deleted the record because a nonnumeric character was identified in cell H13, the log entry might look like the one shown in Figure D-5.

	A	B	C	D	E	F	G	H	I	J	K
1											
2	Non-Numeric Data:										
3	Player ID	First Name	Last Name	Team	Gender	Start Date	At Bats	Hits	Average	Action	Note
4	11 Bruce	Skowron	Robins	M		4/15/2015	160		0.350	Deleted	

FIGURE D-5　Error log entry for nonnumeric cell H13

Duplicate Records

In a small file, duplicate records can be detected by visual inspection, but in a larger file with values that should not be duplicated (for example, a key value), you can search for duplicate keys. First you would sort the file: Select a cell in the range, select the Data tab, and then click the Sort button in the Sort & Filter group. In Figure D-6, you would use Player ID as the sort field and then use an If statement to detect duplicate key values.

| J3 | ▾ | : | × | ✓ | *fx* | =IF(A3=A2,"???","") | | | | |

	A	B	C	D	E	F	G	H	I	J
1	Player ID	First Name	Last Name	Team	Gender	Start Date	At Bats	Hits	Average	
2	1	Pete	Smith	Robins	M	3/6/2015	147	86	0.585	
3	2	Sue	Jones	Penguins	F	4/1/2015	101	68	0.673	

FIGURE D-6   Use of an If statement to detect duplicate key values

The logic of the If statement in cell J3 is as follows: If the key value in cell A3 equals the key value in cell A2, then place "???" in cell J3 to indicate a duplicate; otherwise, place the empty string in cell J3. The formula should be copied down to each cell of the column.

The user could then look for instances of "???" in column J. In the example, there is one duplicate key value (see Figure D-7).

	A	B	C	D	E	F	G	H	I	J
1	Player ID	First Name	Last Name	Team	Gender	Start Date	At Bats	Hits	Average	
2	1	Pete	Smith	Robins	M	3/6/2015	147	86	0.585	
3	2	Sue	Jones	Penguins	F	4/1/2015	101	68	0.673	
4	2	Sue	Jones	Penguins	F	4/1/2015	101	68	0.673	???
5	3	Al	Longoria	Robins	M	3/15/2015	164	165	1.006	
6	4	John	Forsyth	Robins	M	3/6/2015	130	84	0.646	

FIGURE D-7   Duplicate key value found in file

Duplicate keys need to be corrected. Also, they might indicate the existence of duplicate records, as is the case in the example file. You should remove duplicate records and record them in the log file for later inspection.

Incorrect Records

There are many kinds of incorrect entries, and anticipating them is one of the challenges in designing a data cleaning approach. As you will learn in the following sections, common kinds of errors include data type errors, incorrect entries, out-of-range values, and illogical values.

Data Type Errors

Recall that cell values in Excel have data types that a programmer can use to specify what kind of value a cell holds—for example, Text, Date, Time, and Numbers of various kinds. You control data types using the Format Cells window. For instance, with the Home tab active, you can click the Number group's drop-down arrow to bring up the Format Cells window (see Figure D-8) and correct data type errors.

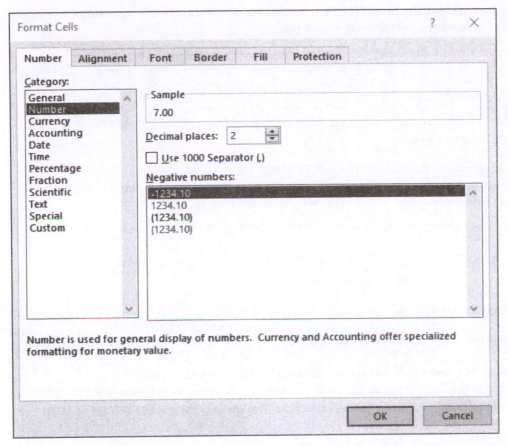

FIGURE D-8   Format Cells window

Incorrect Entries

Data entry errors can occur for any number of reasons, and they are not always caught by data validation filters.

In the example file, assume that dates were supposed to be recorded as 2016, but for some reason the clerk entered 2015 in all cases. How could this error be fixed without manually retyping each entry?

Start Date entries in the file are assigned the Date data type. One approach to correcting the entries would require the following steps:

- Change the values to Text.
- In the resulting text strings, substitute the correct year for the incorrect year.
- Change the new text values to Date integers.
- Use the Format Cells window to change the integer entries back to dates.

These steps are explained in detail next. To begin, you can convert a value to the Text data type using the TEXT function, as shown in Figure D-9.

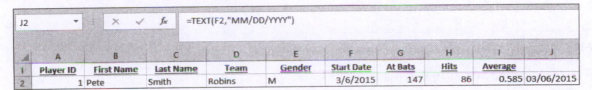

FIGURE D-9   Using the TEXT function

The formula in cell J2 creates a text version of the date in cell F2. The text string format is specified by "MM/DD/YYYY" in the formula. Notice that the text string is left-justified in cell J2—all text strings are left-justified in their cells.

The proper year is inserted using the SUBSTITUTE function, which substitutes one substring for another in a Text value. Figure D-10 shows the substitution, in cell K2.

K2		× ✓ fx	=SUBSTITUTE(J2,"2015","2016")									

	A	B	C	D	E	F	G	H	I	J	K
1	Player ID	First Name	Last Name	Team	Gender	Start Date	At Bats	Hits	Average		
2	1	Pete	Smith	Robins	M	3/6/2015	147	86	0.585	03/06/2015	03/06/2016

FIGURE D-10   Using the SUBSTITUTE function

Notice that the resulting value ("03/06/2016") in cell K2 is still a text string.

The DATEVALUE function changes the text value to a long integer that represents the number of days elapsed since January 1, 1900, for the date in question (see Figure D-11).

L2		× ✓ fx	=DATEVALUE(K2)									

	A	B	C	D	E	F	G	H	I	J	K	L
1	Player ID	First Name	Last Name	Team	Gender	Start Date	At Bats	Hits	Average			
2	1	Pete	Smith	Robins	M	3/6/2015	147	86	0.585	03/06/2015	03/06/2016	42435

FIGURE D-11   Using the DATEVALUE function

The DATEVALUE function converts "03/06/2016" to 42435, which is the number of days from January 1, 1900, to March 6, 2016.

The formulas in cells J2, K2, and L2 should be copied down their respective columns.

The last step is to change the integer values to actual dates. You can make this change using the Format Cells window. With the integers in column L selected, open the window and then select the proper Date format, as shown in Figure D-12.

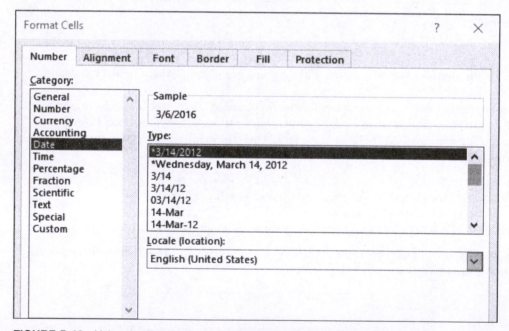

FIGURE D-12   Using the Format Cells window to select the Date data type

Figure D-13 shows the first 2016 date value.

	A	B	C	D	E	F	G	H	I	J	K	L
1	Player ID	First Name	Last Name	Team	Gender	Start Date	At Bats	Hits	Average			
2	1	Pete	Smith	Robins	M	3/6/2015	147	86	0.585	03/06/2015	03/06/2016	3/6/201

FIGURE D-13   First 2016 date value

You can copy and paste the resulting date values in column L to column F. First copy the values, and then select the first cell in the area where you want to paste. Click the arrow next to Paste on the Home tab, click Paste Special, and then click Values in the window that appears. You would also record a log entry that you corrected the Start Date values.

Data entry errors can sometimes be trapped by using pivot tables, as shown in the following example, which includes only two teams. You can use a pivot table to count the number of players on each team. If there are errors in the team name entries, they would be revealed in the pivot table. Figure D-14 shows the pivot table setup.

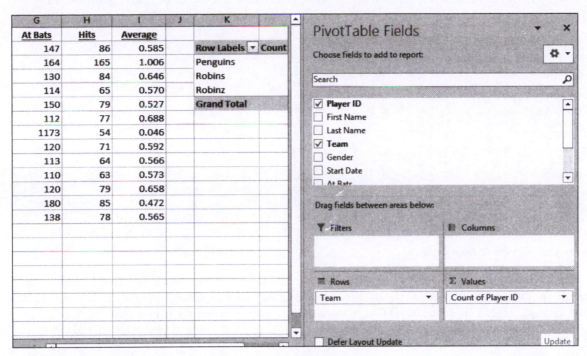

FIGURE D-14   Pivot table set up to search for incorrect team names

The resulting table reveals one error in the team name entries: "Robinz," as shown in Figure D-15.

Average		Row Labels ▾	Count of Player ID	
0.585				
1.006		Penguins	6	
0.646		Robins	6	
0.570		Robinz	1	
0.527		Grand Total	13	
0.688				
0.046				

FIGURE D-15   Incorrect team name revealed by pivot table

You could then search the file for the incorrect record and log the action. In this case, the correction is obvious.

Out-of-Range Values

Numerical values often have associated minimum and maximum values that you can use to check for valid data entry. In the following example, assume that no player can have more than 200 at-bats. You could use an If statement to reveal At Bats entries that violate this rule, as shown in Figure D-16.

| J2 | ▼ | : | × ✓ | fx | =IF(G2>200,"???","") | | | | | |

▲	A	B	C	D	E	F	G	H	I	J
1	**Player ID**	**First Name**	**Last Name**	**Team**	**Gender**	**Start Date**	**At Bats**	**Hits**	**Average**	
2	1	Pete	Smith	Robins	M	3/6/2016	147	86	0.585	

FIGURE D-16   Testing for out-of-range At Bats values

You would copy the formula down the column. Only one At Bats value is out of range, as shown in Figure D-17.

▲	A	B	C	D	E	F	G	H	I	J
1	**Player ID**	**First Name**	**Last Name**	**Team**	**Gender**	**Start Date**	**At Bats**	**Hits**	**Average**	
2	1	Pete	Smith	Robins	M	3/6/2016	147	86	0.585	
3	3	Al	Longoria	Robins	M	3/15/2016	164	165	1.006	
4	4	John	Forsyth	Robins	M	3/6/2016	130	84	0.646	
5	5	John	Bogart	Penguins	M	4/1/2016	114	65	0.570	
6	6	Jean	Cruize	Penguins	F	4/15/2016	150	79	0.527	
7	7	Horace	Dooper	Robins	M	3/15/2016	112	77	0.688	
8	8	Alice	Mantle	Robins	F	3/22/2016	1173	54	0.046	???
9	9	Ajay	Maris	Penguins	M	4/7/2016	120	71	0.592	
10	10	Keefer	Berra	Penguins	M	4/1/2016	113	64	0.566	
11	12	Jenny	Wentz	Robins	F	3/15/2016	110	63	0.573	
12	13	Pat	McAlister	Penguins	M	3/22/2016	120	79	0.658	
13	14	Mary	Lombardi	Penguins	F	4/7/2016	180	85	0.472	
14	15	Tom	Shaw	Robins	M	4/7/2016	138	78	0.565	

FIGURE D-17   Out-of-range At Bats value

Alice Mantle cannot have 1,173 at-bats. If you could determine the proper value, you could enter it and log the correction. Otherwise, you would delete her record and log the action.

Another example of this approach would be to check the Gender column for values that are not "M" or "F." You could use a nested If statement for this purpose:

```
=IF(OR(E2="M", E2="F"),"", "???")
```

The logic would be as follows: If the entry is "M" or "F," enter the empty string in the cell. Otherwise, enter "???".

Logical Errors

Different situations have their own logic that you can test. In this case, Hits values cannot exceed At Bats values. You could use an If statement to check for this possible error:

```
=IF(H2>G2, "???","")
```

Figure D-18 shows the log entries for the actions taken to complete the examples in the preceding exercises.

	A	B	C	D	E	F	G	H	I	J	K
1											
2	**Non-Numeric Data:**										
3	**Player ID**	**First Name**	**Last Name**	**Team**	**Gender**	**Start Date**	**At Bats**	**Hits**	**Average**	**Action**	**Note**
4	11 Bruce		Skowron	Robins	M	4/15/2015	160		0.350	Deleted	
5											
6	**Duplicate Key Values:**										
7	2 Sue		Jones	Penguins	F	42095	101	68	0.673	Deleted	
8	2 Sue		Jones	Penguins	F	42095	101	68	0.673	Deleted	
9											
10	**Start Date Values Corrected to 2016:**										
11		All Start Date values changed from 2015 to 2016.									
12											
13	**Out of Range At Bats Value:**										
14	8 Alice		Mantle	Robins	F	42451	1173	54	0.046	Deleted	>200 AB's
15											
16	**Errorful Team Value Corrected:**										
17	15 Tom		Shaw	Robinz	M	4/7/2016	138	78	0.565		
18	15 Tom		Shaw	Robins	M	4/7/2016	138	78	0.565	Corrected	

FIGURE D-18   Data cleaning log

ANALYTICAL VERSUS OPERATIONAL DATA

Data collected either by people or systems can grow to be quite large and require massive storage facilities. Large amounts of data can pose many problems for a data analyst who needs to transform it into meaningful information for effective reporting. While a simple pivot table can be a lifesaver when you are working with relatively small amounts of data, it can easily become a burden on the system as the stored data increases in size and requires more processing power to manipulate. The issue becomes particularly important for organizations that rely on the same data to carry out daily operations. For this reason, we distinguish between *operational data* and *analytical data*. The split between these two types of data is intended to increase processing efficiency, among other things. Organizations generally separate the two in order to run their businesses and perform analytics without negatively affecting their operations.

For example, picture a large financial institution that issues credit cards for customers, many of whom use their cards a few times a day. Each time a transaction takes place, the data generated must be stored. Data must be retrieved as well:

- The amount of the transaction
- The time and location of the transaction
- Whether the customer has an adequate credit limit to cover the transaction
- Many other details

Customers expect transactions to be completed almost instantaneously, and they often are. Now imagine that during all these daily transactions, a team of analysts is running end-of-month reports on the same data. Running the reports on operational data, which is used to approve or decline transactions, can cause serious bottlenecks, including longer transaction approval times or outright timeouts of approvals. Such delays can lead to unhappy customers, which can lead to lower revenue. Granted, this example is a bit exaggerated, but organizations need to take the division of operational and analytical data very seriously. Depending on the organization's needs, however, the analysts may only have access to "stale" data that is at least a day old. The analytical data is often set up in a mirror image to the operational data environment and updated as often as required by the organization. These two separate environments allow analysts to complete any type of analysis while mitigating the risk of performance degradation on the operational side. The trade-off is that the data might not be completely current; generally, the process of updating analytical data takes place outside business hours, typically overnight. There are two distinct advantages to this approach when creating an analytical data environment:

- The organization mitigates the risk of performance degradation to the operational data. This is extremely important for banks and other organizations that leverage large amounts of data for daily operations.
- The organization can create summarized data sets to expedite analysis and reporting. For example, analysts can be provided a list of total sales by department in addition to the complete list of sales. If data sets are large, analysts might need many hours to summarize data of total sales by department on their own. Summarized tables are easy to visualize using charts in Excel.

The following sections explain how to make full use of the advantages of an analytical environment.

Problem Overview

You have been hired as an intern at a local bookstore for the summer. The owner, Bob Fleck, has run the business for over two decades, and relies heavily on paper records and an antiquated reporting system. Bob is interested in your data analysis skills, but he is worried about giving you too much access to the data used to run his business. Bob is also concerned that the data may become corrupted or that performance issues during sales transactions could ultimately lead to lost customers.

He explains to you that sales are recorded in a simple Microsoft Access database and gives you the data layout, as illustrated in Figure D-19.

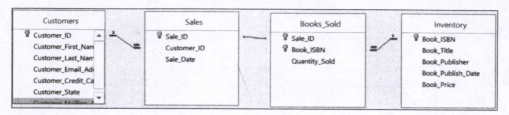

FIGURE D-19   Bookstore database layout

Bob wants to set up monthly reporting for sales and get some insights into where his customers live. Start by examining the database used to log the bookstore's sales (operational data); the filename is **TheBookStore.accdb**. Open each of the four tables in Design view and take a quick look to familiarize yourself with their data structures and attributes. Figures D-20 through D-23 illustrate each of the table structures.

Sales

Field Name	Data Type
Sale_ID	AutoNumber
Customer_ID	Number
Sale_Date	Date/Time

FIGURE D-20   Sales table in the bookstore's database

Inventory

Field Name	Data Type
Book_ISBN	Short Text
Book_Title	Short Text
Book_Publisher	Short Text
Book_Publish_Date	Date/Time
Book_Price	Number

FIGURE D-21   Inventory table in the bookstore's database

Customers

Field Name	Data Type
Customer_ID	AutoNumber
Customer_First_Name	Short Text
Customer_Last_Name	Short Text
Customer_Email_Address	Short Text
Customer_Credit_Card_Number	Short Text
Customer_State	Short Text
Customer_Mailing_Address	Short Text

FIGURE D-22   Customers table in the bookstore's database

Books_Sold

Field Name	Data Type
Sale_ID	Number
Book_ISBN	Short Text
Quantity_Sold	Number

FIGURE D-23   Books_Sold table in the bookstore's database

Creating Analytical Data

Now that you are familiar with the database and its structure, you are ready to create the analytical data sets. The first step is to create copies of the operational data. There are different ways to accomplish this task, depending on how much separation you want between the operational and analytical data. To quell some of Bob's concerns, you want to provide the most separation possible, which will require creating a new database that is different from the one used for sales.

Open a blank Access file and save it as **BookStoreAnalytics.accdb**. In order to copy the data over to the new database, you will need to import the data tables from TheBookStore.accdb using the Access feature shown in Figure D-24.

FIGURE D-24   External data import feature in Access

Follow the prompts and locate TheBookStore.accdb to use as your data, as shown in Figure D-25. Select the option to import tables; do not link to the data source, because it would not achieve the separation you want. Click OK.

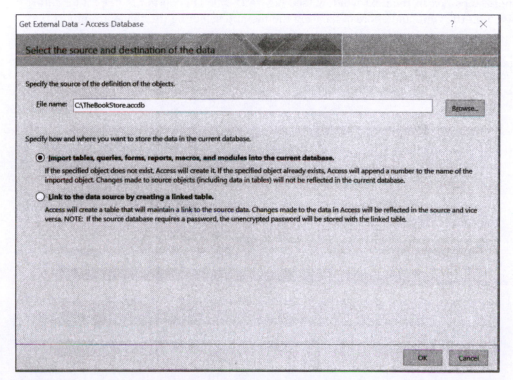

FIGURE D-25   Selecting the source and destination of the data

Select all the tables shown in the Import Objects window and click OK to start the import process. See Figure D-26.

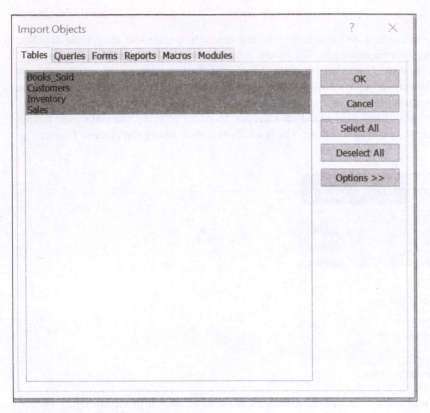

FIGURE D-26   Import Objects window

Check the Save import steps box in the next window (see Figure D-27). This option is helpful for future data updates and will save you the time and effort of locating the file and selecting the tables to import.

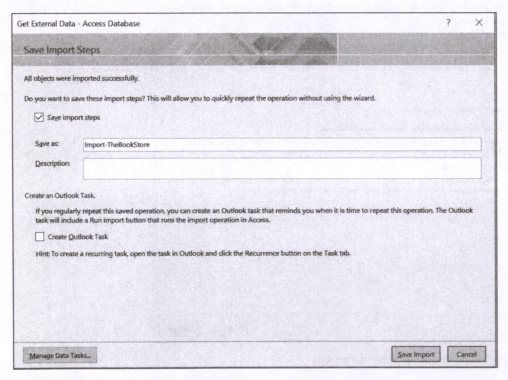

FIGURE D-27   Save Import Steps window

Success! You have created the analytical data sets by copying the operational data.

NOTE

The analytical data is only a snapshot in time, so it will become stale as soon as new data is created in the operational data sets. How often the analytical data is refreshed depends on the organization's needs.

NOTE

While Excel can query directly from Access, the purpose of this exercise is to show the efficiencies you can gain by summarizing data outside of business hours and leveraging Access to expedite analysis in Excel.

From your conversation with Bob, you know he is interested in monthly reporting for sales and in learning where his customers live. Your first step is to create two queries to summarize the data for further reporting in Excel.

Query 1

Summarize the daily sales data by creating a "make table" query (see Figure D-28) that counts the number of sales by date and adds up the total sale amounts. Save the query as Sales_Summary and store the results in a new table labeled Sale_Totals, as shown in Figure D-29.

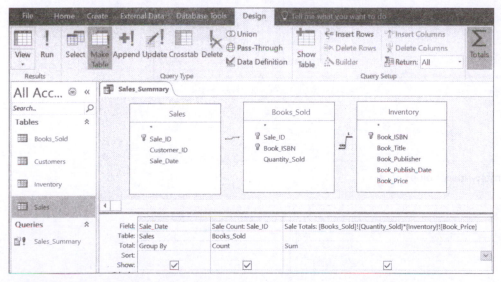

FIGURE D-28 Sales_Summary query setup

FIGURE D-29 Make Table window for sales summary

Before the query is complete, you should see a warning about the number of records you are about to paste into the new table. Figure D-30 shows the warning screen for the Sales_Summary query. If this number is within expectations, click OK to create the new table.

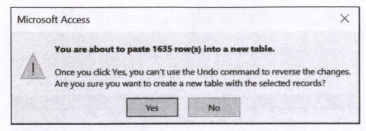

FIGURE D-30 Warning before creating a table

Query 2

Summarize the state sales data by creating a make table query (see Figure D-31) that counts the number of customers by state and adds up the total sale amounts. Save the query as State_Summary and store the results in a new table labeled State_Totals, as shown in Figure D-32.

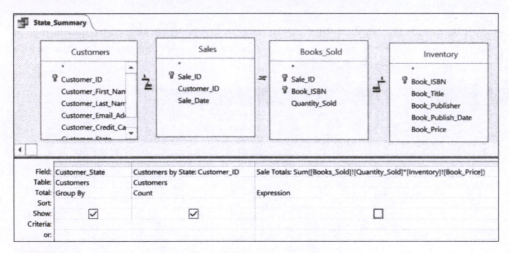

FIGURE D-31 State_Summary query setup

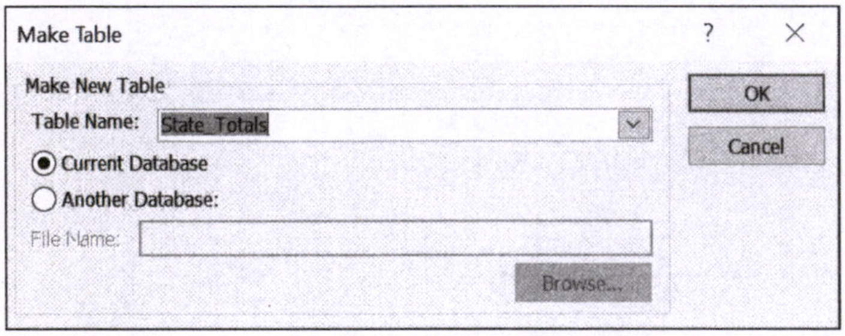

FIGURE D-32 Make Table window for state sales summary

Before the query is complete, you should see another warning about the number of records you are about to paste into the new table. Figure D-33 shows the warning screen for the State_Summary query. If this number is within expectations, click OK to create the new table.

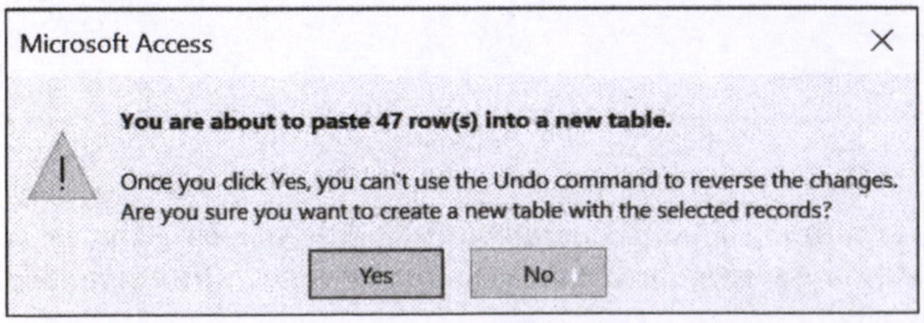

FIGURE D-33 Warning before creating a table

Creating Reports in Excel

Now that you have summarized the analytical data using Access, you are ready to create reports in Excel that give Bob the information he wants. In addition to performance improvements and efficiency gains by summarizing the raw data in the database, this method will result in a rather small spreadsheet that is easy to share.

To begin, open a blank Excel file and save it as **BookStoreReports.xlsx**. Import the summary tables from BookStoreAnalytics.accdb using Excel's data import feature, as shown in Figure D-34.

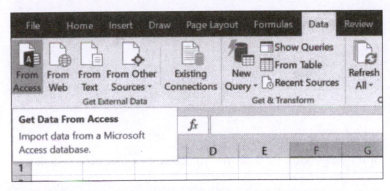

FIGURE D-34   Importing external data into Excel

Follow the prompts and locate BookStoreAnalytics.accdb to use as your data source, as shown in Figure D-35.

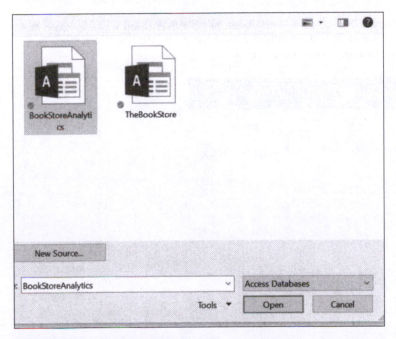

FIGURE D-35   Selecting a data source

The next screen allows you to choose the data you want to import into Excel (see Figure D-36). You need to import both summary tables into your Excel file. To avoid repeating the import process, check the "Enable selection of multiple tables" option and then check the boxes for the Sale_Totals and State_Totals tables. Each of the tables will be imported into a new worksheet. Rename each worksheet tab accordingly.

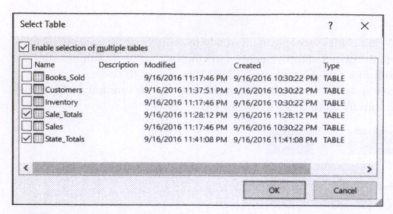

FIGURE D-36   Select Table window

Creating Sales Reports

Bob is interested in different views or "cuts" of the sales data. He asks you to create two charts to visualize the data:

- Total number of sales and dollar amounts by year. This chart will show whether there is a trend in yearly sales totals.
- Total number of sales and dollar amounts by month. This chart will show whether there are any seasonal trends in sales.

Start by creating a new pivot table using the Sale_Totals worksheet, as shown in Figure D-37. Excel will recognize the data and include it in the pivot table. It is generally a good idea to create the pivot table in a new worksheet rather than use the one that contains your source data.

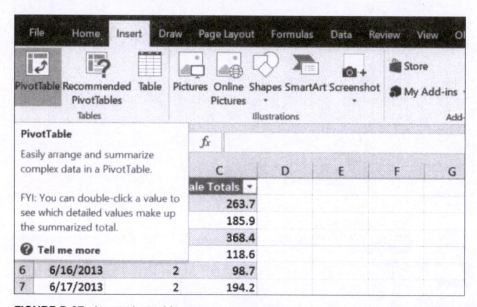

FIGURE D-37   Insert pivot table menu

Notice that entries for Years and Quarters have been added to the pivot table fields. This means that Excel recognizes the Sale Date field as a date and has provided you with some quick groupings (see Figure D-38).

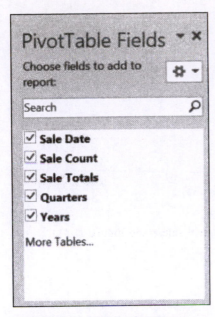

FIGURE D-38 Pivot table fields

Configure the pivot table to show yearly sales totals and change the formatting to Currency where appropriate. Figures D-39 and D-40 illustrate the pivot table configuration and results.

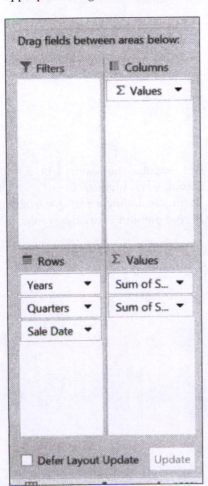

FIGURE D-39 Pivot table configuration

Row Labels ▾	Sum of Sale Count	Sum of Sale Totals
⊞2010	297	$ 30,814.30
⊞2011	1028	$ 104,922.60
⊞2012	963	$ 97,640.10
⊞2013	918	$ 96,683.60
⊞2014	1042	$ 107,881.90
⊞2015	992	$ 105,613.60
⊞2016	742	$ 73,373.00
Grand Total	5982	$ 616,929.10

FIGURE D-40   Yearly sales pivot table

Use the pivot table data to create a meaningful chart that illustrates yearly sales (see Figure D-41).

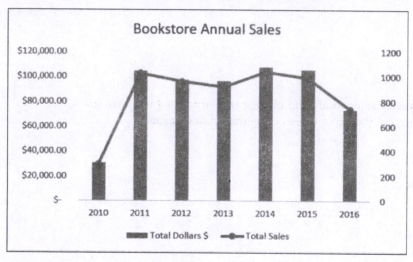

FIGURE D-41   Bookstore annual sales chart

Repeat these steps to create a new pivot table for monthly sales totals and visualize the results with a meaningful chart. The state sales totals are already summarized at the state level, so no pivot table is required. If you wanted to enhance the data, you could group the states by manually adding a region variable, such as New England or Pacific. Otherwise, Bob needs you to produce a clustered column chart that ranks total sales in dollars by state.

You should now know all the basic steps needed to create analytical data sets from operational data in Case 8.

DATA ANALYTICS OF BOUTIQUE HOTEL RESERVATIONS

Data Analytics Using Microsoft Access and Excel

PREVIEW

Boutique hotels are typically not part of a national chain, are often located in a fashionable part of town, and usually have between 10 and 100 rooms. Boutique hotels should not be confused with bed-and-breakfast establishments, which have the look and feel of hotels but are generally smaller. Boutique hotels have been under financial pressure since the inception of online marketplaces like Airbnb, which people can use to book rooms or apartments in parts of town where boutique hotels generally thrive.

The Philadelphia Association of Boutique Hotels is made up of 18 hotels in and around the city. Association members use a central reservation system to book rooms for their customers. The association has noted the threat that online marketplaces pose to its members and has decided to launch a marketing campaign to combat the threat. Before any dollars are invested in the campaign, the association would like to better understand its customer base in order to focus spending on the right geographical areas.

You have been hired as a consultant to analyze reservation data in the association's database. Your analysis will provide valuable insights into reservation trends and help the association determine how to spend its marketing budget.

PREPARATION

- Review spreadsheet concepts discussed in class and in your textbook.
- Complete any exercises that your instructor assigns.
- Complete any part of Tutorial D that your instructor assigns, or refer to it as necessary.
- Review the file-saving procedures for Windows programs in Tutorial C.
- Review Tutorial F as necessary.

BACKGROUND

You will use your data analysis skills to help the association learn about its customers and provide recommendations for how to spend its limited marketing budget. You have been granted access to the reservation system's database in order to complete your analysis. The database diagram is shown in Figure 8-1.

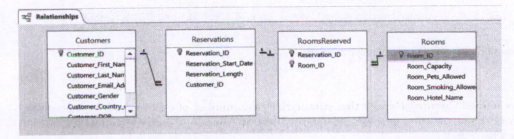

FIGURE 8-1 Layout of reservation system database

The reservation system captures important customer attributes such as:

- Gender
- Country of residence
- Date of birth
- Smoking preferences
- Pet-friendly requests

The reservation system has been known to have performance issues, especially during times of heavy usage. The association's management team is wary of having you work with system data while it is in use and requests that you find an alternative method of retrieving your data for analysis. The association hopes you can research a few basic topics that will help determine how future marketing budgets are segmented:

- Basic customer demographics—Where are the customers from? What are their age groups?
- Current room inventory mix—What hotel rooms can the association offer to tourists?
- Historical occupancy—How successful have the different hotels been in booking reservations, starting in the year 2000?

ASSIGNMENT 1: CREATING ANALYTICAL DATA

In Assignment 1A, you will develop the analytical data sets needed to complete your analysis by creating a series of queries to summarize data and make it easier to manipulate in Microsoft Excel. In Assignment 1B, you will migrate your data to Excel to further summarize it using pivot tables, and then create meaningful charts to help the association visualize your findings.

Assignment 1A: Creating the Analytical Data Sets

Create a new Microsoft Access file and name it **BoutiqueAnalytics.accdb**. You will use this new file to perform queries that would mitigate performance degradation if you used the operational data. (For a review of analytical data versus operational data, see Tutorial D.)

Task 1

Import the data tables from the **Boutique.accdb** source file used by the reservation system. Add the prefix "Analytical_" to each table name to further differentiate the data tables from the operational data source (see Figure 8-2).

FIGURE 8-2 Imported and renamed tables in BoutiqueAnalytics.accdb

Task 2

Create a "make table" query named Country_Gender that summarizes the number of customers by country of residence and gender. Store the results in a new table named Analytical_Country_Gender. The top section of the table should look like Figure 8-3.

Analytical_Country_Gender		
Customer_Country_of_Residence ▼	Customer_Gender ▼	CountOfCustomer_ID ▼
AE	Female	1
AE	Male	2
AF	Female	11
AF	Male	11
AG	Male	2
AL	Female	5
AL	Male	5

FIGURE 8-3 Analytical_Country_Gender table

Task 3

Create a make table query named Capacity_Grid that calculates each hotel's capacity and sorts them by smoking and pet preferences. Store the results in a new table named Analytical_Capacity_Grid. The top section of the table should look like Figure 8-4.

Analytical_Capacity_Grid			
Room_Hotel_Name ▼	Room_Smoking_Allowed ▼	Room_Pets_Allowed ▼	Room Capacity ▼
Avenue of the Arts	FALSE	FALSE	46
Avenue of the Arts	FALSE	TRUE	34
Avenue of the Arts	TRUE	FALSE	42
Avenue of the Arts	TRUE	TRUE	45
Callowhill	FALSE	FALSE	49
Callowhill	FALSE	TRUE	38
Callowhill	TRUE	FALSE	37
Callowhill	TRUE	TRUE	46
Chinatown	FALSE	FALSE	53
Chinatown	FALSE	TRUE	28
Chinatown	TRUE	FALSE	26
Chinatown	TRUE	TRUE	37

FIGURE 8-4 Analytical_Capacity_Grid table

Task 4

Create a make table query named Reservations_Summary that calculates the number of rooms reserved and total capacity used and sorts the data by date of reservation. Store the results in a new table named Analytical_Reservations_Summary. The top section of the table should look like Figure 8-5.

Analytical_Reservations_Summary		
Reservation_Start_Date ▼	Rooms Reserved ▼	Total Capacity Used ▼
1/1/2000	1	5
1/2/2000	2	3
1/3/2000	2	8
1/4/2000	1	5
1/6/2000	2	5
1/8/2000	1	4
1/10/2000	3	8
1/11/2000	1	1
1/13/2000	4	11

FIGURE 8-5 Analytical_Reservations_Summary table

Task 5

Create a make table query named Customer_Age that calculates the average age of customers who have stayed at each hotel. Store the results in a new table named Analytical_Customer_Age. The top section of the table should look like Figure 8-6.

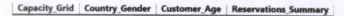

FIGURE 8-6   Analytical_Customer_Age table

Assignment 1B: Working with Summarized Data in Excel

Create a new Excel file and name it **BoutiqueReports.xlsx**. You will use this new Excel file to further manipulate the analytical data sets created in Assignment 1A and create meaningful charts to help the hotel association visualize the results.

Task 1

Open the source file BoutiqueAnalytics.accdb and then import the data tables created in Assignment 1A into different tabs. Rename each tab to match the source data table, as shown in Figure 8-7.

| Capacity_Grid | Country_Gender | Customer_Age | Reservations_Summary |

FIGURE 8-7   Tabs in BoutiqueReports.xlsx

Task 2

Create a pivot table to summarize the number of available rooms that are pet-friendly and smoke-free. Next, add a chart that displays the results (see Figure 8-8). Rename the pivot table tab as PetFriendlySmokeFree.

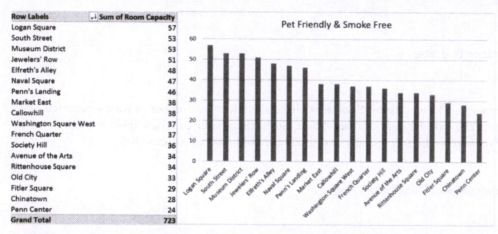

FIGURE 8-8   Pivot table and chart of pet-friendly and smoke-free rooms

Task 3

Add a new column to the Country_Gender tab and label it "North America?" Use a formula to determine if Customer_Country_of_Residence is the United States or Canada. If it is, the formula should return "Yes"; otherwise, the formula should return "No." Create a pivot table that summarizes gender distribution by North American countries and create a meaningful chart to display the results, as shown in Figure 8-9. Rename the pivot table tab as "NorthAmerica."

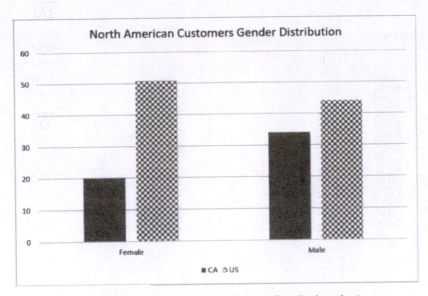

FIGURE 8-9 North American Customers Gender Distribution chart

Task 4

Using the Reservations_Summary tab, create a pivot table that summarizes the hotels' total capacity used by month. Next, create a meaningful chart to visualize the results, as shown in Figure 8-10. Rename the tab "UtilizationbyMonth."

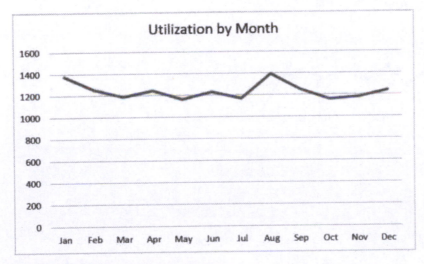

FIGURE 8-10 Utilization by Month chart

Task 5

Using the Reservations_Summary tab, create a pivot table that summarizes the hotels' total capacity used by quarter. Next, create a meaningful chart to visualize the results, as shown in Figure 8-11. Rename the tab "UtilizationbyQuarter."

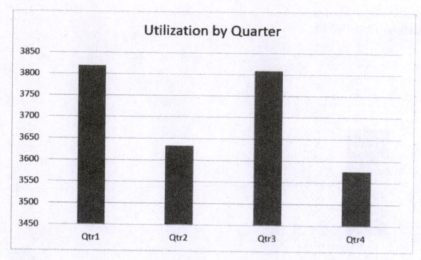

FIGURE 8-11   Utilization by Quarter chart

Task 6

Using the Reservations_Summary tab, create a pivot table that summarizes the hotels' total capacity used by year. Next, create a meaningful chart to visualize the results, as shown in Figure 8-12. Rename the tab "UtilizationbyYear."

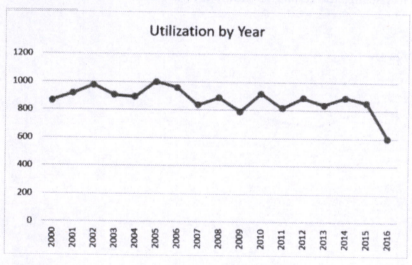

FIGURE 8-12   Utilization by Year chart

Task 7

At this point, it is a good idea to organize the data. One method is to color-code the tabs that contain the data. For this case, create green tabs for your raw data and yellow tabs for the pivot tables. Next, create a new tab named Charts and color-code it as blue. Move each of the charts you created into the new Charts tab, and then organize them in a way that makes sense to you. Figure 8-13 shows an example of how you may choose to align the charts.

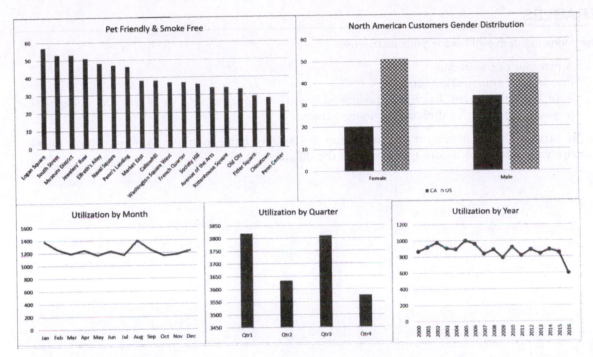

FIGURE 8-13   Charts tab

ASSIGNMENT 2: USING DATA TO DRAW CONCLUSIONS

You have created a series of queries, worksheets, and charts to help the Philadelphia Association of Boutique Hotels learn about its customers and better understand its own business. You will now complete the case by using your findings to make recommendations in a memorandum. Use Microsoft Word to write a memo to the association. State the results of your analysis and make suggestions for additional research topics that have not been covered. Your suggestions should not be limited to the charts you have already produced. Think of the following questions as you complete your analysis:

- Is the gender of the customer base skewed in any way?
- Are the customers primarily from North America?
- Is there a trend in the reservations?
- Is there a seasonal effect on the reservations?
- Are customers asking more for pet-friendly hotels?
- Is there an age difference in smoking preferences?

When preparing the memo, observe the following requirements:

- Set up your memo as described in Tutorial E.
- In the first paragraph, briefly describe the situation and state the purpose of your analysis.
- Next, summarize the results of your analysis and give your recommendations.
- Support your recommendations with appropriate screen shots or Excel objects from the Excel workbook. (Tutorial C describes how to copy and paste Excel objects.)

ASSIGNMENT 3: GIVING AN ORAL PRESENTATION

Your instructor may request that you summarize your analysis and recommendations in an oral presentation. If so, prepare a presentation for the hotel association that lasts 10 minutes or less. When preparing your presentation, use PowerPoint slides or handouts that you think are appropriate. Tutorial F explains how to prepare and give an effective oral presentation.

DELIVERABLES

Prepare the following deliverables for your instructor:

- A printout of the memo
- Printouts of your worksheets
- Your Word document, Excel workbook, and PowerPoint presentation on electronic media or sent to your course site as directed by your instructor

Staple the printouts together with the memo on top. If you have more than one Excel workbook file for your case, write your instructor a note that describes the different files.

THE DATA CLEANSING TASK

Decision Support with Microsoft Excel

PREVIEW

Your company is in the wedding planning business. The company has data for its clients' marriage engagements made in 2010 and 2015. In this case, you will use Microsoft Excel to assess the data's quality and clean the data if possible.

Note that you will use similar data from the same company to answer different questions in Case 12.

PREPARATION

- Review spreadsheet concepts discussed in class and in your textbook.
- Complete any exercises that your instructor assigns.
- Review the Data Cleaning section of Tutorial D.
- Review file-saving procedures for Windows programs.
- Refer to Tutorials E and F as necessary.

BACKGROUND

Your company plans weddings for clients. You help couples pick out wedding rings, and your company's subsidiary, a jewelry firm, can sell rings to them. You help organize bachelor parties, wedding showers, and honeymoons. You help organize weddings at churches and other venues. Your company has operated successfully for 20 years and satisfied thousands of clients throughout the eastern part of your state.

Company management is thinking about expanding into the central part of the state, an area that comprises three large and populous counties. The company sees five marketing regions in this part of the state: northeast (NE), northwest (NW), southeast (SE), southwest (SW), and central (CE).

The company's operations manager wants to analyze data about customer tendencies in the three counties. Therefore, the company hired a marketing research firm to compile data about marriage engagements made in 2010 and 2015 in those counties.

The operations manager calls you in. "The marketing research firm has a reputation for accumulating good data. My counterpart at the firm says he is sure there are no problems with the 2015 data, and I believe him. But he admits he is not so sure about the quality of the 2010 data. We need to look at it and clean it up if possible. Then we can analyze the two years of good data to help us decide if we should expand to the central part of the state."

The operations manager tells you that the data is in an Excel file called EngagementDataCleanup.xlsx. First you should make a copy of the file, called BackupEngagementData.xlsx. It's always a good idea to keep a copy of your starting point. The operations manager says, "You'll notice that the 2010 data is in one worksheet and the 2015 data is in a second worksheet. There is a short note in a Word file that describes the Excel data. The Word file also contains guidance for how to look for problems in the 2010 data. You should read the Word file as a first step."

The operations manager continues describing the assignment. "You will work with the EngagementDataCleanup file. You should create a third worksheet—name it '2010 data error log.' You can accept the 2015 data, but you should challenge the 2010 data. Record any errors you find in the log worksheet. If you must remove a record from the 2010 worksheet, put it into the log worksheet. If you fix any data in the 2010 worksheet, describe the action in your log worksheet. State the error, note the mistaken data, and note the corrected data. When you are done, give me a copy of the cleaned-up file, and write me a short memo about your results."

To get the data file, select Case 9 from your data files and then select **EngagementDataCleanup.xlsx**. The first few rows of the 2010 data are shown in Figure 9-1. An explanation of the data values follows the figure.

	Engagement ID	Region	Date Engaged	Man Age	Woman Age	Months Dated	Church Wedding	Rings Cost
1								
2	1	CE	12/2/1900	30	29	23	0	$ 1,700
3	2	SE	4/3/1900	29	26	1	1	$ 3,025
4	3	CE	4/5/1900	28	26	4	0	$ 2,675
5	4	NE	9/28/1900	28	25	10	0	$ 2,975
6	5	SE	8/27/1900	28	29	21	1	$ 2,425
7	6	CE	3/2/1900	19	20	10	1	$ 1,775
8	7	NW	5/17/1900	22	20	3	1	$ 2,875
9	8	NE	3/4/1900	19	16	22	1	$ 1,475
10	9	SW	4/20/1900	28	28	16	1	$ 2,375
11	10	NE	4/12/1900	26	24	24	0	$ 2,575

FIGURE 9-1   2010 engagement data for cleanup

- Engagement ID—Each row has a unique Engagement ID number.
- Region—The Region field indicates where the person who made the proposal lived at the time. There are five possible valid values: NE, NW, SE, SW, and CE.
- Date Engaged—The date of the engagement is recorded in this column.
- Man Age—The man's age on the date of engagement is recorded in this column.
- Woman Age—The woman's age on the date of engagement is recorded in this column.
- Months Dated—The number of months the couple dated before the proposal is recorded in this column.
- Church Wedding—This column shows whether the wedding was planned for a church. A zero value indicates that the couple did not plan a church wedding. A value of 1 indicates that a church wedding was planned.
- Rings Cost—The total cost of the couple's engagement rings is recorded in this column.

For example, the first record is assigned ID number 1. The couple lived in the central region (denoted by CE). The proposal date was December 2; the man was 30 and the woman was 29 on that date. The couple dated 23 months before the engagement. They did not plan a church wedding and spent a total of $1,700 on their rings.

You will find an analogous worksheet for 2015 engagements in the Excel file.

ASSIGNMENT 1: USING EXCEL FOR DECISION SUPPORT

Your task is to find incomplete records, duplicate records, and erroneous records in the 2010 data. While reviewing the Word file that came with the Excel file, you learn the following things about the data:

- When the data clerk entered the engagement dates, he entered only the month and day. Excel entered the year 1900 as a default value for the rest of the date. All dates should be corrected to show 2010 as the year.
- Engagement ID values should be unique. If there are duplicate Engagement ID values, delete the entire row from the file and log the duplicate values.
- Only CE, NW, NE, SW, and SE are valid values for the Region column. Delete any other Region values from the file and log them. To search for invalid Region values, first use a pivot table to count the number of engagements in each region. In the PivotTable Fields area, drag the Region field into the Rows cell and then drag the Region field into the Values cell. A count of engagements for each region is created in the pivot table. Invalid Region values will be counted along with valid ones. Highlight and copy the pivot table, then paste it into the log file—select the first cell in the area where you want to paste, click the arrow next to Paste on the Home tab, click Paste Special, and then click Values in the window that appears. You can then delete the pivot table from the 2010 data worksheet. If invalid Region values exist, you can sort the data by the Region field to group the problematic rows together.

- Empty cell values are not acceptable. If the empty cell is in the Man Age, Woman Age, Months Dated, or Rings Cost column, keep the record in the file, but log the error and then correct it. To correct the error, compute the column's average 2010 data value for the region and insert the average value into the empty cell. Your log should include a note about the average value you computed and recorded, and the method you used to compute the value (for example, by a pivot table or other means). If you find empty cells in columns other than Man Age, Woman Age, Months Dated, and Rings Cost, delete the record and log it.
- Man Age and Woman Age values that are greater than 99 are assumed to be erroneous. Delete and log such records.
- Months Dated values that are greater than 180 (15 years!) are assumed to be erroneous. Delete and log such records.
- The ages for a couple should not differ by 50 years or more. Delete and log such records.
- Rings Cost values that exceed $50,000 are assumed to be erroneous and require later research. Delete and log such records.
- For generations, survey after survey in your state has shown that the man in an engaged couple is about one year older than the woman. This rule appears to be reflected in the 2015 data averages. Check this rule in the 2010 data that remains after you complete the other checks. Log the averages for each year and state whether the rule is reflected in the 2010 data.

ASSIGNMENT 2: DOCUMENTING FINDINGS IN A MEMO

In this assignment, you write a memo in Microsoft Word that is addressed to the operations manager and documents your findings. In your memo, observe the following requirements:

- Set up the memo as discussed in Tutorial E.
- Briefly outline the situation. However, you need not provide much background—you can assume that readers are familiar with your task.
- In the body of the memo, describe the problems you found and what you did about them.

ASSIGNMENT 3: GIVING AN ORAL PRESENTATION

Assume that the operations manager wants you to present your findings to other members of the management team. Summarize your analysis and results in an oral presentation that lasts 10 minutes or less. Use visual aids or handouts as appropriate. See Tutorial F for guidance on preparing and giving an oral presentation.

DELIVERABLES

Assemble the following deliverables for your instructor:

- Printed copy of your memo and log worksheet
- Spreadsheet printouts, if required by your instructor
- Electronic media such as a flash drive, which should include your Word memo file, your backup Excel file, and your corrected Excel file, including the error log worksheet. Alternatively, your instructor might want you to send the files electronically.

Staple the printouts together with the memo on top. If you have more than one .xlsx file on your electronic media, write your instructor a note that identifies the files for this assignment.

PART 4

DECISION SUPPORT CASE
USING BASIC EXCEL FUNCTIONALITY

THE STATE PENSION FUND ANALYSIS

Decision Support Using Microsoft Excel

PREVIEW

A large Midwestern state has a single pension fund for the state's public school teachers. Many observers think the fund is financially weak. In this case you will use Microsoft Excel to analyze the pension fund's financial condition.

PREPARATION

- Review spreadsheet concepts discussed in class and in your textbook.
- Complete any exercises that your instructor assigns.
- Complete any parts of Tutorials C and D that your instructor assigns, or refer to them as necessary.
- Review Microsoft Windows file-saving procedures.
- Refer to Tutorials E and F as necessary.

BACKGROUND

Many years ago, your state's lawmakers established a pension fund for the state's public school teachers. Under the plan, teachers contribute a portion of their salary each year to the fund. The state is obligated to contribute each year as well. The fund's assets are invested in stocks and bonds; earnings on the investments are put back into the fund. A retired teacher's pension is paid out of fund assets for the rest of the teacher's life. This kind of retirement plan is very common in the United States for public employees, including public school teachers.

Key aspects of the teacher retirement plan are negotiated between state officials and the teachers' union:

- The amount that teachers will contribute to the fund each year
- The amount that the state will contribute to the fund each year
- The formula used to compute the yearly pension payout to retirees

Teachers currently contribute 9.5 percent of their salary to the fund each year. The state agrees to donate 2.5 times as much as the teachers contribute.

A retired teacher's pension is equal to 2.2 percent multiplied by the teacher's salary in his or her final year of work multiplied by the teacher's number of years of service. Thus, a teacher who worked many years and had a high final salary will have a greater pension than a teacher who did not work as many years and had a lower salary in the final year. For example, a teacher who worked 25 years and had a final salary of $100,000 would get a yearly payment of .022 × $100,000 × 25, or $55,000.

In addition, the teachers' union negotiated some inflation protection for retirees years ago. A 3 percent cost of living adjustment is added to the base payout. Continuing the previous example, the teacher's yearly pension payout would be 1.03 × $55,000, or $56,650. The next year, the teacher's pension payout would be 1.03 × $56,650, and so on, as long as the retired teacher receives payouts.

The financial health of a pension fund is assessed by comparing (1) the value of the fund's assets with (2) the amount of benefits the fund is obligated to pay:

1. The value of the assets is relatively easy to compute because stocks, bonds, and other instruments usually have market values for quick reference.

2. The amount of benefits the fund is obligated to pay is harder to estimate. Typically, a 30-year horizon is assumed. The number of covered pensioners is estimated for each year along with the estimated payout for pensioners each year. The present value of each year's estimated obligation is computed. The total of the 30 present values is the estimated total obligation, stated in today's dollars.

3. If the value of the assets is equal to or greater than the present value of the fund's obligations, the fund is said to be fully funded. If the value of the assets is less than the present value of the fund's obligations, the fund is said to be underfunded. In that case, the difference between the present value of the obligations and the assets' value is called the net present value (NPV) of the unfunded liability. The NPV is a measure of how far a pension plan is "in the hole."

Your state's teacher pension fund is thought to be underfunded. In the short term, the problem is not critical—there is enough money in the fund to pay benefits this year and the next few years. However, as time goes on, the fund will not have enough money. The pension payments are a contractual obligation for the state, so the problem must be addressed.

Various factors have contributed to this problem:

- The state assumes that the fund will earn, on average, 7.5 percent of the value of the assets invested each year. However, the financial markets have been volatile in recent years. The average annual rate of return for the last decade has been less than 7.5 percent.

- The state has not always had enough money to make its yearly contribution. For example, the total of the teachers' payroll deductions might be $1 billion, in which case the state would be obligated to pay $2.5 billion into the fund. However, what if the state has more immediate priorities? In several years during the past decade, the state has not written a check for the amount it should have written to the fund.

- Recall that the retirement benefit is a function of the teacher's final annual salary. State officials say that some teachers take on additional tasks in their last year of work to elevate their final annual salary. For example, some teachers might decide to teach summer school. Also, some school districts have "extra pay for extra work" rules. For example, a teacher might decide to be the chairperson of math instruction at his or her school and earn extra money in the final year before retirement. State budget officials estimate that the average teacher earns about $4,000 more in the final year of work than in previous years. State officials want the final salary amount to be reduced, a process that might require union contract negotiation. This reduction would be called the "give-back." For example, a teacher's final salary for pension purposes might be the actual final salary minus $2,000.

- The 3 percent cost of living add-on is an irritant to state budget officials, but union representatives point out that the adjustment remains at 3 percent even in years in which inflation is actually higher. State officials counter by saying that the pension plan was not set up to adjust for inflation, and that 3 percent compounded yearly becomes a lot of money. State budget officials think the plan would be much healthier if the cost of living adjustment did not exist.

- People are living longer these days. On average, a retired teacher in the state draws benefits for 20 years. The plan may not be able to support longer lifespans.

- A decade ago, state education officials launched "productivity" programs with the goal of educating the same number of students with fewer teachers. For example, schools were asked to make better use of technology to deliver educational content. Also, after painful negotiations with the teachers' union, work rules were changed so that administrators could more easily remove incompetent teachers. "Early out" bonuses were put in place to encourage veteran teachers to retire. These productivity programs have been somewhat successful, and the number of teachers has been declining by about 0.5 percent per year.

The teachers' union is quite large, and its members vote. Union officials are questioning the pension plan's viability in meetings with state legislators, who are now convinced the plan is underfunded. A recently passed resolution requires the state to act as quickly as possible to restore the financial health of the teachers' pension fund. The resolution specifies that the ratio of the fund's assets to the present value of the fund's obligations must be raised to at least 80 percent.

The state's budget director has called you in to help analyze the situation. She says she knows the plan is underfunded but does not know how bad the situation is. An Excel model is needed to help her understand the dimensions of the problem and decide how to try to change the plan for the better.

"I do not know where they came up with the 80 percent rule, but I suppose it's not a bad benchmark," she tells you. "We need to figure out a way to get there. I know you are good with Excel models. Run the numbers, and then let's see where we are."

ASSIGNMENT 1: CREATING A SPREADSHEET FOR DECISION SUPPORT

In this assignment, you produce a spreadsheet that models the problem. Then, in Assignment 2, you will use the spreadsheet to gather data and write a memorandum that explains your findings. In Assignment 3, you may be asked to prepare an oral presentation of your analysis.

A spreadsheet has been started and is available for you to use; it will save you time. If you want to use the spreadsheet skeleton, locate Case 10 in your data files and then select **TeachersPensionFund.xlsx**. Your worksheet should contain the following sections:

- Constants
- Inputs
- Summary of Key Results
- Calculations
- Fund Balance Statement
- Fund Liability

A discussion of each section follows.

> **NOTE**
>
> Note that the following figures display values through 2020. However, the TeachersPensionFund file contains 30 years of values, through 2046.

Constants Section

Your spreadsheet should include the constants shown in Figure 10-1. An explanation of the line items follows the figure.

	A	B	C	D	E	F
1	**TEACHERS PENSION FUND**					
2						
3	**CONSTANTS**	_2016_	_2017_	_2018_	_2019_	_2020_
4	Retiree Years of Service	25	25	25	25	25
5	Average Increase in Teacher Salary	0.01	0.01	0.01	0.01	0.01
6	Retiree Rate	0.04	0.04	0.04	0.04	0.04
7	Mortality Rate	0.05	0.05	0.05	0.05	0.05
8	Expected Average Final Salary	$ 82,000	$ 82,820	$ 83,648	$ 84,485	$ 85,330
9	Expected Administrative Expense	NA	$25,000,000	$25,250,000	$25,502,500	$25,757,525

FIGURE 10-1   Constants section

- Retiree Years of Service—On average, teachers work for 25 years before retiring.
- Average Increase in Teacher Salary—Teacher salaries are expected to increase by an average of 1 percent each year for the next 30 years.
- Retiree Rate—On average, 4 percent of teachers are expected to retire each year in the next 30 years.
- Mortality Rate—On average, a pensioner receives payouts for 20 years. On average, 5 percent of pensioners are expected to die each year.
- Expected Average Final Salary—The average final salary for teachers retiring in 2016 was $82,000. The average final salary is expected to increase somewhat each year, as shown.

- Expected Administrative Expense—The pension fund has employees, rents office space, consults with experts in securities markets about investments, and has other expenses. The plan's administrative cost is expected to be $25 million in 2017 and to increase each year, as shown.

Inputs Section

Your spreadsheet should include the inputs shown in Figure 10-2. Possible values are shown in the figure. Each of the inputs applies to each of the 30 years modeled. An explanation of the line items follows the figure.

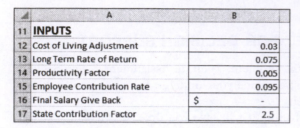

	A	B
11	**INPUTS**	
12	Cost of Living Adjustment	0.03
13	Long Term Rate of Return	0.075
14	Productivity Factor	0.005
15	Employee Contribution Rate	0.095
16	Final Salary Give Back	$ -
17	State Contribution Factor	2.5

FIGURE 10-2   Inputs section

- Cost of Living Adjustment—By union contract, this adjustment is 3 percent. Ideally, plan administrators would like to negotiate this percentage lower.
- Long Term Rate of Return—A 7.5 percent return on investments is assumed. Plan administrators want to see the effects of changing this variable.
- Productivity Factor—The total number of teachers has been declining by 0.5 percent each year in recent years. State officials hope for greater productivity in the future.
- Employee Contribution Rate—Working teachers contribute 9.5 percent of their salary to the pension fund. Some state officials think this rate must increase in the future.
- Final Salary Give Back—State officials want a reduction in the final salary for pension purposes. The reduction would be called the "give-back."
- State Contribution Factor—By contract, the state contributes 2.5 times what the teachers contribute. This factor may need to be increased to ensure there is enough money to pay pensions.

Summary of Key Results Section

Your worksheet should include the key results shown in Figure 10-3. An explanation of the line items follows the figure.

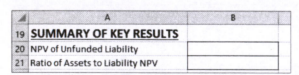

	A	B
19	**SUMMARY OF KEY RESULTS**	
20	NPV of Unfunded Liability	
21	Ratio of Assets to Liability NPV	

FIGURE 10-3   Summary of Key Results section

- NPV of Unfunded Liability—The NPV of the pension fund's unfunded obligation is computed elsewhere in the spreadsheet and can be echoed here.
- Ratio of Assets to Liability NPV—The ratio of the value of fund assets to fund liabilities is computed elsewhere in the spreadsheet and can be echoed here.

Calculations Section

The Calculations section is shown in Figure 10-4. Some 2016 values are provided. Values for 2017 through 2046 are calculated by formula. Use cell addresses when referring to constants in formulas unless otherwise directed. Use absolute addressing properly. An explanation of the line items follows the figure.

	A	B	C	D	E	F
23	**CALCULATIONS**	**2016**	**2017**	**2018**	**2019**	**2020**
24	Average Teacher Salary	$ 68,500				
25	Number of Active Teachers	133,000				
26	Number of New Retirees	NA				
27	Number of Retirees	101,500				
28	Total Teacher Compensation	NA				
29	Employee Contribution to Fund	NA				
30	State Contribution to Fund	NA				
31	Average Retiree Benefit	NA				
32	Expected Benefits Payout	NA				

FIGURE 10-4 Calculations section

- Average Teacher Salary—The average in a year is a function of the prior year's value and the expected rate of increase in the year. The latter value is from the Constants section.
- Number of Active Teachers—This amount is a function of the prior year's value and the expected "productivity factor." The latter value is from the Inputs section.
- Number of New Retirees—This amount is a function of the number of active teachers in the prior year (from the previous row) and the retiree rate for the year (from the Constants section).
- Number of Retirees—The number of retirees in a year is the number of retirees in the prior year plus the number of new retirees in the year, minus the number of retirees who die in the year. The number of retirees who die is a function of the number of retirees in the prior year and the year's mortality rate. The latter value is from the Constants section.
- Total Teacher Compensation—This amount is a function of the average teacher salary in the year and the number of active teachers. Both values are from the Calculations section.
- Employee Contribution to Fund—This value is a function of total teacher compensation (from the previous row) and the contribution rate (from the Inputs section).
- State Contribution to Fund—This value is a function of the employee contribution (from the previous row) and the state contribution factor (from the Inputs section).
- Average Retiree Benefit—The average retiree payout in a year is a function of the expected final salary in the year (from the Constants section), the .022 payout rate (a factor you can hard-code), and the expected years of service (from the Constants section). This amount should be increased by the expected cost of living factor and then reduced by any give-back amount; both values are from the Inputs section.
- Expected Benefits Payout—The total benefits to be paid in a year is a function of the average retiree benefit and the number of retirees in a year. Both values are from the Calculations section.

Fund Balance Statement Section

This section shows a calculation of the pension fund balance at the end of each year, as illustrated in Figure 10-5. The pension fund's balance is increased by employee contributions, state contributions, and earnings on fund assets. The pension fund's balance is decreased by benefits paid and administrative expenses. An explanation of the line items follows the figure.

	A	B	C	D	E	F
34	**FUND BALANCE STATEMENT**	**2016**	**2017**	**2018**	**2019**	**2020**
35	Beginning Balance	NA				
36	Add: Employee Contribution	NA				
37	Add: State Contribution	NA				
38	Add: Income on Investments	NA				
39	Less: Benefits Payout	NA				
40	Less: Administrative Expenses	NA				
41	Ending Balance	$ 40,000,000,000				

FIGURE 10-5 Fund Balance Statement section

- Beginning Balance—The balance at the beginning of a year equals the balance at the end of the prior year.
- Add: Employee Contribution—This amount has been calculated elsewhere in the spreadsheet and can be echoed here.
- Add: State Contribution—This amount has been calculated elsewhere and can be echoed here.
- Add: Income on Investments—This amount equals the fund balance at the beginning of the year multiplied by the expected earnings rate. The latter value is from the Inputs section.
- Less: Benefits Payout—This amount has been calculated elsewhere and can be echoed here.
- Less: Administrative Expenses—This amount is taken from the Constants section and can be echoed here.
- Ending Balance—This amount equals the beginning balance plus the employee contribution, the state contribution, and income on investments, minus the benefits paid and administrative expenses.

Fund Liability Section

This section shows a calculation of the NPV of the pension fund's unfunded liability and the ratio of fund assets to this NPV, as illustrated in Figure 10-6. An explanation of the line items follows the figure.

	A	B	C	D	E	F
43	**FUND LIABILITY**	2016	2017	2018	2019	2020
44	Expected Benefits Payout	NA				
45	Net Present Value of Payouts	NA				
46	NPV of Unfunded Liability	NA				
47	Ratio of Assets to Liability NPV	NA				

FIGURE 10-6   Fund Liability section

- Expected Benefits Payout—The fund's payout in each year has been calculated elsewhere in the spreadsheet and can be echoed here. The series of values will be used in the NPV calculation.
- Net Present Value of Payouts—The NPV of a series of values is calculated using a discount rate applied to those values. Apply the NPV function to the series of expected benefit payouts using .075 as the discount rate. You can hard-code the discount rate.
- NPV of Unfunded Liability—This value is the NPV of payouts minus the fund balance at the end of 2017.
- Ratio of Assets to Liability NPV—This value is the ratio of the fund balance at the end of 2017 to the NPV of payouts.

ASSIGNMENT 2: USING THE SPREADSHEET FOR DECISION SUPPORT

You will now complete the case by (1) using the spreadsheet model to gather data needed to answer the budget director's questions about the plan, (2) documenting your findings in a memo, and (3) giving an oral presentation if your instructor requires it.

Assignment 2A: Using the Spreadsheet to Gather Data

You have built the spreadsheet to create "what-if" scenarios for the model's input values. The inputs represent the logic of a question and the outputs provide information needed to answer the question. The budget director's questions are discussed next.

Question 1 (Base Case)

The budget director asks, "What are the net present value of the unfunded liability and the ratio of assets to the net present value of the unfunded liability, given the current situation? This is the 'base case.' How bad are things right now?" The inputs for the base case are shown in Figure 10-7.

Cost of Living Adjustment	.03
Long-Term Rate of Return	.075
Productivity Factor	.005
Employee Contribution Rate	.095
Final Salary Give-Back	–
State Contribution Factor	2.5

FIGURE 10-7   Question 1 input data

Enter the inputs and then observe the outputs in the Summary of Key Results section. Next, manually record the results in a summary area. You could use a second worksheet for this purpose, as shown in Figure 10-8 (values shown are for illustration only).

	A	B
11	**INPUTS**	
12	Cost of Living Adjustment	0.03
13	Long Term Rate of Return	0.075
14	Productivity Factor	0.005
15	Employee Contribution Rate	0.095
16	Final Salary Give Back	$ –
17	State Contribution Factor	2.5
18		
19	**SUMMARY OF KEY RESULTS**	
20	NPV of Unfunded Liability	$22,000,000,000
21	Ratio of Assets to Liability NPV	70.0%

FIGURE 10-8   Question 1 (base case) inputs and results recorded in summary area

Question 2 (Worst Case)

The budget director says, "In the worst case, we cannot do anything about the cost of living adjustment, the stock market tanks, and we earn very little—say 3 percent. Productivity goes to zero and other factors remain the same. That is the 'worst case.' How bad would that be?" The inputs for the worst case are shown in Figure 10-9.

Cost of Living Adjustment	.03
Long-Term Rate of Return	.03
Productivity Factor	.00
Employee Contribution Rate	.095
Final Salary Give-Back	–
State Contribution Factor	2.5

FIGURE 10-9   Question 2 input data

Enter the inputs and then observe the outputs in the Summary of Key Results section. Next, manually record the results in the summary area.

Question 3 (Aggressive Case)

The budget director says, "In my dreams, I take an aggressive line with the union and I win the battles. The cost of living adjustment is reduced to 1 percent. The productivity factor doubles to 1 percent. The employee contribution rate is increased to 10 percent. The salary give-back is $4,000, and the stock market comes back, so we earn 10 percent on our money. That is the 'aggressive case.' How good would things be? Surely the ratio gets to 80 percent then!" The inputs for the aggressive case are shown in Figure 10-10.

Cost of Living Adjustment	.01
Long-Term Rate of Return	.10
Productivity Factor	.01
Employee Contribution Rate	.10
Final Salary Give-Back	$4,000
State Contribution Factor	2.5

FIGURE 10-10   Question 3 input data

Enter the inputs and then observe the outputs in the Summary of Key Results section. Next, manually record the results in the summary area.

Question 4 (Rescue Case)

The budget director says, "I know the governor is going to ask what the state would have to do to bail out the current system. So, assume the conditions of the base case, except for the state contribution factor." Run a "what-if" scenario with that factor until you reach a ratio of 80 percent. How big a factor is needed? Call this question the "rescue case." How much extra money would the state have to contribute versus the base case contribution by the state? The inputs for the rescue case are shown in Figure 10-11.

Cost of Living Adjustment	.03
Long-Term Rate of Return	.075
Productivity Factor	.005
Employee Contribution Rate	.095
Final Salary Give-Back	–
State Contribution Factor	???

FIGURE 10-11   Question 4 input data

Enter the inputs and then observe the outputs in the Summary of Key Results section. The extra dollar amount that the state would contribute can be calculated by comparing state contribution amounts in the Calculations section in the two scenarios. Next, manually record the results in the summary area.

When you finish gathering data for the four questions, print the model's worksheet with any set of inputs. Print the summary sheet data as well, and then save the spreadsheet for the final time.

Assignment 2B: Documenting your Findings and Recommendation in a Memo

Document your findings in a memo that answers the budget director's four questions. The memo should also state your more general assessment of the fund's financial position: How bad or good is the situation? Use the following guidelines to prepare your memo in Microsoft Word:

- Your memo should have proper and standard headings, such as Date, To, From, and Subject. You can address the memo to the administrators of the state pension fund. Set up your memo as described in Tutorial E.
- Briefly outline the situation. However, you need not provide much background—you can assume that readers are familiar with the situation.

- Answer the four questions in the body of the memo.
- Include tables and charts to support your claims, as your instructor specifies. Tutorial E explains how to create a table in Microsoft Word. Tutorial F explains how to create charts in Excel.

ASSIGNMENT 3: GIVING AN ORAL PRESENTATION

Assume that the budget director asks you to be ready to present your analysis and results in an oral presentation to some key legislators. "These guys are always looking for the silver bullet—you know, trying to fix the problem by changing only one thing. So, they want to see sensitivity data and they want it in chart format," she tells you. "For example, someone will want to know how much the asset-to-liability ratio would change if there was a change in the market rate of return. So get those kinds of charts ready."

Prepare to talk to the group for 10 minutes or less. Tutorial F explains how to prepare and give an oral presentation.

Your instructor will tell you what sensitivity analyses to prepare or may tell you to choose these analyses yourself. The example chart to which the budget director referred should look like the one shown in Figure 10-12.

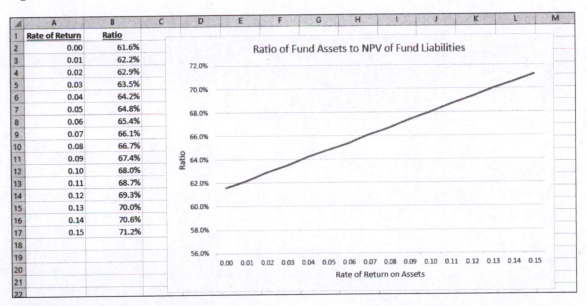

FIGURE 10-12 Chart for presentation

DELIVERABLES

Assemble the following deliverables for your instructor:

- A printout of your memo
- Spreadsheet printouts
- A flash drive or CD that contains your Word file and Excel file

Staple the printouts together with the memo on top. If there is more than one .xlsx file on your flash drive or CD, write your instructor a note that identifies the correct file.

PART 5

INTEGRATION CASES USING MICROSOFT ACCESS AND EXCEL

FAA WILDLIFE HAZARD RESEARCH

Data Analysis and Research with Microsoft Access and Excel

PREVIEW

According to the Federal Aviation Administration (FAA), collisions between aircraft and wildlife during the past century have resulted in the loss of hundreds of lives worldwide, as well as billions of dollars in aircraft damage. The FAA maintains a comprehensive database of wildlife-aircraft strikes; through policy, guidance, and research, it strives to stay ahead of the issue. (For details, see *www.faa.gov/airports/airport_safety/ wildlife/management*.) To take meaningful action and address wildlife management near airports, the FAA first needs to understand what the gathered data means. The types of wildlife generally associated with incidents include birds, mammals, and even reptiles. At established airports, wildlife management techniques include habitat manipulation, such as keeping grass at a specific height to prevent nesting by birds, and the use of predators, such as dogs, to keep runways clear of birds. New airports benefit from data gathered in the analysis of wildlife incidents elsewhere.

Most people don't need to worry about the dangers of wildlife striking airplanes, but for some the experience was unforgettable. You may recall the "Miracle on the Hudson" in 2009, when Captain Chesley B. "Sully" Sullenberger and First Officer Jeffrey Skiles made an unpowered emergency water landing of US Airways Flight 1549 in the Hudson River after the plane hit a flock of Canada geese, causing both jet engines to fail. Captain Sully famously remarked to the air traffic controller, "We're going to be in the Hudson." However lucky the passengers and crew might have been that day, bird strikes are not an isolated event; thousands of incidents are reported annually by airline, private, and military pilots, and many other incidents go unreported. The results of these incidents range from simple nuisances to catastrophic loss of life. Your completed analysis will be used to answer research questions about patterns and behaviors of the wildlife and to provide additional insights about wildlife strike incidents.

PREPARATION

- Review database and spreadsheet concepts discussed in class and in your textbook.
- Complete any exercises that your instructor assigns.
- Complete any parts of Tutorials B, C, and D that your instructor assigns, or refer to them as necessary.
- Review the file-saving procedures for Windows programs in Tutorial C.
- Review Tutorial F as necessary.

BACKGROUND

You will use your Access and Excel skills to analyze wildlife strike incident data gathered over the years and then to identify incident patterns and draw additional conclusions based on your findings. The Access database file is available in the files that come with your casebook. Locate Case 11 in your data files and then select **Wildlife.accdb**.

Using the Database

The database contains four tables with strike reports from January 1, 1990, through December 31, 2015. Figure 11-1 shows the tables in the database file.

FIGURE 11-1   Tables in the database

Additionally, you have been given a data dictionary with the database. This information will prove beneficial because some of the field names in the database might be cryptic at first. You can use Figure 11-2 as a reference throughout your analysis.

Column Name	Explanation of Column Name and Codes
INCIDENT NUMBER	Individual record number
ATYPE	Aircraft
TYPE_ENG	Type of power A = reciprocating engine (piston): B = Turbojet: C = Turboprop: D = Turbofan: E = None (glider): F = Turboshaft (helicopter): Y = Other
INCIDENT_DATE	Date strike occurred
TIME_OF_DAY	Light conditions
TIME	Hour and minute in local time
AIRPORT	Name of airport
STATE	State
HEIGHT	Feet Above Ground Level
SPEED	Knots (indicated air speed)
DISTANCE	Miles from airport
PHASE_OF_FLT	Phase of flight during which strike occurred
PRECIP	Precipitation
SPECIES	Common name for bird or other wildlife

FIGURE 11-2   Database data dictionary

The first step needed to complete any data analysis project is to inspect your data, which generally involves opening tables, looking through table designs, and running a few quick queries. The purpose of the inspections is to identify the overall health or cleanliness of the data. Are the records complete? What about data types? Are date fields formatted as dates? Is there a unique record identifier? These questions will help you get started.

ASSIGNMENT 1: USING ACCESS FOR DATA INSPECTION

In this assignment, you will inspect the data in the database and answer a few questions along the way.

Task 1

How many records are in each of the four tables of the database? Which table has the highest record count? While there are a few ways to answer such questions, you should use queries to create repeatable tasks that can be used to generate reports later. Save the queries as Query 1 through Query 4. Figure 11-3 shows the results of Query 1.

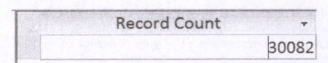

FIGURE 11-3   Query 1 results

Task 2

Open each table in the database, examine them, and determine if any fields in the tables have blank or null values. Figure 11-4 shows that the REG column has some blank fields. Look in the data dictionary; what does the REG field represent? Do other fields have blank values?

INDE	OPID	OPERATOR	ATYPE	AMA	A	EM	EN	AC_(	AC	NU	T\	EN	E	E\	REG	FLT	REMA
100000	AAL	AMERICAN AIRLINES	B-727	148	10	34	10	A	4	3	D	5	6	5	N859AA		
100001	UAL	UNITED AIRLINES	B-737-300	148	24	10	01	A	4	2	D	1	1			1768	
100002	UAL	UNITED AIRLINES	B-737-300	148	24	10	01	A	4	2	D	1	1			1845	
100003	UAL	UNITED AIRLINES	B-757-200	148	26	34	40	A	4	2	D	1	1			306	
100004	UAL	UNITED AIRLINES	A-320	04A	03	23	01	A	4	2	D	1	1			510	
100005	UAL	UNITED AIRLINES	A-320	04A	03	23	01	A	4	2	D	1	1			677	
100006	AAL	AMERICAN AIRLINES	B-727-100	148	10	34	10	A	4	3	D	5	6	5	N977AA		

FIGURE 11-4   Strike Reports (1990–1999) table showing blank values in the REG column

Task 3

Determine whether the INCIDENT DATE field is formatted as a date in all four tables. You can do this by opening each table in Design view. Proper field formatting makes subsequent date manipulation much easier.

ASSIGNMENT 2: USING ACCESS FOR DATA ANALYSIS

Now that you have inspected the data, you are ready to begin your analysis. In this assignment, you will cleanse and organize the data to facilitate your research, and then you will complete a series of queries to further your understanding of the data and shape your research. While the queries are an effective way to summarize data and provide results, you will need to leverage Excel to visually represent data and transform it into meaningful information.

During your inspection you should have noticed that the tables are partitioned into time "chunks," which will prevent you from doing a true longitudinal analysis from 1990 to 2015. In the data's current format, you would need to create separate queries for each time period and find an easy way to merge all the data in a way that makes sense. Fortunately, you can "stack" the tables into a single table and then use it to run your queries. For the stacking to work, the fields in the different tables must be in the same order and have the same names.

Task 4

Although there are many ways to stack all the data tables into one, the most prudent approach is to do it in a series of steps because it facilitates any necessary troubleshooting. You should start this process by creating a copy of one of the tables—it is always a good idea to create a backup copy of your data prior to making irreversible changes. After making the copy, you should now have five tables in the database, two of which are identical except for the name (see Figure 11-5).

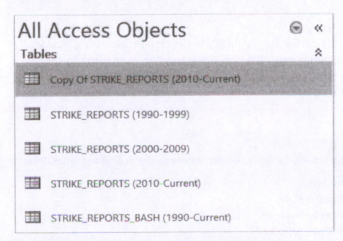

FIGURE 11-5   Tables in the database, including copy

Next, you will create an append query to stack the records of the Strike Reports (1990–1999) table into the Strike Reports (2010–Current) table, as shown in Figure 11-6. Save the results as Query 5.

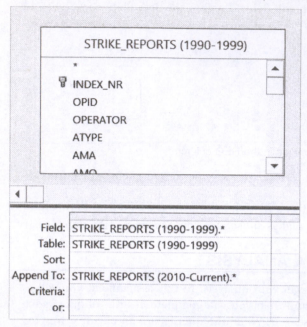

FIGURE 11-6   Query 5 configuration

When you execute the query, you should see a confirmation box that reports how many records are being appended into the table. Does the number match your count during the data inspection tasks? Figure 11-7 shows the confirmation box.

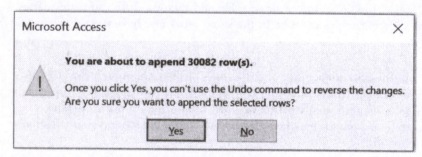

FIGURE 11-7   Append confirmation box for Query 5

Next, you should append the other two tables to the Strike Reports (2010–Current) table using queries. Save these queries as Query 6 and Query 7. Check to make sure that the total number of records in the Strike Reports (2010–Current) table equals the sum of records in all the other tables. In addition, you should rename the table to more accurately describe its contents—for example, you can name the table Master_Strike_Reports.

Task 5

Next, you will run a series of queries to create a quick report in Access that answers the following questions:

- What five states reported the most incidents?
- What five airports reported the most incidents?
- In which five years were the most incidents reported?
- In which five months were the most incidents reported?

For each question, you should write a query to determine the results; save them as Query 8 through Query 11. As you complete the queries, you might encounter blank, null, or "unknown" values, which are generally the result of incomplete incident reports. These blank and unknown values should be included in the query answers only if they are part of the question. For the questions in this task, do not include blank and unknown values. Figure 11-8 shows the result of Query 8.

Query 8

STATE	Incident Count
TX	14998
CA	13277
FL	10715
NY	9133
IL	7519

FIGURE 11-8 Results for Query 8

Task 6

Create a report in Access that displays the results of all four questions. The formatting is up to you, but the results should be neatly displayed and easy for readers to understand.

ASSIGNMENT 3: IMPORTING DATA INTO EXCEL FOR FURTHER ANALYSIS

You will complete your analysis in Excel by using charts that allow you to easily spot trends. First, import the Master_Strike_Reports table into an Excel worksheet. Open a new file in Excel and save it as **strikeanalysis.xlsx**. Next, select cell A1. Then, click the Data tab and select From Access in the Get External Data group. Specify the Access file name, and then specify the query to import. You will import the data into a new sheet and label it as Master Strike Reports, as shown in Figure 11-9.

	A	B	C
1	INDEX_NR	OPID	OPERATOR
2	200009	ABX	ABX AIR
3	200010	ABX	ABX AIR
4	200011	ABX	ABX AIR
5	200012	AMW	AIR MIDWEST
6	200013	UNK	UNKNOWN
7	200014	UNK	UNKNOWN
8	200015	NWA	NORTHWEST AIRLINES
9	200016	AAL	AMERICAN AIRLINES
10	200017	UNK	UNKNOWN
11	200018	UAL	UNITED AIRLINES
12	200019	NWA	NORTHWEST AIRLINES
13	200020	EGF	AMERICAN EAGLE AIRL

Master Strike Reports

FIGURE 11-9 Imported data in Excel

While Access is very effective at manipulating large amounts of data, Excel shines at visually representing results using a wide array of charting tools. Now that you have imported the data into Excel, you need to answer an additional set of questions using pivot tables and charts.

Task 7

Create a series of pivot tables and charts that allow you to determine whether there are any trends or patterns in the data. Create a pivot table to address each of the following points, and name each new tab accordingly.

- Plot the number of incidents by year and create a meaningful chart to display the results. Exclude 2015 because it is not a complete year. See Figures 11-10 and 11-11 for an example.

- Plot the number of incidents by month and create a meaningful chart to display the results. Exclude 2015 because it is not a complete year.
- Plot the number of incidents by time of day and create a meaningful chart to display the results.

Row Labels	Count of INDEX_NR
1990	2099
1991	2672
1992	2816
1993	2849
1994	2938
1995	2989
1996	3215
1997	3651
1998	4131
1999	5385
2000	6351
2001	6216
2002	6659
2003	6485
2004	7122
2005	7591
2006	7750
2007	7992
2008	7993
2009	9848
2010	9934
2011	10363
2012	11264
2013	11666
2014	13981

FIGURE 11-10   Pivot table results for incidents reported by year

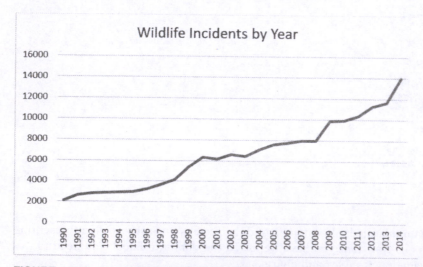

FIGURE 11-11   Line chart that displays incidents reported by year

The tables and charts you created display the results in terms of whole numbers; for example, 2,099 incidents were reported in 1990. Sometimes, however, it is more impactful to display results as a percentage of the overall data set you are examining. For instance, a statement that 2,099 incidents were reported in 1990 is different from saying that only 1.28 percent of all incidents reported since 1990 were reported in 1990. Therefore, add a percentage column to each of the pivot tables you created. See Figure 11-12 for an example.

Row Labels ⏷	Count of INDEX_NR	Count of INDEX_NR2
1990	2099	1.28%
1991	2672	1.63%
1992	2816	1.72%
1993	2849	1.74%
1994	2938	1.79%
1995	2989	1.82%
1996	3215	1.96%
1997	3651	2.23%
1998	4131	2.52%
1999	5385	3.28%
2000	6351	3.87%
2001	6216	3.79%
2002	6659	4.06%
2003	6485	3.96%
2004	7122	4.34%
2005	7591	4.63%
2006	7750	4.73%
2007	7992	4.87%
2008	7993	4.87%
2009	9848	6.01%
2010	9934	6.06%
2011	10363	6.32%
2012	11264	6.87%
2013	11666	7.12%
2014	13981	8.53%

FIGURE 11-12 Pivot table results for incidents reported by year and their percentage of the overall incident count

Are there any patterns you can identify? Do the charts surprise you? What do a large number of bird species do on an annual basis?

ASSIGNMENT 4: DOCUMENTING YOUR FINDINGS IN A MEMO

You have created queries, reports, pivot tables, and charts to perform your analysis. You will now complete the case by using your findings to write a summary memo in Microsoft Word that explains your conclusions. Think of the following questions as you complete your analysis:

- What other questions that were not asked in this case could affect your conclusions?
- According to the data, does the type of plane make a difference? In other words, has one type of aircraft been more prone to wildlife strikes than others?
- Can you confidently say that one aircraft type is safer than others? How?
- Are there different patterns for northern states and southern states? Are there differences for eastern and western states?
- In what part of the year do most incidents occur?
- At what time of day do most incidents occur?
- During what phase of flight do the most incidents occur?
- At what altitude do most incidents occur?

When preparing the memo in Word, observe the following requirements:

- Set up your memo as described in Tutorial E.
- In the first paragraph, briefly describe the situation and state the purpose of your analysis.
- Next, summarize the results of your analysis.
- Support your analysis with appropriate screenshots or Excel objects from the Excel workbook. (Tutorial C describes how to copy and paste Excel objects.)

ASSIGNMENT 5: GIVING AN ORAL PRESENTATION

Your instructor may request that you summarize your analysis and findings in an oral presentation. If so, prepare a presentation that lasts 10 minutes or less. When preparing your presentation, use PowerPoint slides or handouts that you think are appropriate. Tutorial F explains how to prepare and give an effective oral presentation.

DELIVERABLES

Prepare the following deliverables for your instructor:

- A printout of the memo
- Printouts of your worksheets and query designs
- Your Word document, Excel workbook, Access file, and PowerPoint presentation on electronic media or sent to your course site as directed by your instructor

Staple the printouts together with the memo on top. If you have more than one Excel workbook file for your case, write your instructor a note that describes the different files.

THE ENGAGEMENT ANALYSIS

Decision Support with Microsoft Access and Excel

PREVIEW

Your company is in the wedding planning business. The company has data for its clients' marriage engagements made in 2010 and 2015. In this case, you will use Microsoft Access and Excel to examine the details of these engagements and determine whether they changed in any significant ways from 2010 to 2015.

PREPARATION

- Review database and spreadsheet concepts discussed in class and in your textbook.
- Complete any exercises that your instructor assigns.
- Complete any parts of Tutorials B, C, and D that your instructor assigns, or refer to them as necessary.
- Review file-saving procedures for Windows programs.
- Refer to Tutorials E and F as necessary.

BACKGROUND

Your company plans weddings for clients. You help couples pick out wedding rings, and your company's subsidiary, a jewelry firm, can sell rings to them. You help organize bachelor parties, wedding showers, and honeymoons. You help organize weddings at churches and other venues. Your company has operated successfully for 20 years and satisfied thousands of clients throughout three large and densely populated counties in the eastern part of your state.

The company has retained client data in a database, which the operations manager wants to use to review where the business has been and where it might be headed. She has asked for statistics that describe the business in 2010 and in 2015, and has asked for a comparison of the business in those two years.

Here are the kinds of questions that the operations manager has in mind:

- Is it true that Christmas Eve, the day before New Year's Eve (December 30), and Valentine's Day (February 14) are by far the most popular days for popping the question? Are there any other popular days for proposals during the year?
- How much do couples spend on their engagement rings? Have there been changes in this spending from 2010 to 2015? Do people spend more for rings at certain times during the year?
- How long do couples date before becoming engaged? Have there been changes in this length of time over the years?
- Some couples get married in a church, and others do not. How does the behavior of these two groups differ, if at all?
- The three-county area can be divided into five geographical regions—northeast, northwest, southeast, southwest, and central. To some degree, the regions differ ethnically and culturally. Are there regional differences in the behavior of your company's clients?

Knowing the answers to such questions may help the company sharpen its marketing efforts. The operations manager says, "I know you have experience with Access and Excel, and I think you can do the analytical work."

The company has randomly selected 2,500 engagements in 2010 and 2,500 more in 2015 and then compiled the data into an Access database. The database is available for you to use. To get this file, select Case 12 from your data files and then select **EngagementAnalysis.accdb**.

The database tables are discussed next. For example, Figure 12-1 shows the design of the 2010 Engagement Data table.

2010 Engagement Data	
Field Name	**Data Type**
Engagement ID	Number
Region	Short Text
Date Engaged	Date/Time
Months Dated	Number
Church Wedding	Yes/No
Rings Cost	Currency

FIGURE 12-1 Design of 2010 Engagement Data table

The table has 2,500 records. Each record has a unique Engagement ID number. This field is the table's primary key field. The Region field indicates where the person who made the proposal lived at the time of the engagement. The date of the engagement is recorded in the Date Engaged field. The number of months the couple dated before the proposal is shown in the Months Dated field. The Church Wedding field indicates whether the wedding was planned for a church. The total cost of the couple's rings is recorded in the Rings Cost field.

Figure 12-2 shows a few of the table's records.

2010 Engagement Data					
Engagement ID	Region	Date Engaged	Months Dated	Church Wedding	Rings Cost
1	CE	12/2/2010	23	No	$1,700
2	SE	4/3/2010	1	Yes	$3,025
3	CE	4/5/2010	4	No	$2,675
4	NE	9/28/2010	10	No	$2,975
5	SE	8/27/2010	21	Yes	$2,425
6	CE	3/2/2010	10	Yes	$1,775
7	NW	5/17/2010	3	Yes	$2,875
8	NE	3/4/2010	22	Yes	$1,475
9	SW	4/20/2010	16	Yes	$2,375
10	NE	4/12/2010	24	No	$2,575

FIGURE 12-2 Some data records in the 2010 Engagement Data table

For example, the first record is assigned ID number 1. The couple lived in the central region (denoted by CE) of the three-county area. The proposal was given on December 2, after the couple had dated for 23 months. They did not plan a church wedding, and they spent a total of $1,700 on their rings.

An analogous table exists for the 2,500 engagements selected in 2015; the table is called 2015 Engagement Data. Its records are numbered 2501 to 5000.

ASSIGNMENT 1: USING ACCESS AND EXCEL FOR DECISION SUPPORT

The operations manager has several questions, some of which you will attempt to answer using the output of Access queries you will design. You will address other questions by importing Access data into Excel and then using data tables and pivot tables for further analysis.

Access Database Queries

You have been asked to develop a number of queries in Access.

Queries 1-2

What were the most popular days to get engaged in 2010? The operations manager says that on average, each day should have about seven engagements. "That's 2,500 divided by 365," she says. "Let's set the threshold at nearly double that average; in other words, report which days had more than 13 engagements." Create a query that lists each day in 2010 on which more than 13 engagements occurred. Your output should resemble the data shown in Figure 12-3.

Frequency By Day 2010	
Date Engaged	Number of Engagements
12/24/2010	177
2/14/2010	93
12/30/2010	39
6/25/2010	14
3/2/2010	14
1/20/2010	14

FIGURE 12-3 Frequency of engagements by day in 2010

Save the query as Frequency By Day 2010. Note that the output is sorted so the most frequent engagement day is shown first, then the next most frequent day, and so on.

You should create an analogous query for engagements in 2015 and name it Frequency By Day 2015.

Give some thought to the operations manager's questions. Are Christmas Eve, Valentine's Day, and the day before New Year's Eve the most popular days for engagements every year? Are any other days nearly as close in popularity? If so, why do you think they are?

Queries 3-5

The operations manager wants to know the average amount of money spent on engagement rings in 2010 and 2015. "Five years have elapsed. People should be spending a lot more in 2015. Are they? Maybe we can capitalize on that," she says. Create a query that computes those amounts. Your output should look like the data shown in Figure 12-4.

Average Ring Cost Each Year	
Average 2010 Cost	Average 2015 Cost
$2,245.27	$2,263.70

FIGURE 12-4 Average cost of rings in 2010 and 2015

You will need to use both data tables in this query, but you should not link on the Engagement ID field. (Can you see why? There are no common values between the tables in those fields, so there would be no output.) Set up the query without linking, which may require Access to take a bit longer to compute the answer. Save the query as Average Ring Cost Each Year.

The operations manager wants to know if people spend more for engagement rings on some days than on others. "Do they sometimes splurge? If so, we can charge more at those times!" Create a query that computes the average amount of money spent on rings by day of engagement in 2010 and then displays data for days on which more than 13 engagements occurred. Your output should look like the data shown in Figure 12-5.

Ring Cost by Day of Engagement 2010		
Date Engaged	Number of Engagements	Average Cost of Rings
12/24/2010	177	$2,268.79
2/14/2010	93	$2,322.31
12/30/2010	39	$2,194.23
6/25/2010	14	$2,307.14
3/2/2010	14	$2,025.00
1/20/2010	14	$2,367.86

FIGURE 12-5 Average cost of rings by day in 2010

Save the query as Ring Cost by Day of Engagement 2010. Note that the output is sorted so days with the most engagements are shown first. You should create an analogous query for 2015 and name it Ring Cost by Day of Engagement 2015.

Consider the operations manager's question. Do people splurge? In other words, do they spend more than the average on certain days, or is spending by day fairly consistent?

Queries 6-7

You need to create two more queries that gather data you will later import into Excel. The first query summarizes engagement data for 2010. Save the query as 2010 Data Summary. The first few records of the query output should look like the data shown in Figure 12-6.

2010 Data Summary					
Engagement ID ▾	Region ▾	Date Engaged ▾	Months Dated ▾	Church Wedding ▾	Rings Cost ▾
1 CE		12/2/2010	23	No	$1,700
2 SE		4/3/2010	1	Yes	$3,025
3 CE		4/5/2010	4	No	$2,675
4 NE		9/28/2010	10	No	$2,975
5 SE		8/27/2010	21	Yes	$2,425
6 CE		3/2/2010	10	Yes	$1,775
7 NW		5/17/2010	3	Yes	$2,875
8 NE		3/4/2010	22	Yes	$1,475
9 SW		4/20/2010	16	Yes	$2,375
10 NE		4/12/2010	24	No	$2,575

FIGURE 12-6 First part of query output for 2010 engagement data

Notice that the output is sorted by Engagement ID number in ascending order. The second query summarizes the same types of sales data for 2015. Save that query as 2015 Data Summary.

Other Queries

Your instructor might specify that you develop other queries. When you finish creating the queries, close the database file and exit Access.

Importing Summary Data into Excel

Open a new file in Excel and save it as **EngagementAnalysis.xlsx**. Import the 2010 Data Summary query output into Excel. First, click the Data tab and then select From Access in the Get External Data group. Specify the filename of the Access database and then specify the 2010 Data Summary query and where to place the data in the worksheet (cell A1 is recommended).

The data will be imported into Excel as a data table, which is the format you want. To create a totals row for the table, go to the Table Style Options group of the Design tab and click the Totals Row box. Rename the worksheet as 2010 Data. The first few rows of your worksheet should look like those in Figure 12-7.

	A	B	C	D	E	F
1	Engagement ID ▾	Region ▾	Date Engaged ▾	Months Dated ▾	Church Wedding ▾	Rings Cost ▾
2	1	CE	12/2/2010	23	FALSE	1700
3	2	SE	4/3/2010	1	TRUE	3025
4	3	CE	4/5/2010	4	FALSE	2675
5	4	NE	9/28/2010	10	FALSE	2975
6	5	SE	8/27/2010	21	TRUE	2425
7	6	CE	3/2/2010	10	TRUE	1775
8	7	NW	5/17/2010	3	TRUE	2875
9	8	NE	3/4/2010	22	TRUE	1475
10	9	SW	4/20/2010	16	TRUE	2375
11	10	NE	4/12/2010	24	FALSE	2575

FIGURE 12-7 Rows in the 2010 Data summary worksheet

The totals row should look like the one in Figure 12-8.

⊿	A		B	C	D	E	F
2488	2487	CE		10/25/2010	19	TRUE	1875
2489	2488	CE		4/29/2010	5	TRUE	1875
2490	2489	CE		10/2/2010	19	FALSE	2775
2491	2490	CE		6/20/2010	16	TRUE	2875
2492	2491	SW		11/10/2010	3	TRUE	1575
2493	2492	SW		3/4/2010	22	TRUE	2075
2494	2493	NW		5/6/2010	11	FALSE	2175
2495	2494	NW		5/10/2010	16	TRUE	2275
2496	2495	CE		7/2/2010	1	TRUE	1525
2497	2496	SE		2/1/2010	1	TRUE	2775
2498	2497	SE		2/23/2010	13	TRUE	2625
2499	2498	SW		8/29/2010	12	FALSE	2675
2500	2499	CE		8/4/2010	1	TRUE	2875
2501	2500	SW		6/3/2010	1	TRUE	2775
2502	Total						5613175

FIGURE 12-8 Totals row in the 2010 Data summary worksheet

Use the same procedure for the 2015 data summary. Start by clicking the New Sheet button at the bottom of the screen. (The button displays a plus sign.) Then import the query output of the 2015 data summary into the second worksheet. Add a totals row and rename the worksheet 2015 Data.

Using Data Tables to Gather Data

The operations manager wants to know if there are regional differences between couples that chose church weddings in 2010 and 2015. You can use the data tables to develop a frequency table of church weddings. Data tables are discussed in Tutorial E, and some short directions are provided here.

The labels in the data table headings contain drop-down arrows that you can click to filter data under that heading. Click the drop-down arrow in the Region column and then deselect all the boxes in the resulting menu except for the CE box; this action selects only the CE region rows. In the Church Wedding column, use the filter to show only rows with a True value. Click the drop-down arrow in the Church Wedding totals row and then select the Count operation. These filtering operations will report the number of church weddings in the CE region in 2010. Your results should look like those in Figure 12-9.

⊿	A		B	C	D	E	F
2460	2459	CE		1/30/2010	18	TRUE	1775
2471	2470	CE		10/4/2010	17	TRUE	2075
2475	2474	CE		6/30/2010	20	TRUE	1375
2476	2475	CE		3/24/2010	8	TRUE	1475
2478	2477	CE		10/8/2010	13	TRUE	1575
2484	2483	CE		2/16/2010	7	TRUE	2175
2488	2487	CE		10/25/2010	19	TRUE	1875
2489	2488	CE		4/29/2010	5	TRUE	1875
2491	2490	CE		6/20/2010	16	TRUE	2875
2496	2495	CE		7/2/2010	1	TRUE	1525
2500	2499	CE		8/4/2010	1	TRUE	2875
2502	Total					341	735725

FIGURE 12-9 Using data table filters to compute the number of church weddings in a region

If you change the Church Wedding filter to False, your results will look like those in Figure 12-10.

⊿	A	B	C	D	E	F
2307	2306	CE	1/7/2010	18	FALSE	1475
2335	2334	CE	2/14/2010	13	FALSE	2875
2341	2340	CE	1/21/2010	10	FALSE	1775
2358	2357	CE	1/14/2010	1	FALSE	1675
2376	2375	CE	1/19/2010	16	FALSE	1475
2389	2388	CE	7/30/2010	13	FALSE	1475
2405	2404	CE	4/10/2010	4	FALSE	2275
2408	2407	CE	1/18/2010	14	FALSE	2075
2433	2432	CE	1/15/2010	20	FALSE	1375
2455	2454	CE	3/2/2010	4	FALSE	1875
2490	2489	CE	10/2/2010	19	FALSE	2775
2502	Total				150	322275

FIGURE 12-10   Using filters to compute the number of non-church weddings in a region

You can turn off filters by choosing the Clear Filter option in a column's drop-down menu.

Use the same steps to construct a summary of church weddings by region in 2015. In other words, change a filter setting, note a total, and enter the total into your developing frequency table. Put the frequency table at the bottom of the 2010 data table. When you finish, your frequency table should look like the one shown in Figure 12-11. (Note that the values are for illustrative purposes only.)

2501	2500 SW		6/3/2010		1	TRUE	2775		
2502 Total							2500	5613175	
2503									
2504									
2505		2010	2010	2010	2015	2015	2015		
2506	Region	Church	No Church	% Church	Church	No Church	% Church	Difference	
2507	CE	341	150	69.5%	274	217	55.8%	13.6%	
2508	NE	364	158	69.7%	300	222	57.5%	12.3%	
2509	NW	307	177	63.4%	301	183	62.2%	1.2%	
2510	SE	308	185	62.5%	285	208	57.8%	4.7%	
2511	SW	354	156	69.4%	280	230	54.9%	14.5%	
2512	Total	1674	826	67.0%	1530	970	61.2%	5.8%	

FIGURE 12-11   Church wedding data developed from data table filtering

In your summary, the Difference column reports the 2010 church wedding percentage minus the 2015 percentage—in other words, the percentage difference between the two years.

In looking at your data, what conclusions can you draw about the tendency to marry in a church ceremony, both overall and in the various regions of the three-county area? Has the practice changed much in the five years?

Using Pivot Tables to Gather Data

You will develop pivot tables from the summary worksheets. Data in these pivot tables will allow you to compare 2010 results with 2015 results.

Pivot tables are discussed in Tutorial E, but a review of the procedure is in order here. To create a pivot table, first select any cell in the underlying data table range. Select the Insert tab and then select PivotTable in the Tables group. The Create PivotTable window appears. The proper data range should already be shown in the window. A new worksheet is the default destination, but you can specify a location in the Existing Worksheet box. Enter the cell address of the upper-left corner of the pivot table and then click OK.

The right side of the window shows the PivotTable Fields area, which is best explained by an example. Say you want to see the average ring cost for church weddings in 2010. You select the Rings Cost box, which should display this field in the Values cell. If not, you can click the Rings Cost label and drag it into the Values cell. By default, the Sum operator should be displayed in the Values cell, but it is not what you want in this example. Instead, click the drop-down arrow and select Average in the Value Fields menu. Next, click the Church Wedding box, which should display this field in the Rows cell. (Again, click and drag if necessary.) Your PivotTable Fields area should look like the one in Figure 12-12.

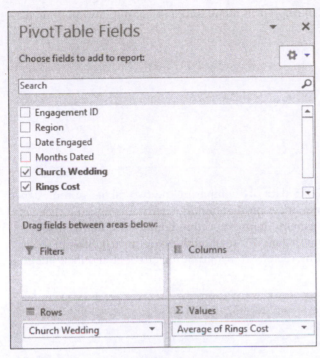

FIGURE 12-12   Setting up the pivot table

The resulting pivot table is shown in Figure 12-13; the average cost column values are formatted for Currency.

	F	G	H	I
1	Rings Cost ▼			
2	1700		Row Labels ▼	Average of Rings Cost
3	3025		FALSE	$ 2,249.42
4	2675		TRUE	$ 2,243.22
5	2975		Grand Total	$ 2,245.27

FIGURE 12-13   Resulting pivot table

Months Dated Pivot Tables

The operations manager wants to know how the number of months a couple dates affects the number of engagements and average amount of money spent on rings. Because there are many values for the number of months dated, she would like to see data just for 5, 10, 15, and 20 months dated. Create pivot tables for each year.

Before filtering, the top part of your 2010 pivot table should look like the one in Figure 12-14. Note that the Average Cost column is formatted for Currency.

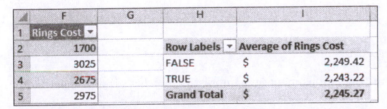

Row Labels ▼	Count	Average Cost
1	261	$ 2,247.80
2	107	$ 2,235.75
3	109	$ 2,207.11
4	93	$ 2,219.09
5	92	$ 2,245.11
6	87	$ 2,206.61
7	81	$ 2,270.06

FIGURE 12-14   Top part of pivot table

You can filter the output by clicking the Row Labels drop-down menu and deselecting unwanted months. Your pivot table would look like the one in Figure 12-15.

Row Labels .T	Count	Average Cost
5	92	$ 2,245.11
10	108	$ 2,193.98
15	105	$ 2,235.00
20	102	$ 2,312.25
Grand Total	407	$ 2,245.76

FIGURE 12-15   Filtered pivot table

You should create a companion pivot table for the 2015 data. By comparing the two tables' output, can you conclude that the number of months of dating has an effect on the amount spent on rings in either year?

Next, the operations manager tells you, "I have the general impression that couples are dating longer before getting engaged, in all regions. Does our data support that?" You should create pivot tables for each year that compute the average number of months dated by region. Your output for 2010 should look like the data in Figure 12-16.

G	H	I
	2010:	
	Row Labels ▼	Average of Months Dated
	CE	11.6
	NE	11.7
	NW	11.1
	SE	11.3
	SW	11.4
	Grand Total	**11.4**

FIGURE 12-16   Average months dated by region in 2010

Compare the 2010 and 2015 outputs. Is the operations manager's impression correct? Did couples date longer in all regions in 2015 than in 2010?

ASSIGNMENT 2: DOCUMENTING FINDINGS IN A MEMO

You have analyzed the data using Access queries, Excel data tables, and Excel pivot tables. In this assignment, you write a memo in Microsoft Word that documents your findings and addresses the questions raised by the operations manager.

In your memo, observe the following requirements:

- Set up the memo as discussed in Tutorial E.
- Briefly outline the situation. However, you need not provide much background—you can assume that readers are generally familiar with your task.
- In the body of the memo, answer the questions posed by the operations manager. Refer to the values in your queries, data tables, and pivot tables to support your answers. Highlight changes in behavior that you see from 2010 to 2015.
- Include any graphical support that your instructor requires, such as copies of query output or pivot tables.

ASSIGNMENT 3: GIVING AN ORAL PRESENTATION

Assume that the operations manager wants you to present your work to other members of the management team. Summarize your analysis and results in an oral presentation that lasts 10 minutes or less. Use visual aids or handouts as appropriate. See Tutorial F for guidance on preparing and giving an oral presentation.

DELIVERABLES

Assemble the following deliverables for your instructor:

- Printed copy of your memo
- Spreadsheet printouts, if required by your instructor
- Query printouts, if required by your instructor
- Electronic media such as flash drive or CD, which should include your Word file, Access file, and Excel file

Staple the printouts together with the memo on top. If you have more than one .xlsx file or .accdb file on your electronic media, write your instructor a note that identifies the files for this assignment.

PART 6

ADVANCED SKILLS
USING EXCEL

TUTORIAL E
Guidance for Excel Cases, 199

GUIDANCE FOR EXCEL CASES

The Microsoft Excel cases in this book require the student to write a memorandum that includes a table. Guidelines for preparing a memo in Microsoft Word and instructions for entering a table in a Word document are provided to begin this tutorial. Also, some of the cases in this book require the use of advanced Excel techniques. Those techniques are explained in this tutorial rather than in the cases themselves:

- Using data tables
- Using pivot tables
- Using built-in functions

You can refer to Sheet 1 of Tutorial E_data.xlsx when reading about data tables. Refer to Sheet 2 when reading about pivot tables.

PREPARING A MEMORANDUM IN WORD

A business memo should include proper headings, such as TO, FROM, DATE, and SUBJECT. If you want to use a Word memo template, follow these steps:

1. In Word, click File.
2. Click New.
3. Enter "memos" in the Search for online templates box, and then click the Start searching button.
4. Click a memo template, such as Memo (elegant) or another memo design of your choice, and then click the Create button to start a new memo document.

The first time you do this, you may need to click Download to install the template. You might also have to search for the memo templates.

ENTERING A TABLE INTO A WORD DOCUMENT

Enter a table into a Word document using the following procedure:

1. Click the cursor where you want the table to appear in the Word document.
2. In the Tables group on the Insert tab, click the Table drop-down menu.
3. Click Insert Table.
4. Choose the number of rows and columns.
5. Click OK.

DATA TABLES

An Excel data table is a contiguous range of data that has been designated as a table. Once you make this designation, the table gains certain properties that are useful for data analysis. (Note that in some previous versions of Excel, data tables were called *data lists*.) Suppose you have a list of runners who have completed a race, as shown in Figure E-1.

	A	B	C	D	E	F
1	RUNNER#	LAST	FIRST	AGE	GENDER	TIME (MIN)
2	100	HARRIS	JANE	O	F	70
3	101	HILL	GLENN	Y	M	70
4	102	GARCIA	PEDRO	M	M	85
5	103	HILBERT	DORIS	M	F	90
6	104	DOAKS	SALLY	Y	F	94
7	105	JONES	SUE	Y	F	95
8	106	SMITH	PETE	M	M	100
9	107	DOE	JANE	O	F	100
10	108	BRADY	PETE	O	M	100
11	109	BRADY	JOE	O	M	120
12	110	HEEBER	SALLY	M	F	125
13	111	DOLTZ	HAL	O	M	130
14	112	PEEBLES	AL	Y	M	63

FIGURE E-1   Data table example

To turn the information into a data table, highlight the data range, including headings, and click the Insert tab. Then click Table in the Tables group. The Create Table window appears, as shown in Figure E-2.

	A	B	C	D	E	F
1	RUNNER#	LAST	FIRST	AGE	GENDER	TIME (MIN)
2	100	HARRIS	JANE	O	F	70
3	101	HILL	GLENN	Y	M	70
4	102	GARCIA	PEDRO			85
5	103	HILBERT	DORIS			90
6	104	DOAKS	SALLY			94
7	105	JONES	SUE			95
8	106	SMITH	PETE			100
9	107	DOE	JANE			100
10	108	BRADY	PETE			100
11	109	BRADY	JOE			120
12	110	HEEBER	SALLY	M	F	125
13	111	DOLTZ	HAL	O	M	130
14	112	PEEBLES	AL	Y	M	63

Create Table ? ×

Where is the data for your table?

=$A$1:$F$14   ↑

☑ My table has headers

OK   Cancel

FIGURE E-2   Create Table window

When you click OK, the data range appears as a table. In the Table Style Options group on the Design tab, click the Total Row check box to add a totals row to the data table. You can also select a light style in the Table Styles list to get rid of the contrasting color in the table's rows. Figure E-3 shows the results.

	A	B	C	D	E	F
1	RUNNER#	LAST	FIRST	AGE	GENDER	TIME (MIN)
2	100	HARRIS	JANE	O	F	70
3	101	HILL	GLENN	Y	M	70
4	102	GARCIA	PEDRO	M	M	85
5	103	HILBERT	DORIS	M	F	90
6	104	DOAKS	SALLY	Y	F	94
7	105	JONES	SUE	Y	F	95
8	106	SMITH	PETE	M	M	100
9	107	DOE	JANE	O	F	100
10	108	BRADY	PETE	O	M	100
11	109	BRADY	JOE	O	M	120
12	110	HEEBER	SALLY	M	F	125
13	111	DOLTZ	HAL	O	M	130
14	112	PEEBLES	AL	Y	M	63
15	Total					1242

FIGURE E-3   Data table example

The headings have acquired drop-down menu tabs, as you can see in Figure E-3.

You can sort the data table records by any field. Perhaps you want to sort by times. If so, click the drop-down menu in the TIME (MIN) heading, and then click Sort Smallest to Largest. You get the results shown in Figure E-4.

	A	B	C	D	E	F
1	RUNNER ▾	LAST ▾	FIRST ▾	AGE ▾	GENDE ▾	TIME (MIN ▾
2	112	PEEBLES	AL	Y	M	63
3	100	HARRIS	JANE	O	F	70
4	101	HILL	GLENN	Y	M	70
5	102	GARCIA	PEDRO	M	M	85
6	103	HILBERT	DORIS	M	F	90
7	104	DOAKS	SALLY	Y	F	94
8	105	JONES	SUE	Y	F	95
9	106	SMITH	PETE	M	M	100
10	107	DOE	JANE	O	F	100
11	108	BRADY	PETE	O	M	100
12	109	BRADY	JOE	O	M	120
13	110	HEEBER	SALLY	M	F	125
14	111	DOLTZ	HAL	O	M	130
15	Total					1242

FIGURE E-4   Sorting list by drop-down menu

You can see that Peebles had the best time and Doltz had the worst time. You can also sort from Largest to Smallest.

In addition, you can sort by more than one criterion. Assume that you want to sort first by gender and then by time (within gender). You first sort by gender from A to Z. Then you again click the Gender drop-down tab, point to Sort by Color, and then click Custom Sort. In the Sort window that appears, click Add Level and choose Time as the next criterion. See Figure E-5.

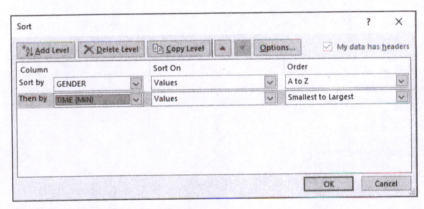

FIGURE E-5   Sorting on multiple criteria

Click OK to get the results shown in Figure E-6.

	A	B	C	D	E	F
1	RUNNER	LAST	FIRST	AGE	GENDE	TIME (MIN)
2	100	HARRIS	JANE	O	F	70
3	103	HILBERT	DORIS	M	F	90
4	104	DOAKS	SALLY	Y	F	94
5	105	JONES	SUE	Y	F	95
6	107	DOE	JANE	O	F	100
7	110	HEEBER	SALLY	M	F	125
8	112	PEEBLES	AL	Y	M	63
9	101	HILL	GLENN	Y	M	70
10	102	GARCIA	PEDRO	M	M	85
11	106	SMITH	PETE	M	M	100
12	108	BRADY	PETE	O	M	100
13	109	BRADY	JOE	O	M	120
14	111	DOLTZ	HAL	O	M	130
15	Total					1242

FIGURE E-6   Sorting by gender and time (within gender)

You can see that Harris had the best female time and that Peebles had the best male time.

Perhaps you want to see the top *n* listings for some attribute; for example, you may want to see the top five runners' times. Select the Time column's drop-down menu, and select Number Filters. From the menu that appears, click Top 10. The Top 10 AutoFilter window appears, as shown in Figure E-7.

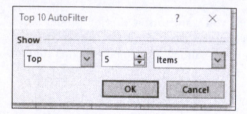

FIGURE E-7   Top 10 AutoFilter window

This window lets you specify the number of values you want. You might see 10 values as a default setting when the window appears. Figure E-7 shows that the user specified five values. Click OK to get the results shown in Figure E-8.

	A	B	C	D	E	F
1	RUNNER	LAST	FIRST	AGE	GENDE	TIME (MIN)
6	107	DOE	JANE	O	F	100
7	110	HEEBER	SALLY	M	F	125
11	106	SMITH	PETE	M	M	100
12	108	BRADY	PETE	O	M	100
13	109	BRADY	JOE	O	M	120
14	111	DOLTZ	HAL	O	M	130
15	Total					675

FIGURE E-8   Top 5 times

The output contains more than five data records because there are ties at 100 minutes. If you want to see all of the records again, click the Time drop-down menu and click Clear Filter From "TIME (MIN)." The full table of data reappears, as shown in Figure E-9.

	A	B	C	D	E	F
1	RUNNER	LAST	FIRST	AGE	GENDE	TIME (MIN)
2	100	HARRIS	JANE	O	F	70
3	103	HILBERT	DORIS	M	F	90
4	104	DOAKS	SALLY	Y	F	94
5	105	JONES	SUE	Y	F	95
6	107	DOE	JANE	O	F	100
7	110	HEEBER	SALLY	M	F	125
8	112	PEEBLES	AL	Y	M	63
9	101	HILL	GLENN	Y	M	70
10	102	GARCIA	PEDRO	M	M	85
11	106	SMITH	PETE	M	M	100
12	108	BRADY	PETE	O	M	100
13	109	BRADY	JOE	O	M	120
14	111	DOLTZ	HAL	O	M	130
15	Total					1242

FIGURE E-9   Restoring all data to window

Each of the cells in the Total row has a drop-down menu. The menu choices are statistical operations that you can perform on the totals—for example, you can take a sum, take an average, take a minimum or maximum, count the number of records, and so on. Assume that the Time drop-down menu was selected, as shown in Figure E-10. Note that the Sum operator is highlighted by default.

	A	B	C	D	E	F
1	RUNNER	LAST	FIRST	AGE	GENDE	TIME (MIN)
2	100	HARRIS	JANE	O	F	70
3	103	HILBERT	DORIS	M	F	90
4	104	DOAKS	SALLY	Y	F	94
5	105	JONES	SUE	Y	F	95
6	107	DOE	JANE	O	F	100
7	110	HEEBER	SALLY	M	F	125
8	112	PEEBLES	AL	Y	M	63
9	101	HILL	GLENN	Y	M	70
10	102	GARCIA	PEDRO	M	M	85
11	106	SMITH	PETE	M	M	100
12	108	BRADY	PETE	O	M	100
13	109	BRADY	JOE	O	M	120
14	111	DOLTZ	HAL	O	M	130
15	Total					1242
16						None
17						Average
18						Count
						Count Numbers
19						Max
						Min
20						Sum
21						StdDev
						Var
22						More Functions...

FIGURE E-10   Selecting Time drop-down menu in Total row

By changing from Sum to Average, you find that the average time for all runners was 95.5 minutes, as shown in Figure E-11.

	A	B	C	D	E	F
1	RUNNER ▾	LAST ▾	FIRST ▾	AGE ▾	GENDE ▾	TIME (MIN ▾
2	100	HARRIS	JANE	O	F	70
3	103	HILBERT	DORIS	M	F	90
4	104	DOAKS	SALLY	Y	F	94
5	105	JONES	SUE	Y	F	95
6	107	DOE	JANE	O	F	100
7	110	HEEBER	SALLY	M	F	125
8	112	PEEBLES	AL	Y	M	63
9	101	HILL	GLENN	Y	M	70
10	102	GARCIA	PEDRO	M	M	85
11	106	SMITH	PETE	M	M	100
12	108	BRADY	PETE	O	M	100
13	109	BRADY	JOE	O	M	120
14	111	DOLTZ	HAL	O	M	130
15	Total					95.53846154 ▾

FIGURE E-11   Average running time shown in Total row

PIVOT TABLES

Suppose you have data for a company's sales transactions by month, by salesperson, and by amount for each product type. You would like to display each salesperson's total sales by type of product sold and by month. You can use a pivot table in Excel to tabulate that summary data. A pivot table is built around one or more dimensions and thus can summarize large amounts of data. Figure E-12 shows total sales cross-tabulated by salesperson and by month.

	A	B	C	D	E
1	**Name**	**Product**	**January**	**February**	**March**
2	Jones	Product1	30,000	35,000	40,000
3	Jones	Product2	33,000	34,000	45,000
4	Jones	Product3	24,000	30,000	42,000
5	Smith	Product1	40,000	38,000	36,000
6	Smith	Product2	41,000	37,000	38,000
7	Smith	Product3	39,000	50,000	33,000
8	Bonds	Product1	25,000	26,000	25,000
9	Bonds	Product2	22,000	25,000	24,000
10	Bonds	Product3	19,000	20,000	19,000
11	Ruth	Product1	44,000	42,000	33,000
12	Ruth	Product2	45,000	40,000	30,000
13	Ruth	Product3	50,000	52,000	35,000

FIGURE E-12   Excel spreadsheet data

You can create pivot tables and many other kinds of tables with the Excel PivotTable tool. To create a pivot table from the data in Figure E-12, follow these steps:

1. Starting in the spreadsheet in Figure E-12, click a cell in the data range, and then click the Insert tab. In the Tables group, choose PivotTable. You see the window shown in Figure E-13.

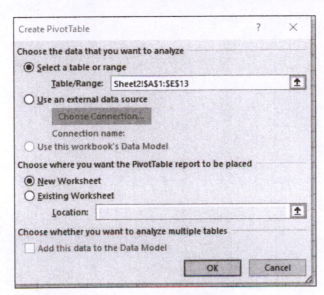

FIGURE E-13   Creating a pivot table

2. Make sure New Worksheet is checked under "Choose where you want the PivotTable report to be placed." Click OK. The window shown in Figure E-14 appears.

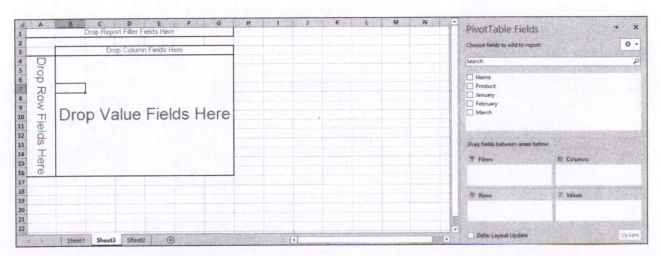

FIGURE E-14   PivotTable design window

The data range's column headings are shown in the PivotTable Field list on the right side of the window. From there, you can click and drag column headings into the Rows, Columns, and Values panes that appear in the lower-right part of the spreadsheet.

3. If you want to see the January sales by product for each salesperson, drag the Name field to the Columns pane, the Product field to the Rows pane, and the January field to the Values pane. By default, the Sum operation will be shown in the Values pane, which is what you want. You should see the result shown in Figure E-15. Your pivot table should look like the one in Figure E-16.

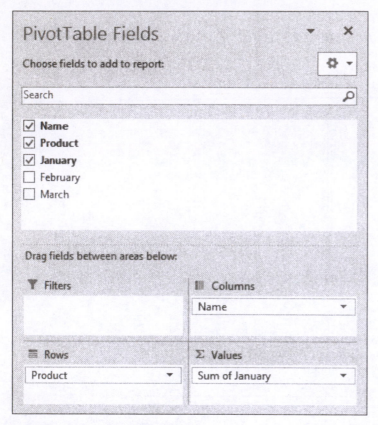

FIGURE E-15   Pivot table fields

	A	B	C	D	E	F
1						
2						
3	Sum of January	Name ▼				
4	Product ▼	Bonds	Jones	Ruth	Smith	Grand Total
5	Product1	25000	30000	44000	40000	139000
6	Product2	22000	33000	45000	41000	141000
7	Product3	19000	24000	50000	39000	132000
8	Grand Total	66000	87000	139000	120000	412000
9						

FIGURE E-16   Pivot table

By default, Excel adds all of the sales for each salesperson by month for each product. At the bottom of the pivot table, Excel also shows the total sales for each month for all products.

Note the four small panes in the lower-right corner. The Values pane lets you easily change from the default Sum operator to another one (Min, Max, Average, Count, and so on). Click the drop-down arrow, select Value Field Settings, and then select the desired operator.

Displaying Pivot Table Results as Percentages

It is often helpful to display pivot table results as percentages of a total. For example, Figure E-16 displays total January sales for each salesperson, but seeing these numbers as percentages would provide a better perspective of the sales numbers. To display the values as percentages, right-click any value in your pivot table and select the Show Values As option from the menu, as shown in Figure E-17. From the submenu that appears, select % of Row Total.

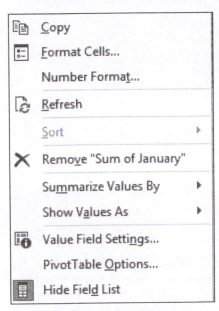

▤	Copy
▤	Format Cells...
	Number Format...
↻	Refresh
	Sort ▸
✕	Remove "Sum of January"
	Summarize Values By ▸
	Show Values As ▸
▤	Value Field Settings...
	PivotTable Options...
▤	Hide Field List

FIGURE E-17 Pivot table menu

Selecting this option allows easier evaluation of January sales, as shown in Figure E-18.

	A	B	C	D	E	F
1	Drop Report Filter Fields Here					
2						
3	Sum of January	Name ▾				
4	Product ▾	Bonds	Jones	Ruth	Smith	Grand Total
5	Product1	17.99%	21.58%	31.65%	28.78%	100.00%
6	Product2	15.60%	23.40%	31.91%	29.08%	100.00%
7	Product3	14.39%	18.18%	37.88%	29.55%	100.00%
8	Grand Total	16.02%	21.12%	33.74%	29.13%	100.00%

FIGURE E-18 Displaying pivot table results as percentages

BUILT-IN FUNCTIONS

You might need to use some of the following functions when solving the Excel cases elsewhere in this text:

- MIN, MAX, AVERAGE, COUNTIF, COUNTIFS, ROUND, ROUNDUP, RANDBETWEEN, TREND, PMT, NPV, ABS, and INT

The syntax of these functions is discussed in this section. The following examples are based on the runner data shown in Figure E-19.

	A	B	C	D	E	F	G
1	RUNNER#	LAST	FIRST	AGE	GENDER	HEIGHT (IN)	TIME (MIN)
2	100	HARRIS	JANE	O	F	60	70
3	101	HILL	GLENN	Y	M	65	70
4	102	GARCIA	PEDRO	M	M	76	85
5	103	HILBERT	DORIS	M	F	64	90
6	104	DOAKS	SALLY	Y	F	62	94
7	105	JONES	SUE	Y	F	64	95
8	106	SMITH	PETE	M	M	73	100
9	107	DOE	JANE	O	F	66	100
10	108	BRADY	PETE	O	M	73	100
11	109	BRADY	JOE	O	M	71	120
12	110	HEEBER	SALLY	M	F	59	125
13	111	DOLTZ	HAL	O	M	76	130
14	112	PEEBLES	AL	Y	M	76	63

FIGURE E-19   Runner data used to illustrate built-in functions

The data is the same as that shown in Figure E-1, except that Figure E-19 includes a column for the runners' height in inches.

MIN and MAX Functions

The MIN function determines the smallest value in a range of data. The MAX function returns the largest. Say that we want to know the fastest time for all runners, which would be the minimum time in column G. The MIN function computes the smallest value in a set of values. The set of values could be a data range, or it could be a series of cell addresses separated by commas. The syntax of the MIN function is as follows:

- MIN(set of data)

To show the minimum time in cell C16, you would enter the formula shown in the formula bar in Figure E-20:

C16   fx =MIN(G2:G14)

	A	B	C	D	E	F	G
1	RUNNER#	LAST	FIRST	AGE	GENDER	HEIGHT	TIME (MIN)
2	100	HARRIS	JANE	O	F	60	70
3	101	HILL	GLENN	Y	M	65	70
4	102	GARCIA	PEDRO	M	M	76	85
5	103	HILBERT	DORIS	M	F	64	90
6	104	DOAKS	SALLY	Y	F	62	94
7	105	JONES	SUE	Y	F	64	95
8	106	SMITH	PETE	M	M	73	100
9	107	DOE	JANE	O	F	66	100
10	108	BRADY	PETE	O	M	73	100
11	109	BRADY	JOE	O	M	71	120
12	110	HEEBER	SALLY	M	F	59	125
13	111	DOLTZ	HAL	O	M	76	130
14	112	PEEBLES	AL	Y	M	76	63
15							
16	MINIMUM TIME:		63				

FIGURE E-20   MIN function in cell C16

(Assume that you typed the label "MINIMUM TIME:" into cell A16.) You can see that the fastest time is 63 minutes.

To see the slowest time in cell G16, use the MAX function, whose syntax parallels that of the MIN function, except that the largest value in the set is determined. See Figure E-21.

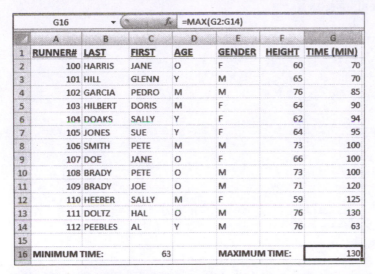

FIGURE E-21 MAX function in cell G16

AVERAGE, ROUND, and ROUNDUP Functions

The AVERAGE function computes the average of a set of values. Figure E-22 shows the use of the AVERAGE function in cell C17:

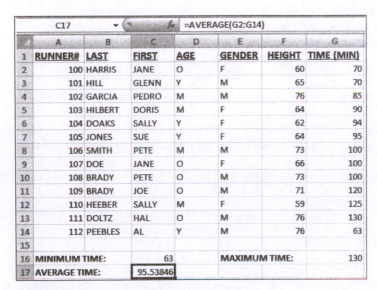

FIGURE E-22 AVERAGE function in cell C17

Notice that the value shown is a real number with many digits. What if you wanted to have the value rounded to a certain number of digits? Of course, you could format the output cell, but doing that changes only what is shown in the window. You want the cell's contents actually to *be* the rounded number. Therefore, you need to use the ROUND function. Its syntax is:

- ROUND(number, number of digits)

Figure E-23 shows the rounded average time (with two decimal places) in cell G17.

	A	B	C	D	E	F	G
				*f*ₓ	=ROUND(C17,2)		
1	RUNNER#	LAST	FIRST	AGE	GENDER	HEIGHT	TIME (MIN)
2	100	HARRIS	JANE	O	F	60	70
3	101	HILL	GLENN	Y	M	65	70
4	102	GARCIA	PEDRO	M	M	76	85
5	103	HILBERT	DORIS	M	F	64	90
6	104	DOAKS	SALLY	Y	F	62	94
7	105	JONES	SUE	Y	F	64	95
8	106	SMITH	PETE	M	M	73	100
9	107	DOE	JANE	O	F	66	100
10	108	BRADY	PETE	O	M	73	100
11	109	BRADY	JOE	O	M	71	120
12	110	HEEBER	SALLY	M	F	59	125
13	111	DOLTZ	HAL	O	M	76	130
14	112	PEEBLES	AL	Y	M	76	63
15							
16	MINIMUM TIME:		63		MAXIMUM TIME:		130
17	AVERAGE TIME:		95.53846		ROUNDED AVERAGE:		95.54

FIGURE E-23   ROUND function used in cell G17

To achieve this output, cell C17 was used as the value to be rounded. Recall from Figure E-22 that cell C17 had the formula =AVERAGE(G2:G14). The following ROUND formula would produce the same output in cell G17: =ROUND(AVERAGE(G2:G14),2). In this case, Excel evaluates the formula "inside out." First, the AVERAGE function is evaluated, yielding the average with many digits. That value is then input to the ROUND function and rounded to two decimal places.

The ROUNDUP function works much like the ROUND function. ROUNDUP's output is always rounded up to the next value. For example, the value 4 would appear in a cell that contained the following formula: =ROUNDUP(3.12,0). In Figure E-23, if the formula in cell G17 had been =ROUNDUP(AVERAGE(G2:G14),0), the value 96 would have been the result. In other words, 95.54 rounded up with no decimal places becomes 96.

COUNTIF and COUNTIFS Functions

The COUNTIF function counts the number of values in a range that meet a specified condition. The syntax is:

- COUNTIF(range of data, condition)

The condition is a logical expression such as "=1", ">6", or "=F". The condition is shown with quotation marks, even if a number is involved.

Assume that you want to see the number of female runners in cell C18. Figure E-24 shows the formula used.

	A	B	C	D	E	F	G
				*f*ₓ	=COUNTIF(E2:E14,"F")		
1	RUNNER#	LAST	FIRST	AGE	GENDER	HEIGHT	TIME (MIN)
2	100	HARRIS	JANE	O	F	60	70
3	101	HILL	GLENN	Y	M	65	70
4	102	GARCIA	PEDRO	M	M	76	85
5	103	HILBERT	DORIS	M	F	64	90
6	104	DOAKS	SALLY	Y	F	62	94
7	105	JONES	SUE	Y	F	64	95
8	106	SMITH	PETE	M	M	73	100
9	107	DOE	JANE	O	F	66	100
10	108	BRADY	PETE	O	M	73	100
11	109	BRADY	JOE	O	M	71	120
12	110	HEEBER	SALLY	M	F	59	125
13	111	DOLTZ	HAL	O	M	76	130
14	112	PEEBLES	AL	Y	M	76	63
15							
16	MINIMUM TIME:		63		MAXIMUM TIME:		130
17	AVERAGE TIME:		95.53846		ROUNDED AVERAGE:		95.54
18	NUMBER OF FEMALES:		6				

FIGURE E-24   COUNTIF function used in cell C18

The logic of the formula is: Count the number of times that "F" appears in the data range E2:E14.

A variation of this function is COUNTIFS. This function applies criteria to cells across multiple ranges and counts the number of times all criteria are met. The syntax is:

- COUNTIFS (range of data 1, condition, range of data 2, condition,...)

Assume that column H shows the rounded ratio of each runner's time in minutes to the runner's height in inches (see Figure E-25).

H2				fx	=ROUND(G2/F2,2)			
	A	B	C	D	E	F	G	H
1	RUNNER#	LAST	FIRST	AGE	GENDER	HEIGHT	TIME (MIN)	RATIO
2	100	HARRIS	JANE	O	F	60	70	1.17
3	101	HILL	GLENN	Y	M	65	70	1.08
4	102	GARCIA	PEDRO	M	M	76	85	1.12
5	103	HILBERT	DORIS	M	F	64	90	1.41
6	104	DOAKS	SALLY	Y	F	62	94	1.52
7	105	JONES	SUE	Y	F	64	95	1.48
8	106	SMITH	PETE	M	M	73	100	1.37
9	107	DOE	JANE	O	F	66	100	1.52
10	108	BRADY	PETE	O	M	73	100	1.37
11	109	BRADY	JOE	O	M	71	120	1.69
12	110	HEEBER	SALLY	M	F	59	125	2.12
13	111	DOLTZ	HAL	O	M	76	130	1.71
14	112	PEEBLES	AL	Y	M	76	63	0.83
15								
16	MINIMUM TIME:		63		MAXIMUM TIME:		130	
17	AVERAGE TIME:		95.53846		ROUNDED AVERAGE:		95.54	
18	NUMBER OF FEMALES:		6					

FIGURE E-25   Ratio of height to time in column H

Assume that all runners whose ratio is less than 1.5 will get an award. How many female runners qualify for the award? If the gender is "F" and the ratio is less than 1.5, an award is warranted. The COUNTIFS function in cell G18 computes the count of female runners with ratios of less than 1.5, as shown in Figure E-26.

G18			✗ ✓	fx	=COUNTIFS(E2:E14,"F",H2:H14,"<1.5")			
	A	B	C	D	E	F	G	H
1	RUNNER #	LAST	FIRST	AGE	GENDER	HEIGHT	TIME (MIN)	RATIO
2	100	HARRIS	JANE	O	F	60	70	1.17
3	101	HILL	GLENN	Y	M	65	70	1.08
4	102	GARCIA	PEDRO	M	M	76	85	1.12
5	103	HILBERT	DORIS	M	F	64	90	1.41
6	104	DOAKS	SALLY	Y	F	62	94	1.52
7	105	JONES	SUE	Y	F	64	95	1.48
8	106	SMITH	PETE	M	M	73	100	1.37
9	107	DOE	JANE	O	F	66	100	1.52
10	108	BRADY	PETE	O	M	73	100	1.37
11	109	BRADY	JOE	O	M	71	120	1.69
12	110	HEEBER	SALLY	M	F	59	125	2.12
13	111	DOLTZ	HALL	O	M	76	130	1.71
14	112	PEEBLES	AL	Y	M	76	63	0.83
15								
16	MINIMUM TIME:		63		MAXIMUM TIME:		130	
17	AVERAGE TIME:		95.53846		ROUNDED AVERAGE:		95.54	
18	NUMBER OF FEMALES:		6		AWARDS NEEDED:		3	

FIGURE E-26   COUNTIFS function used in cell G18

RANDBETWEEN Function

If you wanted a cell to contain a randomly generated integer in the range from 1 to 9, you would use the formula =RANDBETWEEN(1,9). Any value between 1 and 9 inclusive would be output by the formula. An example is shown in Figure E-27.

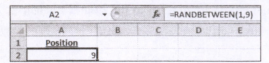

FIGURE E-27   RANDBETWEEN function used in cell A2

Assume that you copied and pasted the formula to generate a column of 100 numbers between 1 and 9. Every time a value was changed in the spreadsheet, Excel would recalculate the 100 RANDBETWEEN formulas to change the 100 random values. Therefore, you might want to settle on the random values once they are generated. To do this, copy the 100 values, click Paste Special, and then click Values to put the values in the same range. The contents of the cells will change from formulas to literal values.

TREND Function

The TREND function can be used to estimate a variable's value based on the values of other variables. For example, you might know the heights, genders, and weights for 20 people. Correlations exist among these three characteristics. You also have height and gender data for 10 other people, and you want to estimate their weights based on the data you have. The data is shown in Figure E-28.

	A	B	C	D	E	F	G	H	I
1	Person	Height	Gender	Weight		Person	Height	Gender	Pred Weight
2	101	70	1	190		130	71	1	
3	102	60	2	110		131	61	2	
4	103	72	1	200		132	70	1	
5	104	62	2	120		133	63	2	
6	105	66	1	175		134	65	1	
7	106	66	2	140		135	65	2	
8	107	64	1	170		136	67	1	
9	108	70	2	155		137	70	2	
10	109	62	1	150		138	61	1	
11	110	66	2	150		139	68	2	
12	111	68	1	186					
13	112	68	2	200					
14	113	70	1	200					
15	114	62	2	100					
16	115	72	1	210					
17	116	63	2	110					
18	117	71	1	200					
19	118	64	2	130					
20	119	70	1	170					
21	120	61	2	120					

FIGURE E-28   Data for people's heights, genders, and weights

The TREND function requires numerical values. In the data, the code for a male is 1 and the code for a female is 2. Height values are measured in inches and weight values are in pounds. For example, person 101 is a male who is 5 feet, 10 inches tall and weighs 190 pounds.

You can use the TREND function to examine a set of data and "learn" the relationship between two or more variables. In this example, the TREND function learns how the heights and genders of 20 people correlate to their weights. Then, given 10 other people's heights and genders, the TREND function applies what it knows to estimate their weights.

The syntax for the TREND function is:

*   =TREND(known Ys, known Xs, new Xs)

In the example, the known Ys are the known weights for 20 people, the known Xs are the related heights and genders, and the new Xs are heights and genders of 10 people for whom you want estimated weights. The formula is shown in Figure E-29.

- =TREND($D$2:$D$21, $B$2:$C$21, G2:H2)

Cells D2 to D21 hold the known weights for 20 people. Cells B2 to C21 hold the values of the two predictor variables (height and gender) for those 20 people. Cells G2 and H2 are the predictor variables for person 130, for whom you want a predicted weight. The predicted weight formula is in cell I2.

FIGURE E-29   Calculation of predicted weight for person 130

When you copy the formula down the cells in column I for the 10 people, you calculate weight predictions for all of them. By using absolute addressing, the only address changes are the predictor height and gender values for the 10 people.

PMT Function

The PMT function calculates a loan payment. The syntax is:

- =PMT(interest rate, number of periods, initial loan principal)

As an example, assume that you have a 6 percent, 30-year loan for $100,000. The calculation of the monthly payment is shown in Figure E-30.

FIGURE E-30   Calculation of monthly loan payment

The formula is in cell B5. The monthly interest rate is the annual rate in cell B1 divided by 12. The number of months covered by the loan is the number of years (see cell B2) multiplied by 12. The loan principal is in cell B3. The PMT function returns a negative number, so the expression is multiplied by −1.

Loan payments for the year are computed by multiplying the monthly payment by 12.

NPV Function

The NPV function calculates the net present value of an investment by using a discount rate and a series of future payments (negative values) and income (positive values). The syntax is:

- NPV(rate, value1, [value2],…)

The function's arguments are as follows:

- **Rate**—This required argument is the rate of discount for one period.
- **value1, value2,…**—value1 is required and subsequent values are optional. You can enter up to 254 arguments that represent the payments and income. The value1, value2,… sequence must be equally spaced in time and occur at the end of each period.

The NPV function uses the order of value1, value2,... to interpret the order of cash flows. Be sure to enter your payment and income values in the correct sequence.

For example, suppose you want to calculate the net present value of a $100,000 investment at a discount rate of 10% after four years. You anticipate returns from each year and use the NPV function to calculate the result, as shown in cell A8 in Figure E-31.

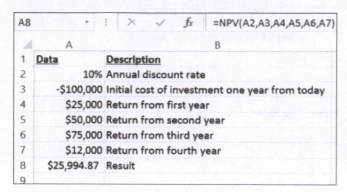

FIGURE E-31   NPV function used in cell A8

ABS Function

The ABS function returns the absolute value of a number. The absolute value of a number is the number without the sign. The syntax is:

- ABS(number)

Figure E-32 shows the results of using the ABS function on different numbers.

	A	B	C
1			
2	Data	Formula	Result
3	4	=ABS(A3)	4
4	-4	=ABS(A4)	4

FIGURE E-32   Using the ABS function

INT Function

The INT function returns a number rounded down to the nearest integer. The syntax is:

- INT(number)

In Figure E-33, the value in cell A2 divided by the value in cell B2 would be the real number 6.4285. The figure shows that using the INT function on the quotient returns the integer 6.

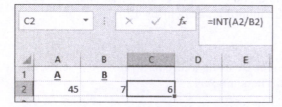

FIGURE E-33   Using the INT function

PART 7

PRESENTATION SKILLS

TUTORIAL **F**

GIVING AN ORAL PRESENTATION

Giving an oral presentation in class lets you practice the presentation skills you will need in the workplace. The presentations you create for the cases in this textbook will be similar to professional business presentations. You will be expected to present objective, technical results to your organization's stakeholders, and you will have to support your presentation with visual aids commonly used in the business world. During your presentation, your instructor might assign your classmates to role-play an audience of business managers, bankers, or employees. They might also provide feedback on your presentation.

Follow these four steps to create an effective presentation:

1. Plan your presentation.
2. Draft your presentation.
3. Create graphics and other visual aids.
4. Practice delivering your presentation.

PLANNING YOUR PRESENTATION

When planning an oral presentation, you need to know your time limits, establish your purpose, analyze your audience, and gather information. This section explores each of these elements.

Knowing Your Time Limits

You need to consider your time limits on two levels. First, consider how much time you will have to deliver your presentation. For example, what are the key points in your material that can be covered in 10 minutes? The element of time is the primary constraint of any presentation. It limits the breadth and depth of your talk and the number of visual aids that you can use. Second, consider how much time you will need for the process of preparing your presentation—drafting your presentation, creating graphics, and practicing your delivery.

Establishing Your Purpose

After considering your time limits, you must define your purpose: what you need to say and to whom you will say it. For the Access cases in this book, your purpose will be to inform and explain. For instance, a business's owners, managers, and employees may need to know how the company's database is organized and how they can use it to fill in forms and create reports. In contrast, for the Excel cases, your purpose will be to recommend a course of action based on the results of your business model. You will make the recommendations to business owners, managers, and bankers based on the results of inputting and running various scenarios.

Analyzing Your Audience

Once you have established the purpose of your presentation, you should analyze your audience. Ask yourself: What does my audience already know about the subject? What do the audience members want to know? What do they need to know? Do they have any biases or personal agendas that I should consider? What level of technical detail is best suited to their level of knowledge and interest?

In some Access cases, you will make a presentation to an audience that might not be familiar with Access or with databases in general. In other cases, you might be giving your presentation to a business owner who started to work on a database but was not able to finish it. Tailor the presentation to suit your audience.

For the Excel cases, you are most often interpreting results for an audience of bankers or business managers. In those instances, the audience will not need to know the detailed technical aspects of how you generated your results. But what if your audience consists of engineers or scientists? They will certainly be more interested in the structure and rationale of your decision models. Regardless of the audience, your listeners need to know what assumptions you made prior to developing your spreadsheets because those assumptions might affect their opinion of your results.

Gathering Information

Because you will have just completed a case as you begin preparing your oral presentation, you will already have the basic information you need. For the Access cases, you should review the main points of the case and your goals. Make sure you include all of the points you think are important for the audience to understand. In addition, you might want to go beyond the requirements and explain additional ways in which the database could be used to benefit the organization, now or in the future.

For the Excel cases, you can refer to the tutorials for assistance in interpreting the results from your spreadsheet analysis. For some cases, you might want to use the Internet or the library to research business trends or background information that can support your presentation.

DRAFTING YOUR REPORT AND PRESENTATION

When you have completed the planning stage, you are ready to begin drafting the presentation. At this point, you might be tempted to write your presentation and then memorize it word for word. Even if you could memorize your presentation verbatim, however, your delivery would sound unnatural because people use a simpler vocabulary and shorter sentences when they speak than when they write. For example, read the previous paragraph out loud as if you were presenting it to an audience.

In many business situations, you will be required both to submit a written report of your work and give a PowerPoint presentation. First, write your report and then design your PowerPoint slides as a "brief" of that report to discuss its main points. When drafting your report and the accompanying PowerPoint slides, follow this sequence:

1. Write the main body of your report.
2. Write the introduction to your report.
3. Write the conclusion to your report.
4. Prepare your presentation (the PowerPoint slides) using your report's main points.

Writing the Main Body

When you draft your report, write the body first. If you try to write the opening paragraph first, you might spend an inordinate amount of time attempting to craft your words perfectly, only to revise the introduction after you write the body of the report.

Keeping Your Audience in Mind

To write the main body, review your purpose and your audience profile. What are the main points you need to make? What are your audience's needs, interests, and technical expertise? It is important to include some technical details in your report and presentation, but keep in mind the technical expertise of your audience.

Remember that the people reading your report or listening to your presentation have their own agendas—put yourself in their places and ask, "What do I need to get out of this presentation?" For example, in the Access cases, an employee might want to know how to enter information on a form, but the business owner might be more interested in generating queries and reports. You need to address their different needs in your presentation. For example, you might say, "And now, let's look at how data entry associates can input data into this form."

Similarly, in the Excel cases, your audience will consist of business owners, managers, bankers, and perhaps some technical professionals. The owners and managers will be concerned with profitability, growth, and customer service. In contrast, the bankers' main concern will be repayment of a loan. Technical professionals will be more concerned with how well your decision model is designed, along with the credibility of the results. You need to address the interests of each group.

Using Transitions and Repetition in Your Presentation

During your presentation, remember that the audience is not reading the text of your report, so you need to include transitions to compensate. Words such as *next, first, second,* and *finally* will help the audience follow the sequence of your ideas. Words such as *however, in contrast, on the other hand,* and *similarly* will help the audience follow shifts in thought. You can use your voice to convey emphasis.

Also consider using hand gestures to emphasize what you say. For instance, if you list three items, you can use your fingers to tick off each item as you discuss it. Similarly, if you state that profits will be flat, you can make a level motion with your hand for emphasis.

You may be speaking behind a podium or standing beside a projection screen, or both. If you feel uncomfortable standing in one place and you can walk without blocking the audience's view of the screen, feel free to move around. You can emphasize a transition by changing your position. If you tend to fidget, shift, or rock from one foot to the other, try to anchor yourself. A favorite technique of some speakers is to come from behind the podium and place one hand on it while speaking. They get the anchoring effect of the podium while removing the barrier it places between them and the audience. Use the stance or technique that makes you feel most comfortable, as long as your posture or actions do not distract the audience.

As you draft your presentation, repeat key points to emphasize them. For example, suppose your main point is that outsourcing labor will provide the greatest gains in net income. Begin by previewing that concept, and state that you will demonstrate how outsourcing labor will yield the biggest profits. Then provide statistics that support your claim and show visual aids that graphically illustrate your point. Summarize by repeating your point: "As you can see, outsourcing labor does yield the biggest profits."

Relying on Graphics to Support Your Talk

As you write the main body, think of how to integrate graphics into your presentation. Do not waste words with a long description if a graphic can bring instant comprehension. For instance, instead of describing how information from a query can be turned into a report, show the query and a completed report. Figures F-1 and F-2 illustrate an Access query and the resulting report.

Order Query 1

Customer Name	City	Product Name	Qty	Price per Unit	Total
Applewood Restaurant	Martinsburg	Frozen Alligator on a Stick	20	$27.99	$559.80
Applewood Restaurant	Martinsburg	Nogales Chipotle Sauce	15	$11.49	$172.35
Applewood Restaurant	Martinsburg	Mom's Deep Dish Apple Pie	12	$12.49	$149.88
Fresh Catch Fishery	Salem	Brumley's Seafood Cocktail Sauce	24	$4.79	$114.96
Fresh Catch Fishery	Salem	NY Smoked Salmon	21	$21.99	$461.79
Fresh Catch Fishery	Salem	Mama Mia's Tiramisu	15	$17.99	$269.85
Jimmy's Crab House	Elkton	Frozen Alligator on a Stick	12	$27.99	$335.88
Jimmy's Crab House	Elkton	Brumley's Seafood Cocktail Sauce	24	$4.79	$114.96
Jimmy's Crab House	Elkton	Mama Mia's Tiramisu	18	$17.99	$323.82
Jimmy's Crab House	Elkton	Mom's Deep Dish Apple Pie	36	$12.49	$449.64

FIGURE F-1   Access query

May 2017 Orders--Fine Foods, Inc.					
Customer Name	City	Product Name	Qty	Price per Unit	Total
Applewood Restaurant	Martinsburg	Frozen Alligator on a Stick	20	$27.99	$559.80
Applewood Restaurant	Martinsburg	Nogales Chipotle Sauce	15	$11.49	$172.35
Applewood Restaurant	Martinsburg	Mom's Deep Dish Apple Pie	12	$12.49	$149.88
Fresh Catch Fishery	Salem	Brumley's Seafood Cocktail Sauce	24	$4.79	$114.96
Fresh Catch Fishery	Salem	NY Smoked Salmon	21	$21.99	$461.79
Fresh Catch Fishery	Salem	Mama Mia's Tiramisu	15	$17.99	$269.85
Jimmy's Crab House	Elkton	Frozen Alligator on a Stick	12	$27.99	$335.88
Jimmy's Crab House	Elkton	Brumley's Seafood Cocktail Sauce	24	$4.79	$114.96
Jimmy's Crab House	Elkton	Mama Mia's Tiramisu	18	$17.99	$323.82
Jimmy's Crab House	Elkton	Mom's Deep Dish Apple Pie	36	$12.49	$449.64
				Total Orders	$2,952.93
					Page 1 of 1

FIGURE F-2   Access report

Also consider what kinds of graphic media are available and how well you can use them. Your employer will expect you to be able to use Microsoft PowerPoint to prepare your presentation as a slide show. Luckily, many college freshmen are required to take an introductory course that covers Microsoft Office and PowerPoint. If you are not familiar with PowerPoint, several excellent tutorials on the Web can help you learn the basics.

Anticipating the Unexpected

Even though you are only drafting your report and presentation at this stage, eventually you will answer questions from the audience. Being able to handle questions smoothly is the mark of a business professional. The first steps to addressing audience questions are being able to anticipate them and preparing your answers.

You will not use all the facts you gather for your report or presentation. However, as you draft your report, you might want to jot down those facts and keep them handy, in case you need them to answer questions from the audience. PowerPoint has a Notes section where you can include notes for each slide and print them to help you answer questions that arise during your presentation. You will learn how to print notes for your slides later in the tutorial.

The questions you receive depend on the nature of your presentation. For example, during a presentation of an Excel decision model, you might be asked why you are not recommending a certain course of action, or why you left it out of your report. If you have already prepared notes that anticipate such questions, you will probably remember your answers without even having to refer to the notes.

Another potential problem is determining how much technical detail you should display in your slides. In one sense, writing your report will be easier because you can include any graphics, tables, or data you want. Because you have a time limit for your presentation, the question of what to include or leave out becomes more challenging. One approach to this problem is to create more slides than you think you need, and then use the Hide Slide option in PowerPoint to "hide" the extra slides. For example, you might create slides that contain technical details you do not think you will have time to present. However, if you are asked for more details on a particular technical point, you can "unhide" a slide and display the detailed information needed to answer the question. You will learn more about the Hide Slide and Unhide Slide options later in the tutorial.

Writing the Introduction

After you have written the main body of your report and presentation, you can develop the introduction. The introduction should be only a paragraph or two, and it should preview the main points you will cover.

For some of the Access cases, you might want to include general information about databases: what they can do, why they are used, and how they can help a company become more efficient and profitable. You will not need to say much about the business operation because the audience already works for the company.

For the Excel cases, you might want to include an introduction of the general business scenario and describe any assumptions you used to create and run your decision support models. Excel is used for decision support, so you should describe the decision criteria you selected for the model.

Writing the Conclusion

Every good report or presentation needs a good ending. Do not leave the audience hanging. Your conclusion should be brief—only a paragraph or two—and it should give your presentation a sense of closure. Use the conclusion to repeat your main points or, for the Excel cases, to recap your findings and recommendations.

On many occasions, information learned during a business project reveals new opportunities for other projects. Your conclusion should provide closure for the immediate project, but if the project reveals possibilities for future improvements, include them in a "path forward" statement.

CREATING GRAPHICS

Visual aids are a powerful means of getting your point across and making it understandable to your audience. Visual aids come in a variety of forms, some of which are more effective than others. The integrated graphics tools in Microsoft Office can help you prepare a presentation with powerful impact.

Choosing Presentation Media

The media you use will depend on the situation and the media you have available, but remember: *You must maintain control of the media or you will lose the attention of your audience.*

The following list highlights the most common media used in a classroom or business conference room, along with their strengths and weaknesses:

- **PowerPoint slides and a projection system**—These are the predominant presentation media for academic and business use. You can use a portable screen and a simple projector hooked up to a PC, or you can use a full multimedia center. Also, although they are not yet universal in business, touch-sensitive projection screens (for example, Smart Board™ technology) are gaining popularity in college classrooms. The ability to project and display slides, video and sound clips, and live Web pages makes the projection system a powerful presentation tool. *Negatives:* Depending on the complexity of the equipment, you might have difficulties setting it up and getting it to work properly. Also, you often must darken the room to use the projector, and it may be difficult to refer to written notes during your presentation. When using presentation media, you must be able to access and load your PowerPoint file easily. Make sure your file is available from at least two sources that the equipment can access, such as a thumb drive, CD, DVD, or online folder. If your presentation has active links to Web pages, make sure that the presentation computer has Internet access.
- **Handouts**—You can create handouts of your presentation for the audience, which once was the norm for many business meetings. Handouts allow the audience to take notes on applicable slides. If the numbers on a screen are hard to read from the back of the room, your audience can refer to their handouts. With the growing emergence of "green" business practices, however, unnecessary paper use is being discouraged. Many businesses now require reports and presentation slides to be posted at a common site where the audience can access them later. Often, this site is a "public" drive on a business network. *Negatives:* Giving your audience reading material may distract their attention from your presentation. They could read your slides and possibly draw wrong conclusions from them before you have a chance to explain them.

- **Overhead transparencies**—Transparencies are rarely used anymore in business, but some academics prefer them, particularly if they have to write numbers, equations, or formulas on a display large enough for students to see from the back row in a lecture hall. *Negatives:* Transparencies require an overhead projector, and frequently their edges are visually distorted due to the design of the projector lens. You have to use special transparency sheets in a photocopier to create your slides. For both reasons, it is best to avoid using overheads.
- **Whiteboards**—Whiteboards are common in both the business conference room and the classroom. They are useful for posting questions or brainstorming, but you should not use one in your presentation. *Negatives:* You have to face away from your audience to use a whiteboard, and if you are not used to writing on one, it can be difficult to write text that is large enough and legible. Use whiteboards only to jot down questions or ideas that you will check on after the presentation is finished.
- **Flip charts**—Flip charts (also known as easel boards) are large pads of paper on a portable stand. They are used like whiteboards, except that you do not erase your work when the page is full—you flip over to a fresh sheet. Like whiteboards, flip charts are useful for capturing questions or ideas that you want to research after the presentation is finished. Flip charts have the same negatives as whiteboards. Their one advantage is that you can tear off the paper and take it with you when you leave.

Creating Graphs and Charts

Strictly speaking, charts and graphs are not the same thing, although many graphs are referred to as charts. Usually charts show relationships and graphs show change. However, Excel makes no distinction and calls both entities *charts*.

Charts are easy to create in Excel. Unfortunately, the process is so easy that people frequently create graphics that are meaningless, misleading, or inaccurate. This section explains how to select the most appropriate graphics.

You should use pie charts to display data that is related to a whole. For example, you might use a pie chart when breaking down manufacturing costs into Direct Materials, Direct Labor, and Manufacturing Overhead, as shown in Figure F-3. (Note that when you create a pie chart, Excel will convert the numbers you want to graph into percentages of 100.)

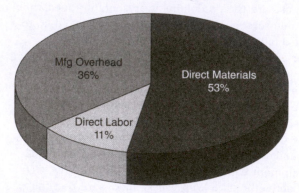

LCD TV Manufacturing Cost

FIGURE F-3   3D pie chart: appropriate use

You would *not*, however, use a pie chart to display a company's sales over a three-year period. For example, the pie chart in Figure F-4 is meaningless because it is not useful to think of the period as a "whole" or the years as its "parts."

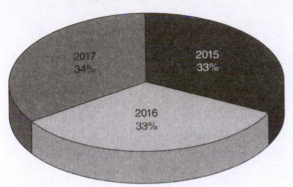

Company Sales–2015 to 2017

FIGURE F-4   3D pie chart: inappropriate use

You should use vertical bar charts (also called column charts) to compare several amounts at the same time, or to compare the same data collected for successive periods of time. The same type of company sales data shown incorrectly in Figure F-4 can be compared correctly using a vertical bar chart (see Figure F-5).

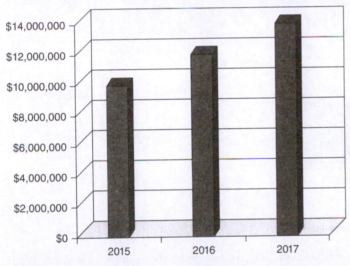

Company Sales–2015 to 2017

FIGURE F-5   3D column chart: appropriate use

As another example, you might want to compare the sales revenues from several different products. You can use a clustered bar chart to show changes in each product's sales over time, as in Figure F-6. This type of bar chart is called a "clustered column" chart in Excel.

When building a chart, include labels that explain the graphics. For instance, when using a graph with an x- and y-axis, you should show what each axis represents so your audience does not puzzle over the graphic while you are speaking. Figures F-6 and F-7 illustrate the necessity of good labels.

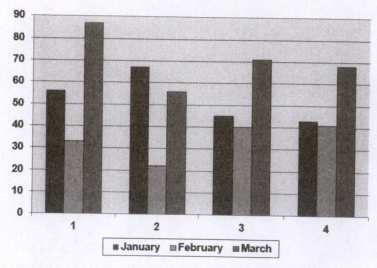

FIGURE F-6 Clustered column graph without title or axis labels

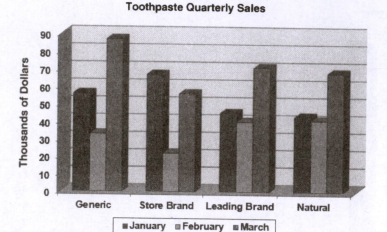

FIGURE F-7 3D clustered column graph with title and axis labels

In Figure F-6, the graph has no title and neither axis is labeled. Are the amounts in units or dollars? What elements are represented by each cluster of bars? In contrast, Figure F-7 provides a comprehensive snapshot of product sales, which would support a talk rather than create confusion. Note also how the 3D chart style adds visual depth to the chart. Using the 3D chart, the audience can more easily discern that February sales were lower across all product categories.

Another common pitfall of visual aids is charts that have a misleading premise. For example, suppose you want to show how sales are distributed among your inventory, and their contribution to net income. If you simply take the number of items sold in a given month, as displayed in Figure F-8, the visual fails to give your audience a sense of the actual dollar value of those sales. It is far more appropriate and informative to graph the net income for the items sold instead of the number of items sold. The graph in Figure F-9 provides a more accurate picture of which items contribute the most to net income.

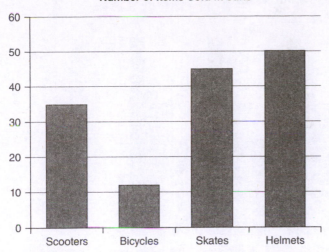

FIGURE F-8   Graph of number of items sold that does not reflect generated income

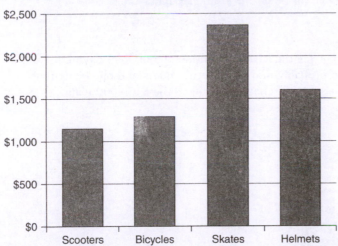

FIGURE F-9   Graph of net income by item sold

You should also avoid putting too much data in a single comparative chart. For example, assume that you want to compare monthly mortgage payments for two loan amounts with different interest rates and time frames. You have a spreadsheet that computes the payment data, as shown in Figure F-10.

	A	B	C	D	E	F	G
1	**Calculation of Monthly Payment**						
2	Rate	6.00%	6.10%	6.20%	6.30%	6.40%	6.50%
3	Amount	$ 100,000	$ 100,000	$ 100,000	$ 100,000	$ 100,000	$ 100,000
4	Payment (360 Payments)	$ 599	$ 605	$ 612	$ 618	$ 625	$ 632
5	Payment (180 Payments)	$ 843	$ 849	$ 854	$ 860	$ 865	$ 871
6	Amount	$ 150,000	$ 150,000	$ 150,000	$ 150,000	$ 150,000	$ 150,000
7	Payment (360 Payments)	$ 899	$ 908	$ 918	$ 928	$ 938	$ 948
8	Payment (180 Payments)	$ 1,265	$ 1,273	$ 1,282	$ 1,290	$ 1,298	$ 1,306

FIGURE F-10   Calculation of monthly payment

In Excel, it is possible (but not advisable) to capture all of the information in a single clustered column chart, as shown in Figure F-11.

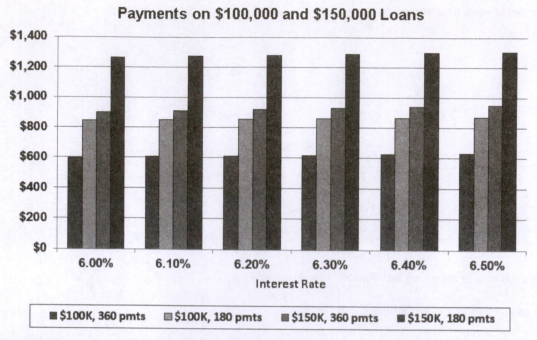

FIGURE F-11 Too much information in one chart

The chart contains a great deal of information. Putting the $100,000 and $150,000 loan payments in the same "cluster" may confuse the readers. They would probably find it easier to understand one chart that summarizes the $100,000 loan (see Figure F-12) and a second chart that covers the $150,000 loan.

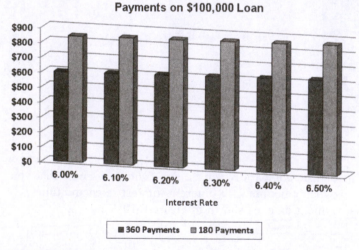

FIGURE F-12 Good balance of information and visual depth

You could then augment the charts with text that summarizes the main differences between the payments for each loan amount. In that fashion, the reader is led step by step through the analysis.

Later versions of Excel no longer have a Chart Wizard; instead, the Insert tab includes a Charts group. Once you create a chart and click it, two chart-specific tabs appear under the Chart Tools heading on the Ribbon to assist you with chart design and formatting. Excel also added three menu buttons to the right of the chart: Chart Elements, Chart Styles, and Chart Filters (see Figure F-13). Click each button to see a menu that helps you edit your chart. If you are unfamiliar with the charting tools in Excel, ask your instructor for guidance or refer to the many Excel tutorials on the Web.

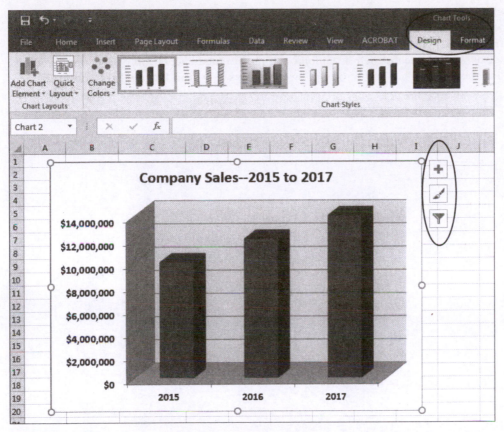

FIGURE F-13   Chart tools and new menu buttons in Excel

Creating PowerPoint Presentations

PowerPoint presentations are easy to create. When you open PowerPoint, click Blank Presentation. You can select from many different themes, styles, and slide layouts by clicking the Design tab. If none of PowerPoint's default themes suit you, you can download theme templates from Microsoft Office Online. When choosing a theme and style for your slides, such as background colors or graphics, fonts, and fills, keep the following guidelines in mind:

- In older versions of PowerPoint, users were advised to avoid pastel backgrounds or theme colors and to keep their slide backgrounds dark. Because of the increasing quality of graphics in both computer hardware and projection systems, most of the default themes in PowerPoint will project well and be easy to read.
- If your projection screen is small or your presentation room is large, consider using boldface type for all of your text to make it readable from the back of the room. If you have time to visit the presentation site beforehand, bring your PowerPoint file, project a slide on the screen, and look at it from the back row of the audience area. If you can read the text, the font is large enough.
- Use transitions and animations to keep your presentation lively, but do not go overboard with them. Swirling letters and pinwheeling words can distract the audience from your presentation.

- It is an excellent idea to animate the text on your slides with entrance effects so that only one bullet point appears at a time when you click the mouse (or when you tap the screen using a touch-sensitive board). This approach prevents your audience from reading ahead of the bullet point being discussed and keeps their attention on you. Entrance effects can be incorporated and managed using the Add Animation button in PowerPoint, as shown in Figures F-14 and F-15.

FIGURE F-14   The Add Animation button on the Ribbon in PowerPoint

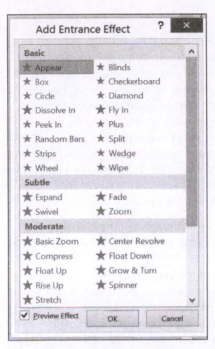

FIGURE F-15 Add Entrance Effect window

- Consider creating PowerPoint slides that have a section for your notes. You can print the notes from the Print dialog box by choosing Notes Pages from the Print menu, as shown in Figure F-16. Each slide will be printed at half its normal size, and your notes will appear beneath each slide, as shown by the print preview on the right side of Figure F-16.

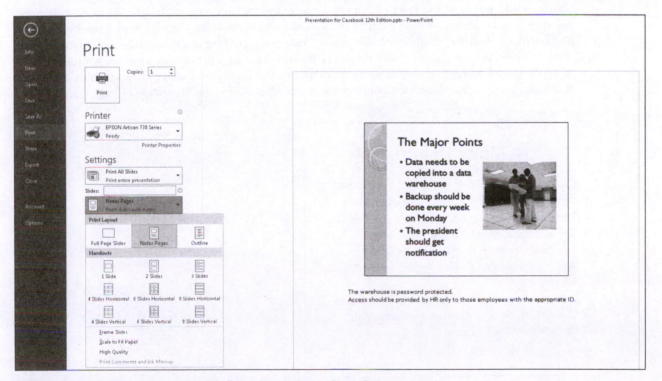

FIGURE F-16 Printing notes page and slide print preview in PowerPoint

- Finally, you should check your PowerPoint slides on a projection screen before your presentation. Information that looks good on a computer display may not be readable on the projection screen.

Using Visual Aids Effectively

Make sure you choose the visual aids that will work most effectively, and that you have enough without using too many. How many is too many? The amount of time you have to speak will determine the number of visual aids you should use, as will your target audience. A good rule of thumb is to allow at least one minute to present each PowerPoint slide. Leave a minimum of two minutes for audience questions after a 10-minute presentation, and allow up to 25 percent of your total presentation time to address questions after longer presentations. (For example, for a 20-minute presentation, figure on taking 5 minutes for questions.) For a 10-minute talk, try to keep the body of your presentation to eight slides or less. Your target audience will also influence your selection of visual aids. For instance, your slides will need more graphics and animation if you are addressing a group of teenagers than if you are presenting to a board of directors. Remember to use visual aids to emphasize your main points, not to detract from them.

Review each of your slides and visual aids to make sure it meets the following criteria:

- The font size of the text is large enough to read from the back of the presentation area.
- The slide or visual aid does not contain misleading graphics, typographical errors, or misspelled words—the quality of your work is a direct reflection on you.
- The content of your visual aid is relevant to the key points of your presentation.
- The slide or visual aid does not detract from your message. Your animations, pictures, and sound effects should support the text. Your visuals should look professional.
- A visual aid should look good in the presentation environment. If possible, rehearse your PowerPoint slides beforehand in the room where you will give the presentation. Make sure you can read your slides easily from the back row of seats in the room. If you have a friend who can sit in, ask her or him to listen to your voice from the back row of seats. If you have trouble projecting your voice clearly, consider using a microphone for your presentation.
- All numbers should be rounded unless decimals or pennies are crucial. For example, your company might only pay fractions of a cent per Web hit, but this cost may become significant after millions of Web hits.
- Slides should not look too busy or crowded. Many PowerPoint experts have a "6 by 6" rule for bullet points on a slide, which means you should include no more than six bullet points per slide and no more than six words per bullet point. Also avoid putting too many labels or pictures on a slide. Clip art can be "cutesy" and therefore has no place in a professional business presentation. A well-selected picture or two can add emphasis to the theme of a slide. For examples of a slide that is too busy versus one that conveys its points succinctly, see Figures F-17 and F-18.

Major Points

- Data needs to be copied into a data warehouse
- Backup should be done every week on Monday
- The president should get notification
- The vice president should get notification
- The data should be available on the Web
- Web access should be on a secure server
- HR sets passwords
- Only certain personnel in HR can set passwords
- Users need to show ID to obtain a password
- ID cards need to be the latest version

FIGURE F-17 Busy slide

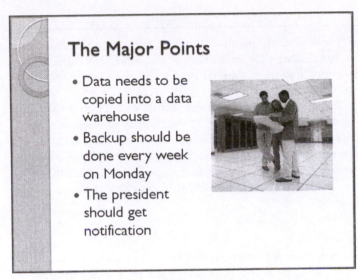

FIGURE F-18   Slide with appropriate number of bullet points and a supporting photo

You may find that you have created more slides than you have time to present, and you are unsure of which slides you should delete. Some may have data that an audience member might ask about. Fortunately, PowerPoint lets you "hide" slides; these hidden slides will not be displayed in Slide Show view unless you "unhide" them in Normal view. Hiding slides is an excellent way to keep detailed data handy in case your audience asks to see it. Figure F-19 shows how to hide a slide in a PowerPoint presentation. Right-click the slide you want to hide and then click Hide Slide from the menu to mark the slide as hidden in the presentation. To unhide the slide, right-click it and then click Hide Slide again from the menu. Click the slide to display it in Slide Show view.

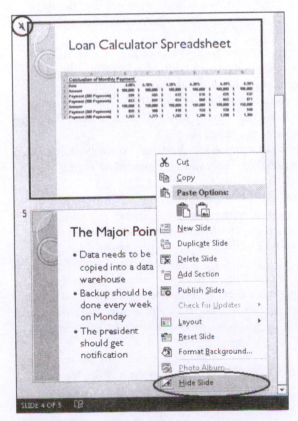

FIGURE F-19   Hiding a slide in PowerPoint

PRACTICING YOUR DELIVERY

Surveys indicate that public speaking is the greatest fear of many people. However, fear or nervousness can be channeled into positive energy to do a good job. Remember that an audience is not likely to think you are nervous unless you fidget or your voice cracks. Audience members want to hear what you have to say, so think about them and their interests—not about how you feel.

Your presentations for the cases in this textbook will occur in a classroom setting with 20 to 40 students. Ask yourself: Am I afraid when I talk to just one or two of my classmates? The answer is probably no. In addition, they will all have to give presentations as well. Think of your presentation as an extended conversation with several classmates. Let your gaze move from person to person, making brief eye contact with each of them randomly as you speak. As your focus moves from one person to another, think to yourself: I am speaking to one person at a time. As you become more proficient in speaking before a group, your gaze will move naturally among audience members.

Tips for Practicing Your Delivery

Giving an effective presentation is not the same as reading a report to an audience. You should rehearse your message well enough so that you can present it naturally and confidently, with your slides or other visual aids smoothly intermingled with your speaking. The following tips will help you hone the effectiveness of your delivery:

- Practice your presentation several times, and use your visual aids when you practice.
- Show your slides at the right time. Luckily, PowerPoint makes this easy; you can click the slide when you are ready to talk about it. Use cues as necessary in your speaker's notes.
- Maintain eye and voice contact with the audience when using the visual aid. Do not turn your back on your audience. It is acceptable to turn sideways to glance at your slide. A popular trick of experienced speakers is to walk around and steal a glance at the slide while moving to a new position.
- Refer to your visual aids in your talk and use hand gestures where appropriate. Do not ignore your own visual aid, but do not read it to your audience—they can read for themselves.
- Keep in mind that your slides or visual aids should support your presentation, not *be* the presentation. Do not try to crowd the slide with everything you plan to say. Use the slides to illustrate key points and statistics, and fill in the rest of the content with your talk.
- Check your time, especially when practicing. If you stay within the time limit when practicing, you will probably finish a minute or two early when you actually give the presentation. You will be a little nervous and will talk a little faster to a live audience.
- Use numbers effectively. When speaking, use rounded numbers; otherwise, you will sound like a computer. Also make numbers as meaningful as possible. For example, instead of saying "in 83 percent of cases," say "in five out of six cases."
- Do not extrapolate, speculate, or otherwise "reach" to interpret the output of statistical models. For example, suppose your Excel model has many input variables. You might be able to point out a trend, but often you cannot say with mathematical certainty that if a company employs the inputs in the same combination, it will get the same results.
- Some people prefer recording their presentation and playing it back to evaluate themselves. It is amazing how many people are shocked when they hear their recorded voice—and usually they are not pleased with it. In addition, you will hear every *um, uh, well, you know,* throat-clearing noise, and other verbal distraction in your speech. If you want feedback on your presentation, have a friend listen to it.
- If you use a pointer, be careful where you wave it. It is not a light saber, and you are not Luke Skywalker. Unless you absolutely have to use one to point at crucial data on a slide, leave the pointer home.

Handling Questions

Fielding questions from an audience can be tricky because you cannot anticipate all of the questions you might be asked. When answering questions from an audience, *treat everyone with courtesy and respect.* Use the following strategies to handle questions:

- Try to anticipate as many questions as possible, and prepare answers in advance. Remember that you can gather much of the information to prepare those answers while drafting your presentation. The Notes section under each slide in PowerPoint is a good place to write anticipated questions and your answers. Hidden slides can also contain the data you need to answer questions about important details.
- Mention at the beginning of your talk that you will take questions at the end of the presentation, which helps prevent questions from interrupting the flow and timing of your talk. In fact, many PowerPoint presentations end with a questions slide. If someone tries to interrupt, say that you will be happy to answer the question when you are finished, or that the next graphic answers the question. Of course, this point does not apply to the company CEO—you *always* stop to answer the CEO's questions.
- When answering a question, a good practice is to repeat the question if you have any doubt that the entire audience heard it. Then deliver your answer to the whole audience, but make sure you close by looking directly at the person who asked the question.
- Strive to be informative, not persuasive. In other words, use facts to answer questions. For instance, if someone asks your opinion about a given outcome, you might show an Excel slide that displays the Solver's output; then you can use the data as the basis for answering the question. In that light, it is probably a good idea to have computer access to your Excel model or Access database if your presentation venue permits it, but avoid using either unless you absolutely need it.
- If you do not know the answer to a question, it is acceptable to say so, and it is certainly better than trying to fake the answer. For instance, if someone asks you the difference between the Simplex LP and GRG solving methods in Excel Solver, you might say, "That is an excellent question, but I really don't know the answer—let me research it and get back to you." Then follow up after the presentation by researching the answer and contacting the person who asked the question.
- Signal when you are finished. You might say that you have time for one more question. Wrap up the talk yourself and thank your audience for their attention.

Handling a "Problem" Audience

A "problem" audience or a heckler is every speaker's nightmare. Fortunately, this experience is rare in the classroom: Your audience will consist of classmates who also have to give presentations, and your instructor will be present to intervene in case of problems.

Heckling can be a common occurrence in the political arena, but it does not happen often in the business world. Most senior managers will not tolerate unprofessional conduct in a business meeting. However, fellow business associates might challenge you in what you perceive as a hostile manner. If so, remain calm, be professional, and rely on facts. The rest of the audience will watch to see how you react—if you behave professionally, you make the heckler appear unprofessional by comparison and you'll gain the empathy of the audience.

A more common problem is a question from an audience member who lacks technical expertise. For instance, suppose you explained how to enter data into an Access form, but someone did not understand your explanation. Ask the questioner what part of the explanation was confusing. If you can answer the question briefly and clearly, do so. If your answer turns into a time-consuming dialogue, offer to give the person a one-on-one explanation after the presentation.

Another common problem is receiving a question that you have already answered. The best solution is to give the answer again, as briefly as possible, using different words in case your original answer confused the person. If someone persists in asking questions that have obvious answers, you might ask the audience, "Who would like to answer that question?" The questioner should get the hint.

PRESENTATION TOOLKIT

You can use the form in Figure F-20 for preparation, the form in Figure F-21 for evaluation of Access presentations, and the form in Figure F-22 for evaluation of Excel presentations.

Preparation Checklist

Facilities and Equipment

☐ The room contains the equipment that I need.
☐ The equipment works and I've tested it with my visual aids.
☐ Outlets and electrical cords are available and sufficient.
☐ All the chairs are aligned so that everyone can see me and hear me.
☐ Everyone will be able to see my visual aids.
☐ The lights can be dimmed when/if needed.
☐ Sufficient light will be available so I can read my notes when the lights are dimmed.

Presentation Materials

☐ My notes are available, and I can read them while standing up.
☐ My visual aids are assembled in the order that I'll use them.
☐ A laser pointer or a wand will be available if needed.

Self

☐ I've practiced my delivery.
☐ I am comfortable with my presentation and visual aids.
☐ I am prepared to answer questions.
☐ I can dress appropriately for the situation.

FIGURE F-20   Preparation checklist

Evaluating Access Presentations

Course: _____ Speaker: _____ Date: _____

Rate the presentation by these criteria:
4=Outstanding   3=Good   2=Adequate   1=Needs Improvement
N/A=Not Applicable

Content

_____ The presentation contained a brief and effective introduction.

_____ Main ideas were easy to follow and understand.

_____ Explanation of database design was clear and logical.

_____ Explanation of using the form was easy to understand.

_____ Explanation of running the queries and their output was clear.

_____ Explanation of the report was clear, logical, and useful.

_____ Additional recommendations for database use were helpful.

_____ Visuals were appropriate for the audience and the task.

_____ Visuals were understandable, visible, and correct.

_____ The conclusion was satisfying and gave a sense of closure.

Delivery

_____ Was poised, confident, and in control of the audience

_____ Made eye contact

_____ Spoke clearly, distinctly, and naturally

_____ Avoided using slang and poor grammar

_____ Avoided distracting mannerisms

_____ Employed natural gestures

_____ Used visual aids with ease

_____ Was courteous and professional when answering questions

_____ Did not exceed time limit

Submitted by: _____

FIGURE F-21   Form for evaluation of Access presentations

Evaluating Excel Presentations

Course: _____ Speaker: _____ Date: _____

Rate the presentation by these criteria:
4=Outstanding   3=Good   2=Adequate   1=Needs Improvement
N/A=Not Applicable

Content

_____ The presentation contained a brief and effective introduction.

_____ The explanation of assumptions and goals was clear and logical.

_____ The explanation of software output was logically organized.

_____ The explanation of software output was thorough.

_____ Effective transitions linked main ideas.

_____ Solid facts supported final recommendations.

_____ Visuals were appropriate for the audience and the task.

_____ Visuals were understandable, visible, and correct.

_____ The conclusion was satisfying and gave a sense of closure.

Delivery

_____ Was poised, confident, and in control of the audience

_____ Made eye contact

_____ Spoke clearly, distinctly, and naturally

_____ Avoided using slang and poor grammar

_____ Avoided distracting mannerisms

_____ Employed natural gestures

_____ Used visual aids with ease

_____ Was courteous and professional when answering questions

_____ Did not exceed time limit

Submitted by: _____

FIGURE F-22   Form for evaluation of Excel presentations

Note: Page numbers in **boldface** indicate key terms